Mass Media and Contemporary Social Issues

Mass Media and Contemporary Social Issues

S.K. Sikka

CYBER TECH PUBLICATIONS
4264/3, Ansari Road, Daryaganj, New Delhi-110002 (India)
Ph.: 011-23244078, 011-43559448 Fax: 011-23280028
E-Mail: cyberpublicationsdelhi@yahoo.com
Website: www.cybertechpublications.com

MASS MEDIA AND CONTEMPORARY SOCIAL ISSUES

S.K. Sikka

First Edition 2010

Published by : Asian Offset Printers

G.S. Rawat for **Cyber Tech Publications**
4264/3, Ansari Road, Daryaganj, New Delhi-110002 (India)
Ph.: 011-23244078, 011-43559448 Fax: 011-23280028
E-Mail: cyberpublicationsdelhi@yahoo.com
Website: www.cybertechpublications.com

Preface

The mass media have an important role in modern society as the main channel of communication. The stronger and more purposeful the communication channels, the more developed the countries and vice versa. The population relies on the news media as the main source of information and the basis on which they form their opinions and voting decisions. Any selection of messages in the mass media will thus have a profound effect on the entire society.

Media Today is the product of over three decades of teaching the introductory course, talking to colleagues around the country about course trends and issues, and writing about mass media industries and issues in the scholarly and popular press. The hope is that readers will become critical, media literate consumers of mass media and, if they go on to work in mass media industries, more alert, sensitive practitioners.

The present volume is devoted to the discussion of the role of the media in presenting contemporary social issues. Specific instance of media coverage of issues related to human rights, women, environment, consumerism etc., are duly discussed. The potential of media to improve our social situation is contrasted with the actual trends in addressing these issues. It also attempts to identify the areas in which media can bring about radical changes for the better future.

— *Author*

CONTENTS

1

INTRODUCTION

The commission on Freedom of the press (1947) has listed most political and legal controls that have commonly been applied to the media. They include licensing in advance; censorship of offending material before publication; seizure of offending material; injunctions against publication of a newspaper or book or of specified content; requirement of surety bonds against libel or other offense; compulsory disclosure of ownership and authority; post publication criminal penalties for objectionable matter; post publication collection of damages in a civil action; post publication correction of libel and other misstatements; discrimination in granting access to news source and facilities; discrimination and denial in the use of communications facilities for distribution; taxes; discriminatory subsidies; and interference with buying, reading and listening.

TRANSFORMATION

Habermas believed that society becomes increasingly polarised into spheres of "public authority"-referring to the emergence of the state and associated political activity-and the "private"-the intimate domain of private relationships and the family. Jürgen Habermas believed that the development of mass media was a crucial factor in the transition from an absolutist regime to liberal-democratic society. With the invention of the printing press and then the availability of newspapers and other forms of printed literature, Habermas claimed the emergence of an intermediate sphere which according to him is the bourgeois public sphere.

This space will provide individuals with a chance to gather together to critically access, discuss and evaluate important contemporary issues of utmost importance for the people. He claimed that this will resemble the Greek agora. Habermas claims that this public use of reason not only acts as a regulatory mechanism over the state, which is now highly visible, but also as a catalyst for the replacement of the absolutist regime with a liberal democratic government.

Frankfurt School

The Frankfurt School came into existence in order to explain the success of Nazism in Weimar Germany. It sees the loss of individuality through decline of privacy as the main cause of dependence on great mass organisations. Habermas to a certain extent depends on some early critiques of the media from the 'Frankfurt School', such as that of Max Horkheimer, Theodor Adorno and Herbert Marcuse. For these three, media was a 'culture industry' which was creating an impact on passive individuals. These individuals merely absorb any information they are exposed to.

According to Thompson, the cause of this is the commodification of art and culture, which allows the possibility of "manipulation by demagogues". Emile Durkheim claimed that the interdependence of highly specialised individuals, or what is known as 'organic solidarity', is seen as being succeeded by a new and barbarous homogeneity. Due to this, only a 'mechanical' cohesion is possible, dependent on similarity and standardisation. Horkheimer thus argued that, paradoxically, individuality was impaired by the decline in the impulse for collective action. According to him, 'As the ordinary man withdraws from participating in political affairs, society tends to revert to the law of the jungle, which crushes all vestiges of individuality.' In this analysis the Frankfurt school saw totalitarianism emerging as a result of corrupt social institutions and the decline of liberal principles.

Thus Horkheimer claimed that: "Just as the slogans of rugged individualism are politically useful to large trusts in society seeking exemption from social control, so in mass culture the rhetoric of individuality, by imposing patterns for collective imitation, subverts the very principle to which it gives lip service." Adorno in The Jargon of Authenticity claimed that "mass media can create an aura which makes the spectator seem to experience a non-existent actuality". Thus a mass-produced, artificial culture replaces what went before.

MASS MEDIA AND MODERN SOCIETY

In political behaviour, opinion leading tends to correlate positively with status, whereas this is not the case in consumer behaviour. So for political behaviour, the general conclusion that the media merely fixes (confirms) people's opinion is not supported. Hovland, using experimental psychology, found significant effects of information on longer-term behaviour and attitudes, particularly in areas where most people have little direct experience (e.g. politics) and have a high degree of trust in the source (e.g. broadcasting). Since class has become a less reliable indicator of party (since the surveys of the 40s and 50s) the floating voter today is no longer the apathetic voter, but likely to be more well-informed than the consistent voter-and this mainly through the media.

There is also some very persuasive and empirical evidence suggesting that it is 'personal contact, not media persuasiveness' which counts. For example, Trenaman and McQuail (1961) found that 'don't knows' were less well informed than consistent voters, appearing uninterested, showing a general lack of information, and not just ignorance of particular policies or policies of one particular party. During the 1940 presidential election, a similar view was expressed by Katz and Lazarsfeld's theory of the two-step flow of communication, based on a study of electoral practices of the citizens of Erie County, Ohio. This examined the political propaganda prevalent in the media at the time during the campaign period to see whether it plays an integral role in influencing people's voting.

The results contradict this: Lazarsfeld et. al. (1944) find evidence for the Weberian theory of party, and identify certain factors, such as socio-economic circumstances, religious affiliation and area of residence, which together determine political orientation. The study claims that political propaganda serves to re-affirm the individual's pre-disposed orientation rather than to influence or change one's voting behaviour.

Thompson does not see 'mediated quasi-interaction' (the monological, mainly one-way communication of the mass media) as dominant, but rather as intermingling with traditional face-to-face interactions and mediated interactions (such as telephone conversations). Contrary to Habermas' pessimistic view, this allows both more information and discussion to come into the public domain (of mediated quasi-interaction) and more to be discussed within the private domain (since the media provides information individuals would not otherwise have access to).

FREE ENTERPRISE SOCIETY

Although a sizeable portion of mass media offerings-particularly news, commentaries, documentaries, and other informational programmes-deal with highly controversial subjects, the major portion of mass media offerings are designed to serve an entertainment function. These programmes tend to avoid controversial issues and reflect beliefs and values sanctified by mass audience. This course is followed by Television networks, whose investment and production costs are high. Jerry Mander's work has highlighted this particular outlook. According to him, the atomised individuals of mass society lose their souls to the phantom delights of the film, the soap opera, and the variety show.

They fall into a stupor; an apathetic hypnosis Lazarsfeld was to call the 'narcotizing dysfunction' of exposure to mass media. Individuals become 'irrational victims of false wants'-the wants which corporations have thrust upon them, and continue to thrust upon them, through both the advertising in the media (with its continual exhortation to consume) and through the individualist consumption culture it promulgates. Thus, according to the Frankfurt School, leisure has been industrialised. The production of culture had become standardised and dominated by the profit motive as in other industries. In a mass society leisure is constantly used to induce the appropriate values and motives in the public. The modern media train the young for consumption. 'Leisure had ceased to be the opposite of work, and had become a preparation for it.'

MASS MEDIA, MASS CULTURE AND ELITE

The relation of the mass media to contemporary popular culture is commonly conceived in terms of dissemination from the elite to the mass. There are periods when this process is reversed. During the 18th century it was the utmost chic for the aristocrats of the French Court to assume the guise of shepherds and peasants in their restive outings.

The long-term consequences of this are significant in conjunction with the continuing concentration of ownership and control of the media, leading to accusations of a 'media elite' having a form of 'cultural dictatorship'. Thus the continuing debate about the influence of 'media barons' such as Conrad Black and Rupert Murdoch. For example, the UK Observer reported the Murdoch-owned HarperCollins' refusal to publish Chris Patten's East and West, because of the former Hong Kong Governor's description of the Chinese leadership as "faceless Stalinists" possibly being damaging to Murdoch's Chinese broadcasting interests. In this case, the author was able to have the book accepted by another publisher, but this kind of censorship may point the way to the future. A related, but more insidious, form is that of self-censorship by members of the media in the interests of the owner, in the interests of their careers.

MODERN MASS MEDIA

During the recent years mass media has invaded the life of a common man in a big way. Upto seventies, mass media mainly remained confined to cinema, newspaper and radio. It was in the early eighties that audio-visual electronic medium in the form of television invaded the Indian scenario in a big way. The Government created huge infrastructure for spread of television network in the country. During this decade itself, advent of computers and Video Cassette Recorders (VCR) also supplemented the audio-visual media, putting well established medium of cinema to shade. During the early nineties, satellite television revolutionised the audio-visual media by reaching most of the households in the urban areas.

The latest invasion of audio-visual electronic media has suddenly increased the demand for professionals in journalism, technicians and other service individuals. These careers not only offer excellent opportunities, salaries, challenge and satisfaction of work, but also provide an opportunity for self-employment in various fields.

PRINT MEDIA

An old saying goes "pen is mightier than sword". The saying is not just a rhetoric. It reflects the power of print media. Being the most important media, print media pertains to broad activity of publication of newspapers, magazines and books and all persons connected with this activity have their contribution in successful running of this medium. While writing of books and contributing to magazines is largely a self-employment occupation, publication of newspapers and magazines involves a huge work force such as editors, technicians, printing technicians, composers, etc.

In all these jobs the options of either working on desk or working in the field are available to the candidates. Reporters and correspondents generally operate in the field and submit their reports or stories on local, national or international issues pertaining to politics, trade, commerce, defence, sports, etc. One special category of reporters and correspondents operates in the field of investigative journalism.

This category of reporting pertains to investigation on the issues of public importance. This type of journalism and reporting attracts public attention instantaneously. Special attention in such reporting is required in the authenticity of information, selection of issues of public interest and succinct reporting in interesting and convincing language. In case of magazine reporting, many a times the reports, stories and features are contributed by free-lance reporters and part-time amateur writers. To pursue the career as a reporter one may attain bachelor's degree or post-graduate diploma in journalism.

Some of the universities offer post graduate diplomas of 9-month duration while others offer post-graduate one-year diploma in Public Relations or post graduate degree in mass-communication.

Latest trend in this regard is that big groups of newspapers advertise the posts of trainees in any of the above categories for which all graduates are eligible. After conducting the entrance examination, suitable graduate trainees, with flair for writing are selected and employed. In other words, now the formal academic qualification for being a reporter, copy writer or correspondent is not an essential qualification. Similarly, for writing features or analytical articles in magazines, one need not have any formal and professional academic qualification.

What is required is in-depth knowledge, command over the language concerned and outstanding analytical capability. Broadly speaking, anyone keen to pursue this career in any capacity must have outstanding general awareness, good perception, an eye for details and very keen observation. In turn, the career offers challenge, immense job satisfaction and fairly good compensation. For acquiring general awareness regular reading of newspapers, magazines and books on variety of topics is a must. Discussions on current topics also go a long way in widening the horizons of knowledge.

For the beginners, it is better to consult a good book on the background to current affairs so that further knowledge is strengthened after acquiring fundamental knowledge. Latest edition of "Current Affairs and Backgrounders" published by M/s Khanna Brothers (Publishers) Pvt Ltd is an ideal book for this purpose. Command over the concerned language is not a capability which can be acquired overnight. Regular and intensive reading as well as regular writing practice not only improves the command over the language, but also improves the flair for writing.

Candidates seriously pursuing this career should also go in for academic degree/diploma in Journalism/Public Relations/ Mass Communication from a good university or institute to have an edge over others.

AUDIO-VISUAL MEDIA

The requirement of personnel for the audio and audio-visual media is a little different than that for the print media. Traditionally, Radio has been the audio media having farthest reach. It was only with effect from the early eighties that Radio started getting replaced by Television. In most of the cases TV just supplemented the Radio. Despite the recent invasion by Doordarshan channels and Satellite and Cable TV, importance of Radio has not been undermined. The percentage of population covered by Radio is much more than the TV, mainly due to better technical infrastructure, longer range of short wave radio and cheaper cost and running cost of radio and transistors. Hence, Radio still remains very important medium.

Radio needs various types of personnel which includes announcers, news-readers, news-composers, writers, producers, commentators, and various categories of radio artists like singers, musicians, drama artists, narrators, etc. There is also a growing demand for good programmes and producers of such programmes. Audio-visual media is the strongest form of medium, but has limited reach. The earliest form of audio-visual medium was cinema which had very limited reach and people had to spend some money to have an access to it. Cinema, however, still enjoys the most glamorous place in the entire media. In this feature, Cinema as career in audio-visual media has been left out and will be covered later in a separate feature on careers.

Television, satellite and cable TV offer varied opportunities for career seekers. This medium offers excellent opportunities for newsreaders, composers, announcers, technicians, commentators, producers, models, actors, cameramen, script writers, etc. In addition to the Government-run Doordarshan, all other companies in the field of television, be it in production, direction, acting, cable operation and satellite TV operation, are handled by the individuals or private companies.

The choice of career is available in a variety of fields, not only with Doordarshan but with commercially-run media companies also. Candidates seeking any type of career in audio-visual electronic media must have characteristics like artistic inclination, expertise in own field of activity, pleasing personality, adaptability, general awareness, quick reflexes, flexibility and imagination. All these qualities must be coupled with the required technical and academic qualifications and professional competence. In case of announcers and newsreaders the qualities of good voice and presentable and photogenic face are additional requirements.

Good flow of spoken language and command over the language concerned are also pre-requisites in these cases. Capabilities to compare and compose become added qualifications. In addition to programmes and news, three other aspects of advertisement, engineering and management are also of paramount importance in TV and other electronic media. Technical and professional staff provide engineering services and act from behind the screen. These personnel are responsible for providing support services so essential for good quality of transmission, colour combinations, creation of support infrastructure for transmission, day-to-day management of video recording, time-management and other related aspects.

JOURNALISM

Journalism fascinates many young people who have a keen desire of seeing their name in print. Anyone who has written something for the college paper believes a career in journalism can be pursued. This feature points out that a career in journalism means more than merely writing well. As we receive a number of queries from our readers who want to become famous journalists and editors, we decided to describe in detail the requirements of newspapers and television channels today. This feature describes the skills required, as also the upside and the downside of the field. It also gives information about how one can become a journalist, the qualities that are required to be a successful one and addresses of some of the well known institutes. To an outsider, journalism is an exciting field in which fame and fortune can be achieved if one is able to write well. The names of some famous journalists come easily to mind. Khushwant Singh, who writes columns in several newspapers; M.J. Akbar, the editor of The Asian Age; and

Shobha De, former editor of Stardust and now a celebrated writer. Opportunities in the field have also multiplied with the boom in magazines and television channels.

Each of these requires people who can report and interpret events in a coherent and interesting manner. To assess whether you can be a famous journalist, you have to first know the skills that are required. The first is a good command over language. You must be able to express yourself well. A course in journalism will help sharpen these skills.

But this is not all. What is required is the ability to collect information and report events quickly. If you are in a television channel, it may mean going on camera as the event is happening, often a difficult task. In newspapers one has to write out the story before the deadline and it must contain all the correct information and the drama. Even a small error can destroy the credibility of the journalist. So journalism is just not about being able to write well alone.

The nature of a journalist's job is also changing. With news becoming competitive and personality-oriented, the job of a TV journalist often means waiting outside the offices or homes of politicians for hours and trying to catch a "sound byte" as the leader comes out.

The pursuit of truth does not extend beyond getting a small segment in the news programme. In this race, there is no room for being creative or following stories that one may like to. Threats of law-suits have made news channels and newspapers increasingly wary about publishing scoops and many of the investigative stories are just killed. There is little room for creativity in today's news organisations.

Increasing Scope

Once you accept these limitations, a career in journalism may be a good option. Some years back there was a boom in television channels which led to an increase in opportunities for aspiring journalists. Many print journalists shifted to television. Salaries had jumped. Today, there is a shakeout among the channels, which has led to the opportunities being reduced drastically. Newspapers and magazines continue to employ journalists, but with circulations and profitability under stress, three has been a decrease in opportunities somewhat. However, this situation may be linked to the economic slowdown and things may become better once the economy picks up. It may be mentioned that there are over 4,000 newspapers in 100 languages registered in India and the scope for employment will always exist, despite difficulties.

Avenues in journalism have multiplied because of unexpected growth in two new areas: (a) Niche publications; and (b) Web editing. We explain these below: Niche Publications: This means special purpose publications catering to particular industries, for example, travel and tourism, hotels, textiles or computers. Many such publications have been started in the past few years. These "niche" publications may not have the mass circulations of newspapers but are highly profitable. However, to work in them one needs to have journalistic skills as well as industry knowledge. Hence, MBAs are employed in business publications while computer experts find jobs in information technology magazines. The idea is to develop a specialisation and build on it. In the future, journalists with specialised skills in an industry may be more in demand than those with mere writing skills.

CULTURE AND DEMOCRACY

The Dominant Social Paradigm and Culture

A fruitful way to start the discussion of the significance of culture and its relationship to the mass media would be to define carefully our terms. This would help to avoid the confusion, which is not rare in discussions on the matter. Culture is frequently defined as the integrated pattern of human knowledge, belief, and behaviour. This is a definition broad enough to include all major aspects of culture: language, ideas, beliefs, customs, taboos, codes, institutions, tools, techniques, works of art, rituals, ceremonies and so on. However, in what follows, I am not going to deal with all these aspects of culture unless they are related to what I call the dominant social paradigm. By this I mean the system of beliefs, ideas and the corresponding values which are dominant in a particular society at a particular moment of its history. It is clear that there is a significant degree of overlapping between these two terms although the meaning of culture is obviously broader than that of the social paradigm.

But, let us see first the elements shared by both terms. Both culture and the social paradigm are time- and space-dependent, i.e. they refer to a specific type of society at a specific time. Therefore, they both change from place to place and from one historical period to another. This implies that there can be no 'general theory' of History, which could determine the relationship between the cultural with the political or economic elements in society.

In other words, our starting point is the rejection not only of the crude economistic versions of Marxism (the economic base determines the cultural superstructure) but also of the more sophisticated versions of it (the economic base determines 'in the last instance' which element is to be dominant in each social formation).

In my view, which I expanded elsewhere, the dominant element in each social formation is not determined, for all time, by the economic base, or any other base. The dominant element is always determined by a creative act, i.e. it is the outcome of social praxis, of the activity of social individuals. Thus, the dominant element in theocratic societies was cultural, in the societies of 'actually existing socialism' political and so on.

Similarly, the dominant element in market economies is economic, as a result of the fact that the introduction of new systems of production during the Industrial Revolution in a commercial society, where the means of production were under private ownership and control, inevitably led to the transformation of the socially- controlled economies of the past (in which the market played a marginal role in the economic process) into the present market economies (defined as the self-regulating systems in which the fundamental economic problems—what, how, and for whom to produce—are solved 'automatically', through the price mechanism, rather than through conscious social decisions).

Still, the existence of a dominant element in a social formation does not mean that the relationship between this element and the other elements in it is one of heteronomy and dependence. Each element is autonomous and the relationship between the various elements is better described as one of interdependence. So, although it is the economic element which is the dominant one in the system of the market economy, this does not mean that culture is determined, even 'in the last instance' by this element. But, there are also some important differences between culture and the dominant social paradigm. Culture, exactly because of its greater scope, may express values and ideas, which are not necessarily consistent with the dominant institutions. In fact, this is usually the case characterising the arts and literature of a market economy, where, (unlike the case of 'actually existing socialism', or the case of feudal societies before), artists and writers have been given a significant degree of freedom to express their own views. But this is not the case with respect to the dominant social paradigm. In other words, the beliefs, ideas and the corresponding values which are dominant in a market economy and the corresponding market society have to be consistent with the economic element in it, i.e. with the economic institutions which, in turn, determine that the dominant elites in this society are the economic elites (those owning and controlling the means of production).

This has always been the case in History and will also be the case in the future. No particular type of society can reproduce itself unless the dominant beliefs, ideas and values are consistent with the existing institutional framework. For instance, in the societies of 'actually existing socialism' the dominant social paradigm had to be consistent with the dominant element in them, (which was the political), and the corresponding political institutions, which determined that the dominant elites in this society were the political elites (party bureaucracy). Similarly, in the democratic society of the future, the dominant social paradigm had to be consistent with the dominant element in them, which would be the political, and the corresponding democratic institutions, which would secure that there would be no formal elites in this kind of society (although, of course, if democracy does not function properly the emergence of informal elites could not be ruled out).

So, culture and, in particular, the social dominant paradigm play a crucial role in the determination of individual and collective values. As long as individuals live in a society, they are not just individuals but social individuals, subject to a process, which socialises them and induces them to internalise the existing institutional framework as well as the dominant social paradigm. In this sense, people are not completely free to create their world but are conditioned by History, tradition and culture. Still, this socialisation process is broken, at almost all times-as far as a minority of the population is concerned-and in exceptional historical circumstances even with respect to the majority itself.

In the latter case, a process is set in motion that usually ends with a change of the institutional structure of society and of the corresponding social paradigm. Societies therefore are not just "collections of individuals" but consist of social individuals, who are both free to create their world, (in the sense that they can give birth to a new set of institutions and a corresponding social paradigm), and are created by the world, (in the sense that they have to break with the dominant social paradigm in order to recreate the world).

VALUES OF THE MARKET ECONOMY

As the dominant economic institutions in a market economy are those of markets and private ownership of the means of production, as well as the corresponding hierarchical structures, the dominant social paradigm promoted by the mainstream mass media and other cultural institutions, (e.g. universities) has to consist of ideas, beliefs and values which are consistent with them. Thus, the kind of social 'sciences' which are taught at universities and the kind of articles which fill academic journals, explicitly, or usually implicitly, take for granted the existing economic institutions.

Therefore, their search for 'truth' in the analysis of major economic or social problems is crucially conditioned by this fundamental characteristic. The causes of world-wide unemployment, for instance, or of massive inequality and concentration of economic power, will not be related to the system of the market economy itself; instead, the malfunctioning of the system or bad policies will be blamed, which supposedly can be tackled by the appropriate improvement of the system's functioning, or the 'right' economic policies.

In economics, in particular, the dominant theory/ideology since the emergence of the market economy has been economic liberalism, in its various versions: from the old classical and neo-classical schools up to the modern versions of it in the form of supply-side economics, new classical macro-economics etc. But, from Adam Smith to Milton Friedman, the values adopted are the same: competition and individualism, which, supposedly, are the only values that could secure freedom.

Thus, for Adam Smith, the individual pursuit of self-interest in a market economy will guarantee social harmony and, therefore, the main task of government is the defence of the rich against the poor. So, in Smith's system, as Canterbery puts it, 'individual self-interest is the motivating force, and the built-in regulator that keeps the economy from flying apart is competition'. Similarly, for Milton Friedman, the Nobel-prize winner in economics (note: the Nobel Prize in economics was never awarded to an economist who challenged the very system of the market economy) the capitalist market economy is identified with freedom:

> The kind of economic organisation that provides freedom directly, namely, competitive capitalism, also promotes political freedom because it separates economic power from political power and in this way enables the one to offset the other...The two ideas of human freedom and economic freedom working together came to their greatest fruition in the United States

It is obvious that in this ideology, which passes as the 'science' of economics, the values of individualism and competition are preferred over the values of collectivism and solidarity/co-operation, since freedom itself is identified with the former values as against the latter. But, it 'happens' also that the same values are the only ones, which could secure the production and reproduction of the market economy. No market economy can function properly unless those in control of it, (i.e., the economic elites), at least, and as many of the rest as possible, are motivated by individualism and competition.

This is because the dynamic of a market economy crucially depends on competition and individual greed. Furthermore, the fact that often the economic elites resort to state protection against foreign competition, if the latter threatens their own position, does not in the least negate the fact that competition is the fundamental organising principle of the market economy. It is therefore no historical accident that, as Polanyi has persuasively shown, the establishment of the market economy implied sweeping aside traditional cultures and values and replacing the values of solidarity, altruism, sharing and co-operation (which usually marked community life) with the values of individualism and competition as the dominant values. As Ray Canterbery stresses:

The capitalistic ethic leans toward the extreme of selfishness (fierce individualism) rather than toward altruism. There is little room for collective decision making in an ethic that argues that every individual should go his or her own way. As we have seen, the idea that capitalism protects 'individual rights' would have been rejected during the early Middle Ages. 'Individual rights' were set in advance by the structure of feudalism, governed by the pull of tradition and the push of authority. Economics was based upon mutual needs and obligations.

A good example of the enthusiastic support for these values today is, again, the Nobel-prize winner in economics Milton Friedman. According to him:

Few trends could so thoroughly undermine the very foundations of our free society as the acceptance by corporate officials of a social responsibility other than to make as much money for their stockholders as possible. This (social responsibility) is a fundamentally subversive doctrine.

Indeed, it is not Friedman who supports values which are inconsistent with the market economy system but the various social democrats and Green economists, who, taking for granted the market economy system, proceed to argue in favour of utopian economic institutions incorporating values which are inconsistent with this system (*e.g.*'stakeholding' capitalism, 'social investment' etc).

As I attempted to show elsewhere, the basic cause of the failure of both the 'actually existing socialism' in the East and social democracy in the West was exactly that they attempted to merge two fundamentally incompatible elements: the 'growth' element, (which implies the concentration of economic power and expresses the logic of the market economy), with the social justice element (which is inherently linked to equality and expresses socialist ethics).

Chomsky's Views

However, quite apart from social democrats and reformist Greens, there is an alternative view about the values of the market economy proposed by Noam Chomsky, which, however, ends up with similar conclusions about the feasibility and desirability of state action with respect to controlling today's market economy.

Thus, for Chomsky, the values which motivate today's elites in advanced capitalist countries are not individualism and competition; instead, these elites simply use such values as propaganda in their attempt to 'persuade' their own public and the countries in the periphery and semi-periphery to implement them whereas they themselves demand and enjoy the protection of their own states:

For the general public, individualism and competition are the prescribed values. Not for elites, however. They demand and obtain the protection of a powerful state, and insist on arrangements that safeguard them from unfettered competition or the destructive consequences of individualism. The process of corporatization is a standard illustration, as is the reliance in every economy—crucially, the US—on socialisation of risk and cost. The need to undermine the threat of competition constantly takes new forms: today, one major form, beyond corporatization, is the development of a rich network of "strategic alliances" among alleged competitors: IBM-Toshiba-Siemens, for example, or throughout the automotive industry.

This has reached such extremes that prominent analysts of the business world now speak of a new form of "alliance capitalism" that is replacing the managerial/corporate capitalism that had largely displaced proprietary capitalism a century ago in advanced sectors of the economy.

Chomsky has recently expanded on the same theme in a New Left Review article in which it is made clear that his views above about the values of the market economy are perfectly consistent with his views on the nature of today's capitalism. In this article he first states that the word 'capitalist' does not mean capitalist but rather it refers to state subsidised and protected private power centres, or 'collectivist legal entities,' which embody today's corporatization of the market economy. He then goes on to describe corporatization and the role of the state as follows:

The corporatization process was largely a reaction to great market failures of the late nineteenth century, and it was a shift from something you might call proprietary capitalism to the administration of markets by collectivist legal entities-mergers, cartels, corporate alliances-in association with powerful states...the primary task of the states-and bear in mind that, with all the talk about minimising the state, in the OECD countries the state continues to grow relative to GNP, notably in the 1980s and 1990s-is essentially to socialise risk and cost, and to privatise power and profit.

Furthermore, Chomsky's views about the market economy's values and the nature of present capitalism are, in turn, entirely consistent with his present views on the potential role of the state in controlling today's market economy. Thus, as Chomsky stresses in the aforementioned article: The long-term goal of such initiatives (like the Multilateral Agreement on Investment-MAI) is clear enough to anyone with open eyes; an international political economy which is organised by powerful states and secret bureaucracies whose primary function is to serve the concentrations of private power which administer markers through their own internal operations, through networks of corporate alliances, including the intra-firm transactions that are mislabelled 'trade'. They rely on the public for subsidy, research and development, for innovation and for bailouts when things go wrong. They rely on the powerful states for protection from dangerous 'democracy openings'. In such ways, they seek to ensure that the 'prime beneficiaries' of the world's wealth are the right people: the smug and prosperous 'Americans'; the 'domestic constituencies and their counterparts elsewhere. The scale of all of this is nowhere near as great or, for that matter, as novel as claimed; in many ways it's a return to the early twentieth century. And there's no reason to doubt that it can be controlled even within existing formal institutions of parliamentary democracy.

One, however, could object on several grounds this stand, as portrayed by the above extracts. First, the argument about the values of the economic elites, as I attempted to show above, is contestable; second, the nature of today's market economy could be seen in a very different analytical framework than the one suggested by Chomsky and, finally, it could be shown that the way out of the present multi-dimensional crisis and the related huge concentration of power can not be found in fragmented and usually 'monothematic' defensive battles with the elites. Such battles, even if sometimes victorious, are never going to win the war, as long as they are not an integral part of a new popular movement's fight against the system of the market economy itself, which is the ultimate cause of the concentration of economic power.

Shift from proprietary (or entrepreneurial) capitalism to the present internationalised market economy, where a few giant corporations control the world economy, did not happen, as Chomsky presents it, as the outcome of 'a reaction to great market failures of the late nineteenth century.' What Chomsky omits is that it was competition, which led from simple entrepreneurial firms to the present giant corporations.

The market failures he mentions are not a God-given calamity. Excepting the case of monopolies, almost all market failures in history have been directly or indirectly related to competition. It is competition, which creates the need for expansion, so that the best (from the profit of view of profits) technologies and methods of organising production (economies of scale etc) are used. It is the same competition, which has led to the present explosion of mergers and take-overs in the advanced capitalist countries, as well as the various 'strategic alliances'. For instance, the recently announced merger of giant oil companies, in a sense, is the result of a 'market failure' because of the fall in their profits. But, in a deeper sense, this merger, as well as the take-overs, strategic alliances etc going on at the moment, are simply the result of self-protective action taken by giant corporations, in order to survive the cut-throat competition launched by the present internationalisation of the market economy. Therefore, it is competition, which has led to the present corporate (or 'alliance') capitalism, not 'market failures' and/or the associated state activity, which just represent the effects of competition.

Similarly, the present internationalisation of the market economy is not just the result of state action to liberalise financial and commodity markets. In fact, the states were following the de facto internationalisation of the market economy, which was intensified by the activities of multinationals, when, (in the late seventies), under pressure from the latter, started the process of liberalising the financial markets and further deregulating the commodity markets (through the GATT rounds). Therefore, the present internationalisation is in fact the outcome of the grow-or-die dynamics, which characterises the market economy, a dynamics that is initiated by competition, the crucial fact neglected by Chomsky.

It is also the same internationalisation of the market economy, which became incompatible with the degree of state control of the economy achieved by the mid seventies, that made necessary the present neoliberal consensus. The latter, therefore, is not just a policy change, as socialdemocrats and their fellow travellers suggest, but represents an important structural change. So, minimising the state is not just 'talk', as Chomsky assumes basing his argument on the assumption that 'the state continues to grow relative to GNP, notably in the 1980s and 1990s'. However, not only the fall in the growth rate of government spending in OECD countries was higher than that of the other parts of aggregate demand in the period 1980-93 but, in fact, the (weighted average) general government consumption of high income economies was lower in 1995, at 15% of GNP, than in 1980 (17%). All this, not taking into account the drastic reduction in the overall public sectors in the last twenty years, as a result of the massive privatisation of state industries. Therefore, minimising the state, far from being 'talk' is a basic element of the present neoliberal consensus.

Also, strategic alliances, mergers and take-overs do not represent a movement away from the market economy but a movement towards a new form of it. Away from a market economy, which was geared by the internal market and towards a market economy, which is geared by the world market. This means further and further concentration of economic power not only in terms of incomes and wealth but also in terms of concentration of the power to control world output, trade and investment in fewer and fewer hands. However, the oligopolisation of competition does not mean lack of competition.

Furthermore, it will be wrong to assume that the main characteristic of the present period is an 'assault against the markets', as the purist neoliberal argument goes, which Chomsky accepts. The present period of neoliberal consensus can be characterised instead, as an assault against social controls on markets, particularly those aiming at the protection of humans and nature against the effects of marketization, (the historical process that has transformed the socially controlled economies of the past into the market economy of the present). Such controls have been introduced as a result of social struggles undertaken by those who are adversely affected by the market economy's effects on them (social security legislation, welfare benefits, macro-economic controls to secure full employment etc).

What is still debated within the economic elites is the fate of what I call social controls in the broad sense, i.e. those primarily aiming at the protection of those controlling the market economy against foreign competition (tariffs, import controls, exchange controls—in the past, and non-tariff barriers, massive public subsidy for R&D, risk-protection (bailouts), administration of markets etc—at present). Thus, pure neoliberal economists, bankers, some politicians and others are against any kind of social controls over markets (in the narrow or broad sense above). On the other hand, the more pragmatic governments of the neoliberal consensus, from Reagan to Clinton and from Thatcher to Blair, under the pressure of the most vulnerable to competition sections of their own economic elites, have kept many social controls in the broad sense and sometimes even expanded them (not hesitating to go to war to secure their energy supplies) giving rise to the pure neoliberal argument (adopted by Chomsky) about an assault on markets.

In this context, one should not confuse liberalism/neoliberalism with laissez-faire. As I tried to show elsewhere, it was the state itself that created the system of self-regulating markets. Furthermore, some form of state intervention has always been necessary for the smooth functioning of the market economy system. The state, since the collapse of the socialdemocratic consensus, has seen a drastic reduction in its economic role as it is no longer involved in a process of directly intervening in the determination of income and employment through fiscal and monetary policies.

However, even today, the state still plays an important role in securing, through its monopoly of violence, the stability of the market economy framework and in maintaining the infrastructure for the smooth functioning of it. It is within this role of maintaining the infrastructure that we may see the activities of the state in socialising risk and cost and in maintaining a safety net in place of the old welfare state. Furthermore, the state is called today to play a crucial role with respect to the supply-side of the economy and, in particular, to take measures to improve competitiveness and to train the working force to the requirements of the new technology, in supporting research and development and even in subsidising export industries wherever required.

Therefore, the type of state intervention which is compatible with the marketization process not only is not discouraged but, instead, is actively promoted by most of the professional politicians of the neoliberal consensus.

It is true that the economic elites do not like the kind of competition which, as a result of the uneven development of the world market economy, threatens their own interests and this is why they have always attempted (and mostly succeeded) to protect themselves against it.

But, it is equally true that it was the force of competition which has always fuelled the expansion of the market economy and that it was the values of competition and self-interest which have always characterised the value system of the elites which control the market economy. Chomsky, however, sometimes gives the impression that, barring some 'accidents' like the market failures he mentions, as well as the aggressive state support that economic elites have always enjoyed, the 'corporatization' of the market economy might have been avoided.

But, of course, neither proprietary capitalism (or any other type of it) is desirable—since it cannot secure covering the basic needs of all people—nor can we deny all radical analysis of the past hundred and fifty years or so, from Marx to Bookchin, and all historical experience since then, which leads to one conclusion: the market economy is geared by a grow-or-die dynamic fuelled by competition, which is bound to lead to further and further concentration of economic power.

Therefore, the problem is not the corporatization of the market economy which, supposedly, represents 'an attack on markets and democracy', and which was unavoidable anyway within the dynamic of the market economy. In other words, the problem is not corporate market economy/capitalism, as if some other kind of market economy/capitalism was feasible or desirable, but the market economy/capitalism itself. Otherwise, one may easily end up blaming the elites for violating the rules of the game, rather than blaming the rotten game itself!

If the above analytical framework is valid then obviously it is not possible, within the existing institutional framework of parliamentary democracy and the market economy to check the process of increasing concentration of economic power. This is a process that is going since the emergence of the market economy system, some two centuries ago, and no social-democratic governments or grassroots movements were ever able to stop it, or even to retard it, apart from brief periods of time. In fact, even the grass root 'victory' hailed by Chomsky against the MAI proposals is doubtful whether it would have been achieved had there been no serious divisions among the economic elites about it.

Furthermore, the 'victory' itself has already started showing signs that it was hollow, as it is now clear that the MAI agreement was not, in fact, set aside, but it is simply implemented 'by installments', through the 'back door' of the IMF at present, and possibly the World Trade Organisation in the future. The basic reason why such battles are doomed is that they are not an integral part of a comprehensive political program to replace the institutional framework of the market economy itself and, as such, they can easily be marginalised or lead to simple (easily reversible) reforms.

The inevitable conclusion is that only the struggle for the building of a new massive movement aiming at fighting 'from without' for the creation of a new institutional framework, and the development of the corresponding culture and social paradigm, might have any chances to lead to a new society characterised by the equal distribution of power.

CULTURAL HOMOGENISATION

The establishment of the market economy implied sweeping aside traditional cultures and values. This process was accelerated in the twentieth century with the spreading all over the world of the market economy and its offspring the growth economy. As a result, today, there is an intensive process of culture homogenisation at work, which not only rules out any directionality towards more complexity, but in effect is making culture simpler, with cities becoming more and more alike, people all over the world listening to the same music, watching the same soap operas on TV, buying the same brands of consumer goods, etc.

The establishment of the neoliberal consensus in the last twenty years or so, following the collapse of the socialdemocratic consensus, has further enhanced this process of cultural homogenisation. This is the inevitable outcome of the liberalisation and de-regulation of markets and the consequent intensification of commercialisation of culture.

As a result, traditional communities and their cultures are disappearing all over the world and people are converted to consumers of a mass culture produced in the advanced capitalist countries and particularly the USA. In the film industry, for instance, even European countries with a strong cultural background and developed economies have to effectively give up their own film industries, unable to compete with the much more competitive US industry. Thus, in the early 1990s, US films' share amounted to 73% of the European market. Also, indicative of the degree of concentration of cultural power in the hands of a few US corporations is the fact that, in 1991, a handful of US distributors controlled 66% of total cinema box office and 70% of the total number of video rentals in Britain.

Thus, the recent emergence of a sort of "cultural" nationalism in many parts of the world expresses a desperate attempt to keep a cultural identity in the face of market homogenisation. But, cultural nationalism is devoid of any real meaning in an electronic environment, where 75 percent of the international communications flow is controlled by a small number of multinationals. In other words, cultural imperialism today does not need, as in the past, a gunboat diplomacy to integrate and absorb diverse cultures.

The marketization of the communications flow has already established the preconditions for the downgrading of cultural diversity into a kind of superficial differentiation akin to a folklorist type.

Furthermore, it is indicative that today's 'identity movements', like those in Western Europe (from the Flemish to the Lombard and from the Scots to the Catalans) which demand autonomy as the best way to preserve their cultural identity, in fact, express their demand for individual and social autonomy in a distorted way.

The distortion arises from the fact that the marketization of society has undermined the community values of reciprocity, solidarity and co-operation in favour of the market values of competition and individualism. As a result, the demand for cultural autonomy is not founded today on community values which enhance co-operation with other cultural communities but, instead, on market values which encourage tensions and conflicts with them. In this connection, the current neoracist explosion in Europe is directly relevant to the effectual undermining of community values by neoliberalism, as well as to the growing inequality and poverty following the rise of the neoliberal consensus.

Finally, one should not underestimate the political implications of the commercialisation and homogenisation of culture. The escapist role traditionally played by Hollywood films has now acquired a universal dimension, through the massive expansion of TV culture and its almost full monopolisation by Hollywood subculture.

Every single TV viewer in Nigeria, India, China or Russia now dreams of the American way of life, as seen on TV serials (which, being relatively inexpensive and glamorous, fill the TV programmes of most TV channels all over the world) and thinks in terms of the competitive values imbued by them. The collapse of existing socialism has perhaps more to do with this cultural phenomenon, as anecdotal evidence indicates, than one could imagine.

As various TV documentaries have shown, people in Eastern European countries, in particular, thought of themselves as some kind of 'abnormal' compared with what western TV has established as the 'normal'.

In fact, many of the people participating in the demonstrations to bring down those regimes frequently referred to this 'abnormality', as their main incentive for their political action. In this problematique, one may criticise the kind of cultural relativism supported by some in the Left, according to which almost all cultural preferences could be declared as rational (on the basis of some sort of rationality criteria), and therefore all cultural choices deserve respect, if not admiration, given the constraints under which they are made. But, obviously, the issue is not whether our cultural choices are rational or not. Nor the issue is to assess 'objectively' our cultural preferences as right or wrong. The real issue is how to make a choice of values which we think is compatible with the kind of society we wish to live in and then make the cultural choices which are compatible with these values.

This is because the transition to a future society based on alternative values presupposes that the effort to create an alternative culture should start now, in parallel with the effort to establish the new institutions compatible with the new values. On the basis of the criterion of consistency between our cultural choices and the values of a truly democratic society, one could delineate a way beyond post-modern relativism and distinguish between 'preferable' and 'non-preferable' cultural choices.

So, all those cultural choices involving films, videos, theatrical plays etc, which promote the values of the market economy and particularly competition for money, individualism, consumerist greed, as well as violence, racism, sexism etc should be shown to be non-preferable and people should be encouraged to avoid them. On the other hand, all those cultural choices, which involve the promotion of the community values of mutual aid, solidarity, sharing and equality for all (irrespective of race, sex, ethnicity) should be promoted as preferable.

2

CONTRIBUTION OF MEDIA IN SOCIETY

INTRODUCTION

A basic issue in the discussion of the role of the mass media in today's society is whether they do reflect social reality in a broad sense, or whether, instead, the elites which control them filter out the view of reality which they see fit to be made public. To my mind, the answer to this question is that the media do both, depending on the way we define reality.

To take, first, political reality, mass media, in one sense, do not provide a faked view of it. Taking into account what is considered as politics today, i.e. the activity of professional politicians 'representing' the people, one may argue that it is politics itself, which is faked, and mass media simply reproduce this reality. In this sense, the issue is not whether the mass media manipulate democracy, since it is democracy itself, which is faked, and not its mass media picture, which simply reflects the reality of present 'democracy'.

But, at the same time, if we give a different definition to political reality, mass media do provide, in general, a distorted picture of it. In other words, if we define as real politics the political activity of people themselves (for instance, the collective struggles of various sectors of the population around political, economic or social issues) rather than that of professional politicians, then, the mass media do distort the picture they present about political reality. They do so, by minimising the significance of this type of activity, by distorting its meaning, by marginalising it, or by simply ignoring it completely.

Furthermore, mass media do provide a distorted picture of political reality when they come to report the causes of crises, or of the conflicts involving various sections of the elites. In such cases they faithfully reflect the picture that the sections of the elites controlling them wish to reproduce. The latest example of this was the way in which the Anglo-American media, in particular, distorted the real meaning of the criminal bombardment of the Iraqi people at the end of 1998. Thus, exactly, as in their reporting during the war in the Gulf, the real cause of the conflict, (i.e. who controls the world's oil, irrespective of where the oil stocks are located—the elites of the North versus those in the South), was distorted as a conflict between the peace loving regimes in the North versus the rogue regimes in the South, or, in more sophisticated versions supported by socialdemocrat intellectuals, as a conflict between the 'democracies' in the North versus the 'despotic regimes' in the South over the control of oil.

Under these circumstances, it is obvious that the mass media usually offer a true glimpse of reality only when the elites are divided with respect to their conception of a particular aspect of political reality. From this point of view, concentration in the mass media industry is significant and whether the media are owned by 100 or 10 owners does indeed matter in the struggle for social change. It is for instance such divisions among the European elites over the issue of joining the European Monetary Union which have allowed a relatively wide media discussion on the true meaning of European integration, particularly in countries like Britain where the elites were split.

It was also similar divisions between the Anglo-American and the European elites over the latest war crime in the Gulf which made a bit clearer the directly criminal role of the former (support for the bombardments), as well as the indirectly criminal role of the latter (support for the embargo). It is not accidental that in the USA and UK, where the media played a particularly despicable role in distorting the truth and misinforming the public, the polls showed consistently vast majorities in favour of the criminal activities of their elites. Of course, this does not mean that decentralisation of power in the mass media industry (or anywhere else) represents by itself, even potentially, a radical social change leading to an authentic democracy. Still, the significance of decentralisation in the media industry with respect to raising consciousness should not be ignored.

THE ECONOMIC REALITY

As regards economic reality, mass media, in one sense again, do provide a relatively accurate picture of what counts as economic reality today. This is when the media, taking for granted the system of the market economy, end up with a partial picture of economic reality where what matters is not whether the basic needs of the population are covered adequately but whether prices (in commodity and stock markets), interest rates, exchange rates and consequently profit rates are going up or down. Still, in another sense, the very fact that mass media take for granted the system of the market economy means that they cannot 'see' the 'systemic' nature of most of the real economic problems (unemployment, poverty and so on) and therefore inevitably end up with a faked image of economic reality. This way of seeing economic reality is not imposed on the media by their owners, important as their influence may otherwise be, or by their internal hierarchical structure etc. The media simply reflect the views of orthodox economists, bankers, businessmen and professional politicians, i.e. of all those who express the dominant social paradigm.

But if the picture of political and economic reality offered by the media is mixed this is not the case with respect to ecological reality. As no meaningful reporting of the ecological crisis is possible unless it refers to the systemic causes of it, which by definition are excluded by the discourse in the mainstream media, the result is a complete misinformation, or just straightforward description of the symptoms of the crisis. The mass media are flooded by the 'realist' Greens who fill the various ecological parties and who blame technology, consumerist values, legislation etc—anything but the real cause of the crisis, i.e. the very system of the market economy.

Similarly, the reporting of the present social crisis never links the explosion of crime and drug abuse, for instance, with their root cause, i.e. the increasing concentration of political, economic and social power in the hands of various elites. Instead, the symptoms of the social crisis are distortedly reported as its causes and the media blame, following the advice of the establishment 'experts', the breaking of the traditional family, or of the school, as the causes of crime. Similarly, various 'progressive' intellectuals (like the lamentable ex 'revolutionary' and now well promoted by the mainstream media Euro-parliamentarian Con Bendit) blame the prohibitive legislation on drugs for the massive explosion of drug abuse!

However, there is another approach being promoted recently by system theorists, according to which mass media do not just either reflect or distort reality but also manufacture it. This is not said in the usual sense of manufacturing consent described by Chomsky and Herman or, alternatively, by Bourdieu, which is basically a one-way process whereby the elites controlling the mass media filter out the information, through various control mechanisms, in order to create consent around their agenda. Instead, system theorists talk about a two-way process whereby social reality and mass media are seen as two interdependent levels, the one intruding into the other. This is based on the valid hypothesis that reality is not just something external to the way it is conceived. TV watching is a constituent moment of reality since our information about reality consists of conceptions that constitute reality itself. At the same time, the conception of reality is conditioned by the media functioning, which is differentiated in relation to the other social systems (political, economic etc).

In the systems analysis problematique, it is not the economic, or the political systems, which control the media functioning. What determines their functioning, as well as their communicative capability, is their ability to generate irritation- a fact that could go a long way to explain the high ratings of exciting or irritating TV programs.

The diversified functioning of mass media creates, in turn, the conditions for a social dynamic which, in a self-reflective and communicative way, reproduces, as well as institutes, society. Thus, whereas the early modern society is instituted through a transcendental subjectivity and a material mode of production, the present post-modern society's reproduction depends on the processes of communicative rationality. The mass media are an integral and functional part of the communicative processes of post-modern society.

However, one may point out here that although it is true that social reality and mass media are interacting, i.e. that our conception of TV news is a constituent element of reality and at the same time our conception of reality is conditioned by TV functioning, this does not imply that the diversified functioning of mass media creates the conditions for a social dynamic which acts for the institution of society, although it does play this role as far as its reproduction is concerned. The meaning we assign to TV reporting is not determined exogenously but by our world view, our own paradigm, which in turn, as we have seen above, is the result of a process of socialisation that is conditioned by the dominant social paradigm.

Furthermore, TV functioning plays a crucial role in the reproduction of the dominant social paradigm and the socialisation process generally. So, the diversified functioning of TV does indeed create the conditions for a social dynamic leading to the reproduction of the status quo, but in no way could be considered as doing the same for instituting society.

AIMS AND ACHIEVEMENTS

The goals of the mass media are determined by those owning and controlling them, who, usually, are members of the economic elites that control the market economy itself. Given the crucial role that the media could play in the internalisation of the dominant social paradigm and therefore the reproduction of the institutional framework which secures the concentration of power in the hands of the elites, it is obvious that those owning and controlling the mass media have broader ideological goals than the usual goals pursued by those owning and controlling other economic institutions, i.e. profit maximising.

Therefore, an analysis that would attempt to draw conclusions on the nature and significance of media institutions on the basis of the profit dimension alone, (i.e. that they share a common goal and consequently a similar internal hierarchical structure with all other economic institutions and that they just sell a product, the only difference with other economic institutions being that the product is the audience,) is bound to be one-dimensional. Profit maximising is only one parameter, often not even the crucial one, which conditions the role of mass media in a market economy. In fact, one could mention several instances where capitalist owners chose even to incur significant losses (which they usually cover from other profitable activities) in order to maintain the social influence (and prestige), which ownership of an influential daily offers to them (Murdoch and The Times of London is an obvious recent example).

Given the ultimate ideological goal of mass media, the main ways in which they try to achieve it are:

- first, by assisting in the internalisation of the dominant social paradigm and,
- second, by marginalising, if not excluding altogether, conceptions of reality which do not conform with the dominant social paradigm.

But, what are the mechanisms through which the media can achieve their goals? To give an answer to this question we have to examine a series of mechanisms, most of them 'automatic' built-in mechanisms, which ensure effective achievement of these goals. It will be useful here to distinguish between 'internal' and 'external' control mechanisms, which function respectively as internal and external constraints on the freedom of media workers to reproduce reality.

Both internal and external mechanisms work mainly through competition which secures homogenisation with respect to the media's main goals. Competition is of course the fundamental organisational principle of a market economy; but, it plays a special role with respect to the media. As Bourdieu points out, competition 'rather than automatically generating originality and diversity tends to favour uniformity'. Still, competition is not the only force securing homogenisation. In a similar way as with the market economy itself, competition provides only the dynamic mechanism of homogenisation.

It is the fact that owners of mass media, as well as managers and the highest paid journalists, share the same interest in the reproduction of the existing institutional framework which constitutes the 'base', on which this competition is developed.

But, let us consider briefly the significance of the various control mechanisms. The main 'internal control' mechanisms are ownership and the internal hierarchical structure, which are, both, crucial in the creation of the conditions for internal competition among journalists, whereas the 'ratings' mechanism plays a similar role in the creation of the conditions for external competition among media.

Starting with ownership, it matters little, as regards the media's overall goals defined above, whether they are owned and controlled by the state and/or the state-controlled institutions or whether, instead, they are owned and controlled by private capital.

However, there are certain secondary differences arising from the different ownership structures which may be mentioned. These secondary differences have significant implications, particularly with respect to the structure of the elites controlling the media, their own organisational structure and their 'image' with respect to their supposedly 'objective' role in the presentation of information.

As regards the elite structure, whereas under a system of state ownership and control the mass media are under the direct control of the political elite and the indirect control of the economic elites, under a system of private ownership and control, the media are just under the direct control of the economic elites.

This fact, in turn, has some implications on whether filtering out of information takes place directly through state control, or indirectly through various economic mechanisms (e.g. ratings).As regards the media organisational structure, whereas state-owned media are characterised by bureaucratic rigidity and inefficiency, privately owned media are usually characterised by more flexibility and economic efficiency. Finally, the 'objective' image of mass media suffers less in case of private ownership compared to the case of state ownership. This is because in the latter case control of information is more direct and therefore more obvious than in the former.

Another important internal control mechanism is the hierarchical structure which characterises all media institutions (as it does all economic institutions in a market economy) and which implies that all-important decisions are taken by a small managerial group within them, who are usually directly responsible to the owners.

The hierarchical structure creates a constant internal competition among journalists as to who will be more agreeable to the managerial group (on which their career and salary prospects depend).

Similarly, people in the managerial group are in constant competition as to who will be more agreeable to the owners (on which their highly paid position depends). So, everybody in this hierarchical structure knows well (or soon learns) what is agreeable and what is not and acts accordingly.

Therefore, the filtering of information works through self-censorship rather than through any kind of 'orders from above'. The effect of the internal hierarchical structure is to impose, through the internal competition that it creates, a kind of homogenisation in the journalists' performance.

But, does this exclude the possibility that some media workers may have incentives other those determined by career ambitions? Of course, not. But, such people, as Chomsky points out, will never find a place in the corridors of media power and, one way or another, will be marginalised:

They (journalists) say, quite correctly, "nobody ever tells me what to write. I write anything I like. All this business about pressures and constraints is nonsense because I'm never under any pressure." Which is completely true, but the point is that they wouldn't be there unless they had already demonstrated that nobody has to tell them what to write because they are going to say the right thing... it is not purposeful censorship. It is just that you don't make it to those positions. That includes the left (what is called the left), as well as the right. Unless you have been adequately socialised and trained so that there are some thoughts you just don't have, because if you did have them, you wouldn't be there.

But, how is it determined what is agreeable? Here it is where the 'external' control mechanisms come into play. It is competition among the various media organisations, which homogenises journalists' behaviour.

This competition takes the form of a struggle to improve ratings (as regards TV channels) or circulation (as regards newspapers, magazines etc). Ratings or circulation are important not per se but because the advertising income of privately owned mass media (which is the extra income determining their survival or death) depends on them. The result is, as Pierre Bourdieu points out that: Ratings have become the journalist's Last Judgement... Wherever you look, people are thinking in terms of market success.

Only thirty years ago, and since the middle of the nineteenth century—since Baudelaire and Flaubert and others in avant-garde milieux of writers' writers, writers acknowledged by other writers or even artists acknowledged by other artists—immediate market success was suspect. It was taken as a sign of compromise with the times, with money... Today, on the contrary, the market is accepted more and more as a legitimate means of Iegitimation.

The pressures created by the ratings mechanism, as Bourdieu points out, have nothing to do with the democratic expression of enlightened collective opinion or public rationality, despite what media ideologues assert. In fact, as the same author points out, the ratings mechanism is the sanction of the market and the economy, that is, of an external and purely market law.

I would only add to this that given how 'public opinion' is formed within the process of socialisation and internalisation of the dominant social paradigm, it is indeed preposterous to characterise the ratings mechanism as somehow expressing the democratic will of the people. Ratings, as well as polls generally, is the 'democracy of the uninformed'. They simply reflect the ignorance, the half-truths, or the straightforward distortions of the truth which have been assimilated by an uninformed public and which, through the ratings mechanism, reinforce the role of the mass media in the reproduction of the dominant social paradigm.

One may therefore conclude that the role of the media today is not to make the system more democratic. In fact, one basic function of the media is, as Chomsky stresses, to help in keeping the general population out of the public arena because 'if they get involved they will just make trouble.

Their job is to be "spectators," not "participants". Furthermore, the media can play a crucial role in offsetting the democratic rights and freedoms won after long struggles. This has almost always been the case when there was a clash between the elites and trade unions, or popular movements generally. Walter Lippmann, the revered American journalist was explicit about it, as Chomsky points out. For Lippmann, there is a new art in the method of democracy, called "manufacture of consent." By manufacturing consent, you can overcome the fact that formally a lot of people have the right to vote. We can make it irrelevant because we can manufacture consent and make sure that their choices and attitudes will be structured in such a way that they will always do what we tell them, even if they have a formal way to participate. So we'll have a real democracy. It will work properly. That's applying the lessons of the propaganda agency. Within this analytical framework we may explore fruitfully the particular ways through which the filtering of information is achieved, as, for instance, is described by Chomsky and Herman in their 'propaganda model'. Similarly Bourdieu shows in a graphic way how the filtering of information takes place in television, through the structuring of TV debates, the time limits, the methods of hiding by showing etc. Particularly important is the way in which the media, particularly television, control not just the information flow, but also the production of culture, by controlling the access of academics as well as of cultural producers, who in turn, as a result of being recognised a public figures, gain recognition in their own fields.

Thus, at the end, the journalistic field, which is structurally very strongly subordinated to market pressures and as such is a very heteronomous field, applies pressure, in turn, to all other fields. An illustrative application of the above analytical framework is the crucial contribution of the mass media in the creation of the subjective conditions for the neoliberal consensus. Thus, the mass media have played a double ideological role with respect to the neoliberal consensus. On the one hand, they have promoted directly the neoliberal agenda:

- by degrading the economic role of the state,
- by attacking the 'dependence' on the state which the welfare state supposedly creates,
- by identifying freedom with the freedom of choice, which is supposedly achieved through the liberation of markets etc. (talk radio and similar TV shows play a particularly significant role in this respect).

On the other hand, the media have also attempted to divert attention from the consequences of the neoliberal consensus (in terms of growing inequality and poverty, the explosion of crime and drug abuse and so on):

- by promoting irrational beliefs of all sorts (religion, mystical beliefs, astrology etc). The film and video explosion on the themes of exorcism, supernatural powers etc (induced mainly by Hollywood) has played a significant role in diverting attention from the evils of neoliberalism.
- by manufacturing irrelevant and/or insignificant 'news stories' (e.g. Monica Lewinsky affair), which are then taken over by opposition politicians who are eager to find fictitious ways (because of the lack of real political differences within the neoliberal consensus) to differentiate themselves from those in power.
- by creating a pseudo 'general interest' (for instance around a nationalist or chauvinist cause) in order to

unite the population around a 'cause' and make it forget the utterly dividing aspects of neoliberalism.

At the same time, the creation of the neoliberal conditions at the institutional level had generated the objective conditions for the mass media to play the aforementioned role. This was because the deregulation and liberalisation of markets and the privatisation of state TV in many European countries had created the conditions for homogenisation through the internal and external competition, which I mentioned above. It is not accidental anyway that major media tycoons like Murdoch in the Anglo-Saxon world, Kirsch in Germany, or Berlusconi in Italy have also been among the main exponents of the neoliberal consensus agenda.

3

Television an Effective Communication Channel

HISTORY

Television first came to India (named as Doordarshan or DD) as the National Television Network of India. The first telecast started on September 15, 1959 in New Delhi. After a gap of about 13 years, second television station was established in Mumbai (Maharashtra) in 1972 and by 1975 there were five more television stations at Srinagar (Kashmir), Amritsar (Punjab), Calcutta (West Bengal), Madras (Tamil Nadu) and Lucknow (Uttar Pradesh). For many years the transmission was mainly in black & white. Television industry got the necessary boost in the eighties when Doordarshan introduced colour TV during the 1982 Asian Games.

1980s: Indian small screen programming started off in the early 1980s. At that time there was only one national channel Doordarshan, which was government owned. The Ramayana and Mahabharata was the first major television series produced. This serial notched up the world record in viewer ship numbers for a single program.

By the late 1980s more and more people started to own television sets. Though there was a single channel, television programming had reached saturation. Hence the government opened up another channel which had part national programming and part regional. This channel was known as DD 2 later DD Metro. Both channels were broadcast terrestrially.

Post Liberalization Television: The central government launched a series of economic and social reforms in 1991 under Prime Minister Narasimha Rao. Under the new policies the government allowed private and foreign broadcasters to engage in limited operations in India. This process has been pursued consistently by all subsequent federal administrations. Foreign channels like CNN, Star TV and domestic channels such as Zee TV and Sun TV started satellite broadcasts. Starting with 41 sets in 1962 and one channel (Audience Research unit, 1991) at present TV in India covers more than 70 million homes giving a viewing population more than 400 million individuals through more than 100 channels. A large relatively untapped market, easy accessibility of relevant technology and a variety of programmes are the main reasons for rapid expansion of Television in India.

Cable Television: In 1992, the government liberated its markets, opening them up to cable television. Five new channels belonging to the Hong Kong based STAR TV gave Indians a fresh breath of life. MTV, STAR Plus, BBC, Prime Sports and STAR Chinese Channel were the 5 channels. Zee TV was the first private owned Indian channel to broadcast over cable. A few years later CNN, Discovery Channel, National Geographic Channel made its foray into India. Star expanded its bouquet introducing STAR World, STAR Sports, ESPN and STAR Gold. Regional channels flourished along with a multitude of Hindi channels and a few English channels. By 2001 HBO and History Channel were the other international channels to enter India. By 2001-2003, other international channels such as Nickelodeon, Cartoon Network, VH1, Disney and Toon Disney came into foray. In 2003 news channels started to boom.

THE SPECTATOR AS SPECTACLE

In April last year, a banner appeared on the terraces of the Newlands cricket ground in Cape Town, South Africa, during a one-day international. It was a blow-up of a dollar bill bearing a picture of the disgraced South African captain Hansie Cronje's face. The legend above the photo read: Rally Round the Green Machine.

The banner appeared a few days after Cronje had been sacked for lying about his involvement with an illegal Indian bookmaking ring, and it raised a few wry laughs. It reflected fairly accurately the public cynicism over the entire affair, soon nicknamed Hansiegate. But the banner had also hijacked one of cricket's most triumphal chants "Rally Round the West Indies" and turned it into a cruel dig at the state of the game itself.

Back in the 1970s, the West Indies cricket team was close to unbeatable, playing cricket with a flair and a freedom that disguised its tactical heart and discipline. Everywhere they played, whenever a handful of their supporters turned up at grounds, the cry would go out, "Rally Round the West Indies!"

In the year 2000, as West Indies cricket struggles for survival and the credibility of cricket and some of its most celebrated names has been called to question, the banner at Newlands speaks of many truths. Not just about the current crisis, but about the distance that the sport has travelled from the era of "Rally Round The West Indies" to the present day, when cricket has turned into an entertainment industry. Particularly in South Asia, where its liaison with satellite television and big business has led to a financial boom, prompting an image make-over and now, in the light of the match-fixing scandal, something approaching overkill.

Banners like the one at Newlands may seem like the graffiti of the sport, a medium for off-the-cuff and irreverent comment. The individuals who think up and display such banners may even be considered a late 20th century version of the legendary barrackers who flocked to the cheap stands at grounds in England and Australia before the advent of television and passed deafening comment on the state of the game. Caribbean grounds still feature characters who try to puncture superstar egos and lighten the atmosphere, but these men have now shrunk to a handful; in the popular culture of modern cricket, it is the banner that rules over the banter.

The world has absorbed this change over 25 years. In India, it has taken place in less than ten and the stresses are still with us. Until the late 1980s, the slow pace of Test cricket was believed to be ideally suited to the Indian temperament (it was open-ended, and had a casual disregard for time), one scholar stating that it was an Indian game invented by the British. Yet today, that theory stands on shaky ground as the Indian temperament has become an addict to the culture of the insta-thrill one-day game, which is both a product of television and now a force driven by it. This spatial and territorial shift has not only changed the way Indians watch cricket, but also the way they see themselves as its spectators.

The country has staged two World Cups of Cricket, almost ten years apart: the first in 1987, organised with Pakistan, was hugely popular, a subcontinental financial success story. In 1987, spectators would pack into grounds, carrying food and drink and do as they always did: behave with sobriety and restraint in Bangalore and Madras, risk being lathi-charged in Delhi and take up chanting in Bombay. What astonished overseas visitors most was the fact that Australia played England in the final in front of a vociferous capacity crowd. In no other country in the world, it was said, would such an enthusiastic non-partisan reception have been possible. (Indeed, when India played Pakistan in the 1985 World Championship of Cricket final in Australia, the stadium was far from full, and a banner described the final thus: "Bus Drivers vs. Tram Conductors," a snide reference to the most common image of the Indian and Pakistani presence in Australia.

Nine years later, the second World Cup, organised by India, Pakistan and Sri Lanka in 1996, marked the zenith of the sport's popularity and marketability. But for the Indian team, it ended in a crowd riot at the Eden Gardens, caused by the knowledge that the national heroes were going to lose.

The period between these two World Cups is virtually a case study of the effect of television on a sport and on its fans. The end result? The growth of a very large, easily-manipulated spectator mass with a low tolerance for failure and a large appetite for jingoism. The elevation of cricket to a vehicle of National self-esteem, the sensitive index of urban morale.

A street performer tries to attract spectators for viewing a snake-mongoose fight, but with little success.

The chief catalyst in this process was the advent, in 1993, of satellite television: for the first time in a long and colourful history, there were banners, and the Indian flag made its appearance at cricket grounds.

At the same time, cricket on television began to resemble the slick, much-envied coverage on Australia's Channel 9 in the days when Doordarshan's best efforts were black and white blurs. The banners and face-painting were imported adaptations of what Indians saw Australians doing in Melbourne or Sydney (minus, of course, two cultural no-nos: streakers and sunbathers in bikinis). Shrewd Australian marketing men now pay $500 prizes for the wittiest banners picked out by the TV cameras at a match provided they include the logo of the company sponsoring the prize; it is a practice which will no doubt soon be latched on to by Indian sponsors.

The Indian flags, again imitative of fan behaviour overseas, have come to represent an angry and aggressive nationalism; the old, somewhat harmless practice of a century-maker being garlanded by someone jumping the fence at grounds is now abandoned for orgies of bottle-throwing. Indian cricket is no stranger to crowd disturbances, but the frequency and the venom have increased manifold.

Perhaps this has something to do with the fact that the pot of public sentiment is kept boiling by promotional ad campaigns in which Indian cricketers no longer bat or bowl in advertisements: they leap over burning tyres to make stops in the field, hurl balls of fire at opposition batsmen and bat against bowlers shooting machine guns. Westernised accents promote cricket series nicknamed Badla, Qayamat, and Sarfarosh. The imagery and vocabulary smoothly subvert Orwell's analogy of sport as war minus the shooting and justify themselves by the ominous reminder that only two things bring India together: cricket and war. Defeat, therefore, is not an option. This may sound like the hackneyed MTV Theory of Social Change: how traditional Indian values (here, institutions like cricket) are being corrupted by the impact of television. In most cases, blaming the media may be the easiest option, but in the case of sport it is perhaps the most valid one.

A soccer fan stabbing a supporter of a rival team. Live sport cricket in India, football in Europe or basketball in the U.S. is the highest-revenue earner on television. The sale and purchase of TV "rights" is a multi-million dollar business, and sporting events are turned into "properties" sold for terrestrial and satellite television, radio and now the internet.

Such an exhaustive dissemination of sport spawns imitative but largely homogeneous behaviour over large swathes of the globe. It could spark off a trend in street fashion (e.g. the baggy shorts of NBA basketball superstars), teach Indian cricket spectators to do the Mexican wave and pass on to the athletes themselves, who turn any key moment on the field-a goal, a catch, a three-pointer-into an elaborate celebratory ritual.

The high-five, the chest-butt, the mass pile-up of bodies near the football goal-mouth... no matter what their tribalistic origins, where or why they were actually "invented" or first used, this elaborate sign language of sport is always "discovered" by the media, mostly television, and returned to the public as a legitimised, desirable code of behaviour. This phenomenon of crowd participation, largely for the benefit of the all-seeing eyes of television in the form of celebrations, chanting, banners, has turned the spectator from a witness into an element of the spectacle itself. It is a self-perpetuating cycle, a mass of flag-waving, banners, Mexican waves, each gesture magnified time after time to catch the attention of the camera.

The Indian Board's drive to take cricket and its revenue-earning television cameras to all corners of the country, including smaller metros, has created and perpetuated the image (more like an orientalist caricature) of the Indian cricket crowd: large, "colourful" "passionate" "volatile"-words sprinkled all over television commentary from a group of distinguished English or Australian experts, who have turned into the eyes and mind of the crowd. It sees what they want it to see, it believes what they tell it. With little work for the powers of imagination or interpretation, it acts the way they would like it to act.

Television companies know that the tempo of a match, no matter how humdrum, can now be cranked up merely by turning a television camera on a section of the crowd. The temperature of a crowd can be raised by replaying a controversial umpiring decision over and over again on a giant screen. The whole production, its mechanics and its "look" is under control.

Mark Mascarenhas, chief of World Tel, which brought the 1996 World Cup live to television, told Sportstar that his company's television coverage changes from nation to nation, the Indian formula being ridiculously simple: "In India spend much more time on the crowd because they are so animated, so colourful. We spend more time on the VIPs because in India people like to be seen on television... If you try to do this Indian type of coverage in England it won't go over very well."

Such commodification and codification of public space has left little room for spontaneity or candour, which is really the heart of a spectator's response. During the Australian Open tennis tournament a few years ago, "fans" of French tennis player Mary Pierce showed up in the stands wearing all her trademark tennis dresses and naturally caught the cameras. They turned out to be employees of Nike, whose tennis clothing is endorsed by the statuesque Frenchwoman, planted in the stands to do precisely that.

Hansie Cronje's disgrace was made complete, again by "fans" who blackened his face on an advertising hoarding a few days after his admission of dishonesty. But the fans (in reality, members of the "youth" wing of a political party) made sure that they did so in the presence of television cameras. Cronje's descent from role model to persona non grata was formalised in footage. Other hoardings featuring Cronje and the South African team were pulled down; in the age of the media, removal from the public gaze is akin to punishment, humiliation and exile. In India, cricket's sign language may appear to become more varied, more elaborate, richer in colour and bolder in gesture. But its words today, as part of a pre-determined script written by someone else, come up empty.

A SNAPSHOT OF INDIAN TELEVISION HISTORY

Television in India has been in existence for nigh on four decades. For the first 17 years, it spread haltingly and transmission was mainly in black & white. The thinkers and policy makers of the country, which had just been liberated from centuries of colonial rule, frowned upon television, looking on at it as a luxury Indians could do without. In 1955 a Cabinet decision was taken disallowing any foreign investments in print media which has since been followed religiously for nearly 45 years. Sales of TV sets, as reflected by licences issued to buyers were just 676,615 until 1977.

Television has come to the forefront only in the past 21 years and more so in the past 13. There were initially two ignition points: the first in the eighties when colour TV was introduced by state-owned broadcaster Doordarshan (DD) timed with the 1982 Asian Games which India hosted. It then proceeded to install transmitters nationwide rapidly for terrestrial broadcasting. In this period no private enterprise was allowed to set up TV stations or to transmit TV signals.

The second spark came in the early nineties with the broadcast of satellite TV by foreign programmers like CNN followed by Star TV and a little later by domestic channels such as Zee TV and Sun TV into Indian homes. Prior to this, Indian viewers had to make do with DD's chosen fare which was dull, non-commercial in nature, directed towards only education and socio-economic development. Entertainment programmes were few and far between. And when the solitary few soaps like Hum Log (1984), and mythological dramas: Ramayana (1987-88) and Mahabharata (1988-89) were televised, millions of viewers stayed glued to their sets.

When, urban Indians learnt that it was possible to watch the Gulf War on television, they rushed out and bought dishes for their homes. Others turned entrepreneurs and started offering the signal to their neighbours by flinging cable over treetops and verandahs. From the large metros satellite TV delivered via cable moved into smaller towns, spurring the purchase of TV sets and even the upgradation from black & white to colour TVs.

DD responded to this satellite TV invasion by launching an entertainment and commercially driven channel and introduced entertainment programming on its terrestrial network. This again fuelled the purchase of sets in the hinterlands where cable TV was not available. The initial success of the channels had a snowball effect: more foreign programmers and Indian entrepreneurs flagged off their own versions. From two channels prior to 1991, Indian viewers were exposed to more than 50 channels by 1996. Software producers emerged to cater to the programming boom almost overnight. Some talent came from the film industry, some from advertising and some from journalism.

More and more people set up networks until there was a time in 1995-96 when an estimated 60,000 cable operators were existing in the country. Some of them had subscriber bases as low as 50 to as high as in the thousands. Most of the networks could relay just 6 to 14 channels as higher channel relaying capacity required heavy investments, which cable operators were loathe to make. American and European cable networks evinced interest, as well as large Indian business groups, who set up sophisticated headends capable of delivering more than 30 channels.

These multi-system operators (MSOs) started buying up local networks or franchising cable TV feeds to the smaller operators for a fee. This phenomenon led to resistance from smaller cable operators who joined forces and started functioning as MSOs. The net outcome was that the number of cable operators in the country has fallen to 30,000.

The rash of players who rushed to set up satellite channels discovered that advertising revenue was not large enough to support them. This led to a shake-out. At least half a dozen either folded up or aborted the high-flying plans they had drawn up, and started operating in a restricted manner. Some of them converted their channels into basic subscription services charging cable operators a carriage fee.

Foreign cable TV MSOs discovered that the cable TV market was too disorganised for them to operate in and at least three of them decided to postpone their plans and got out of the market..

The government started taxing cable operators in a bid to generate revenue. The rates varied in the 26 states that go to form India and ranged from 35 per cent upwards. The authorities moved in to regulate the business and a Cable TV Act was passed in 1995. The apex court in the country, the Supreme Court, passed a judgement that the air waves are not the property of the Indian government and any Indian citizen wanting to use them should be allowed to do so. The government reacted by making efforts to get some regulation in place by setting up committees to suggest what the broadcasting law of India should be, as the sector was still being governed by laws which were passed in 19th century India. A broadcasting bill was drawn up in 1997 and introduced in parliament. But it was not passed into an Act. State-owned telecaster Doordarshan and radiocaster All India Radio were brought under a holding company called the Prasar Bharati under an act that had been gathering dust for seven years, the Prasar Bharati Act, 1990. The Act served to give autonomy to the broadcasters as their management was left to a supervisory board consisting of retired professionals and bureaucrats.

A committee headed by a senior Congress (I) politician Sharad Pawar and consisting of other politicians and industrialist was set up to review the contents of the Broadcasting Bill. It held discussions with industry, politicians, and consumers and a report was even drawn up. But the United Front government fell and since then the report and the Bill have been consigned to the dustbin. But before that it issued a ban on the sale of Ku-band dishes and on digital direct-to-home Ku-band broadcasting, which the Rupert Murdoch-owned News Television was threatening to start in India. ISkyB, the Murdoch DTH venture, has since been wallowing in quicksand and in recent times has even shed a lot of employees. But News Corp has been running a C-band DTH venture in the country which has around 20,000 subscribers.

INDIA: CHANGING LIVES THROUGH TV PROGRAMMING

Nothing can be more devastating for a father than not being able to touch his own children. And that is exactly what happened to Panchu Bhol, a villager in the southeastern state of Orissa, India. Many men from this poverty-stricken hinterland of Puri district migrate seasonally to Gujarat in search of livelihood. Panchu had also embarked on this migration route, regularly sending money to his family, until he contracted HIV in Surat, the port city of Gujarat.

News of Panchu's HIV status spread like a wildfire. His family was excommunicated, and his village declared Panchu a curse. Even Panchu himself started to believe it. He lost the courage to pick up his daughter, fearing that he might infect her. Banned from the village life, Panchu cried at his fate, seeing death as the only way out.

But an extraordinary event in December 2005 turned his life around. Panchu still remembers the mild afternoon breeze on the day when the Kalyani team came to his hamlet. Kalyani-meaning the one who provides welfare-is a television health telecast on Doordarshan, the national television of India. Since May of 2002 when it was launched, the program about building positive health behaviours has been reaching nearly 50% of India's population.

Doordarshan national television is the world's largest public broadcaster and a signatory to the Global AIDS Media Summit. Providing localized content, Doordarshan produces its key messages in consultation with the National AIDS Control Organisation and the Ministry of Health. Its telecasts feature short spots, folk songs, and informative segments with experts, in an attempt to tackle themes of HIV related stigma, discrimination and treatment. Kalyani program also provides follow up action through expert visits to rural areas to interact with the target audiences.

Actors playing Kalyani characters 'Sehri Didi and Chakulia Panda', along with the rest of the Kalyani team, reached Panchu's village. The team met an emaciated, bearded and confused Panchu. And as the villagers gathered to catch a glimpse of the movie stars, tears rolled out of Panchu's eyes. It was the first time that someone had visited him since he had been diagnosed with HIV. Informed of Panchu's situation, Sehri Didi (the character portraying the sister's role in the programme) offered to become Panchu's "sister" in real life and tied him a raakhi, the traditional auspicious red thread. She also shared some sweets with him.

Sehri Didi challenged the villagers not to stigmatize her new "brother" Panchu. An elderly man from the crowd summed up the sentiments of the village: "You told us that HIV does not spread by touching people living with HIV or eating with them. Why should we hate Panchu? We are sorry we did not know this before."

Panchu was finally accepted. Having learned about means of HIV transmission, Panchu took his daughter into his arms for the first time. For Sehri Didi, accustomed to crying with glycerine on screen, it was difficult to control her tears.

When the Kalyani team visited Panchu's village three months later, they could hardly recognize him-now a clean shaven and confident young man championing HIV prevention. The doctor treating Panchu thanked the Kalyani team for removing a major hurdle in Panchu's recovery-the social stigma.

Kalyani program airs in the capital cities of eight highly populated Indian states and there now exist nearly 2,000 community level Kalyani Health Clubs, with close to half million members.

A CLIENT-CENTRED NETWORKING PROJECT IN RURAL INDIA

TV Firms Gear up for Rural Market: When Oscar Television made it to ORG-Gfk's list of 10 top-selling colour television brands earlier this year, there was one person who wasn't satisfied.

Arpita Khurana, Oscar's youthful director, insisted that the ORG-Gfk survey didn't tell half the story because it collected figures only in the metropolitan areas.

Oscar, she said, was flying off the shop-shelves in semi-urban and rural India. What's more, Khurana predicted that semi-urban and rural demand would zoom by around 80 per cent this year. That, say her rivals, may be an overestimate. But the other colour television and consumer electronics manufacturers aren't disagreeing loudly. In fact, they are also gearing for a buying spree in rural and semi-urban India.

The industry association too is bullish about sales this year. Cetma (the Consumer Electronics and TV Manufacturers Association) has projected sales of 10 million sets in 2004 compared to around 8 million to 8.25 million TVs likely to be sold this year. That's compared to 6.7 million sets sold in 2002.

- Cetma believes that between 8 million and 8.25 million TV sets will be sold this year compared to 6.7 million last year
- In 2002 63.1 per cent of sales came from cities and smaller regions with a population of less than 1 million
- Companies like LG and Philips are almost doubling distribution networks in the rural areas
- To attract rural buyers 14-inch televisions are being sold for as little as Rs 3,500

Most amazingly, about 70 per cent of this will come from the semi-urban and rural market. "This means the rural market will grow by as much as 25 per cent compared to 5 per cent growth in the urban markets," says an association executive.

What's fuelling the rural optimism? There's a growth in awareness, say the manufacturers. Also, they have boosted penetration in semi-urban and rural areas. And this year there have been good monsoons followed by good harvests. Diwali sales have been robust and the feel-good factor in the economy is boosting buying.

It's important to keep one thing in mind. This isn't the first year when rural demand has climbed sharply. Market research firm Francis Kanoi recently said in a report (on consumer electronic market growth and projections) that the top seven metros contributed 24.1 per cent of total sales in 2002. That was followed by towns with a population of over 1 million where 12.0 per cent of the sets were bought. The remaining 63.1 per cent of sales in 2002 came from cities and smaller regions with a population of less than 1 million.

The tilt towards the smaller towns and rural areas is becoming more pronounced with each passing year. This year, for instance, it has been reckoned that buying in the top seven metros will contribute only 22.6 per cent a fall from last year. Smaller towns and regions will be 64.3 per cent of total sales.

"Barely five years ago, the contribution from semi-urban and rural markets for us was 20 per cent. Today we get 70 per cent of our volumes from these markets," says Chandramani Singh, product group head (consumer electronics) at LG Electronics India.

But another subtle change is taking place this year, according to industry analysts. Until now, the market transformation has happened primarily because owners of radios and B&W televisions were upgrading to colour televisions. As per Francis Kanoi data, the upgrades from B&W to the colour TV segment forms over 60 per cent of total CTV purchases.

But now the industry is talking of other factors, which will drive growth like the booming rural economy. Also, they feel consumers will be making up for lost time: the feel-good factor has been distinctly missing for the last two years so rural consumers have held back on big ticket purchases.

But there's an additional factor that's likely to fuel growth. Loans for products like televisions have become easier in the rural areas because the public sector banks are moving in with offers of easy credit.

Add to that the fact that prices of televisions have fallen steeply and companies are taking extra initiatives to promote sales.

"Rural consumption is linked with agricultural output and the availability of cash. Untill very recently, financing was available to the rural people at very high interest rates and that too, not made available by any financing agents or banks but by the village sahukars (money lender). Thus, the trend in the rural areas still is to make cash purchases, which links to good harvests and ready availability of cash," says Ravinder Zutshi, director (sales) of Samsung India Electronics Ltd.

Zutshi is convinced that buying will climb even more sharply in coming years because of cheap financing. Banks such as the State Bank of India are pushing their loan schemes in the rural areas and so are financing companies like Bajaj Finance.

"The manufacturers too are expanding both their penetration as well as the products for the rural markets, all of which should help boost rural sales," he says.

Says LG's Singh, "Electrification of villages and an increase in awareness among the people, a good harvest and a booming economy will help drive growth. The rural market should see a growth that is three to four times that in the urban markets."

"The potential is high as the penetration levels are low, and hence our efforts towards creating a bigger market here," adds Devender Saini, senior product manager (television), Philips India Ltd.

"If we look at the penetration levels in rural markets, it is less than 10 per cent. This is lower than the all-India average of 21 per cent and the urban markets which are at 35 per cent to 40 per cent."

The increase in penetration levels in the rural markets has also shown the way to the Oscars and Belteks of the world, which are carving out a niche by positioning themselves as price warriors. And their cut-price tactics have forced LG, Samsung and Philips, among others, to launch products targeted only at these markets.

These products have fewer frills, and are hence, cheaper. As a result, the rural masses are being tempted by the lower prices offered by all manufacturers. The entry of the bigger players in these market segments has forced the smaller ones to squeeze margins and reduce prices further.

R K Caprihan, an old industry hand and the chief executive of The Kelon Corporation, claims he is selling 14-inch for as low as Rs 3,600 and a 20-inch for only Rs 5,500.

In fact, the success of the smaller brands and the entry of the bigger players have started a war on many fronts. It's not restricted to pricing, but it's also about visibility and value for money.

Oscar, for instance, which derives 40 per cent of its sales from the semi-urban and rural sectors, has launched a battery-operated television model in the 14" segment to cater to parts of Eastern UP and Bihar. This has boosted the company's sales by 5 per cent to 7 per cent. It is planning to come out with a similar 21" model this month. Says Arpita Khurana: "Since electricity is a problem in these areas we felt the model would be a success."

LG is putting more emphasis on dealership network. The company had only one distributor in Jaipur. But it now has distributors in Jodhpur, Jaisalmer, Udaipur and several other places. Over the past year, the company's direct dealers have risen from 1,000 to 1,500 and the number of sub-dealers has climbed from 2,800 to 5,000.

The company, which is the market leader in the colour television segment, has focused on decentralising its operations to increase its rural penetration this year. It has increased its 'remote area offices', which function at district levels, from 27 earlier to 62 this year. Similarly, Philips is planning to double its retail presence. From an existing network of 6,000, the company plans to have 12,000 retailers. About 75 per cent of this increase will take place in the rural areas.

Companies are also spending on huge sums on advertising, especially in local vernacular newspapers. Philips has fallen back on some unconventional advertising media like wall-writing and radio advertising. Says D Shivakumar, vice-president, consumer electronics, Philips India: "We have a strong base of loyal consumers of transistor sets as well as B/W TVs who are now ready to upgrade. We will try and tap these consumers for our rural scheme."

Companies are also organising rural melas and haats and use mobile hoardings to reach potential customers in villages and semi-urban markets. And, if the rural customers are switching on in larger numbers the picture can only get brighter for all the companies.

SOCIOLINGUISTIC DISTINCTION OF TV

In sociolinguistics, a T-V distinction describes the situation wherein a language has second-person pronouns that distinguish varying levels of politeness, social distance, courtesy, familiarity, or insult toward the addressee.

History and Usage

The expressions T-form and V-form were introduced by Brown and Gilman (1960), with reference to the initial letters of these pronouns in Latin, tu and vos. In Latin, tu was originally the singular, and vos the plural, with no distinction for honorific or familiar. According to Brown and Gilman, usage of the plural to the Roman emperor began in the fourth century AD.

They mention the possibility that this was because there were two emperors at that time (in Constantinople and Rome), but also mention that "plurality is a very old and ubiquitous metaphor for power". This usage was extended to other powerful figures, such as Pope Gregory I (590-604). But Brown and Gilman note that it was only between the twelfth and fourteenth centuries that the norms for the use of T-and V-forms crystallized. Less commonly, the use of the plural may be extended to other persons, such as the "royal we" (pluralis majestatis) in English.

Brown and Gilman argued that the choice of form is governed by either relationships of 'power' and/or 'solidarity', depending on the culture of the speakers, showing that 'power' had been the dominant predictor of form in Europe until the twentieth century. Thus it was quite normal for a powerful person to use a T-form but expect a V-form in return. However in the twentieth century the dynamic shifted in favour of solidarity, so that people would use T-forms with those they knew, and V-forms in service encounters, with reciprocal usage being the norm in both cases.

Modern English has no T-V distinction. It can often be confusing for an English speaker learning a language with a T-V distinction to assimilate the rules surrounding when to call someone with the formal or the informal pronoun. Students are often advised to err on the side of caution by using the formal pronouns. However, this risks sounding snobbish or ridiculous. Though English has no syntactic T-V distinction, there are semantic analogies, such as whether to address someone by first name or last name (or using sir and ma'am). However the boundaries between formal and informal language differ from language to language, and most languages use formal speech more frequently, and/or in different circumstances than English. In some circumstances it is not unusual to call other people by first name and the respectful form, or last name and familiar form. For example, German teachers use the former construct with upper-secondary students.

The use of these forms calls for compensating translation of dialogue into English. For example, a character in a French film or novel saying "Tutoie-moi!" ("Use [the informal pronoun] tu when addressing me!") might be translated "Don't be so formal!"

Examples

In many languages, the formal singular pronoun derives from a plural form. Many Romance languages have familiar forms derived from the Latin singular tu and formal forms derived from Latin plural vos, sometimes via a circuitous route. Sometimes, singular V-form derives from a third person pronoun. Some languages have separate T and V forms for both singular and plural; others have the same form; others have a T-V distinction only in the singular.

Different languages distinguish pronoun uses in different ways. Even within languages, there are differences between groups (older people and people of higher status tending to both use and expect more formal language) and between various aspects of one language. For example, in Dutch, u is slowly falling into disuse in the plural, and thus one could sometimes address a group as jullie when one would address each member individually as u.

In Latin American Spanish, the opposite change has occurred-having lost vosotros, Latin Americans address all groups as ustedes, even if the group is composed of friends whom they would call tú or vos (mostly in Argentina). In Standard Peninsular Spanish, however, vosotros is still regularly employed in familiar conversation. In some cases, V-forms are likely to be capitalized when written.

TRADITIONAL MEDIA

For generations, rural populations living in isolated villages without access to modern means of communication have relied on the spoken word and traditional forms of communication as a means of sharing knowledge and information and providing entertainment.

For illiterate rural women in particular, occasions for information exchange have consisted solely in local festivities, family gatherings, traditional and religious associations, interaction with itinerant merchants and encounters at marketplaces or water wells.

However, women have made use of the oral tradition to ensure their own as well as their families' survival and, as a result, have developed a rich communication environment. They have lived creative lives, transmitting culture, knowledge, customs and history through traditional forms of communication such as poetry, proverbs, songs, stories, dances and plays.

Within their communities, women are active participants in social communication networks. They use indigenous communication methods for information exchange, knowledge sharing and the dissemination of strategies for mutual assistance and survival.

Culture and history play an important role in the social development of a community. The preservation of traditional forms of communication and social change are not mutually exclusive. Traditional communication methods can be important channels for facilitating learning, behavioural change, people's participation and dialogue for development purposes.

Indigenous media have been successfully adopted by change agents to promote rural development issues of relevance to women. They have been used, for instance, to influence attitudes towards family size, female genital mutilation, teenage pregnancies, unsettling lifestyles and HIV/AIDS.

They have also been applied in health care, environmental protection and women's literacy programmes as well as in teaching mothers about child nutrition and in introducing new agricultural practices. Traditional forms of communication can also be integrated with other media such as radio, television, video and audio cassettes.

Communication is a product of culture, and culture determines the code, structure, meaning and context of the communication that takes place. The participation of local folk artists, storytellers and performers in the production and use of traditional media ensures respect for traditional values, symbols and realities and, at the same time, ensures that such media productions appeal to rural audiences.

By tapping the community's creative pool of traditional culture, expressions and formats, women can maintain their cultural identity while gaining social self-reliance. Women's use of local media and communication channels also increases the credibility of media programmes and thus their effectiveness and impact on the knowledge, attitudes and behaviour of other women.

Grassroots Artists for Population Communication in Malawi

Population communication teams working in the Comoros, Burundi, Rwanda, Kenya, Uganda and the Philippines have tapped a variety of artistic expressions: the beat of drums, the sound of three-string guitars, the rhythm of skiffle bands, women's dance groups, village clowns, storytellers, theatre groups and puppets.

Building on those experiences, a population communication project in Malawi invited grassroots artists (including women) from the project's target audience to a communication workshop. The participants then worked together to produce a coherent multimedia package of songs and dances, stories and plays, village clowneries and drum shows addressing a variety of population issues and lifestyles.

The productions were pretested and integrated into a multimedia campaign, which also used radio, visual materials, drama and print. Yet it was the talent, creativity and intuition of the artists that triggered a process of village participation in the rural areas of southern Malawi.

The emotional excitement created by the launching of village campaigns gave way to the spontaneous development of traditional songs, dances and popular plays by other village artists. The Malawi experience proves the potential that traditional forms of communication have to involve and reach women audiences.

MULTIMEDIA

Communication programmes should make use of all media infrastructures and channels available in a country, both modern and traditional, in an orchestrated and mutually reinforcing fashion.

The combination of several media approaches and tools with interpersonal channels multiplies the impact of communication campaigns, which are being used increasingly to support clearly defined development priorities.

Some striking examples include a health campaign in the United Republic of Tanzania; nutrition programmes in Nicaragua, the Philippines and Tunisia; a breast-feeding campaign in Trinidad and Tobago; family planning programmes in China, Colombia, Egypt, Honduras, Pakistan and Thailand; and a campaign against female genital mutilation in Ethiopia.

Multichannel communication approaches can also help in identifying appropriate agricultural technologies for women as well as in disseminating the required knowledge and skills.

A recent evaluation of the Soul City "edutainment" programme in South Africa has demonstrated the added value and effectiveness of using a multichannel approach.

This communication campaign aimed at delivering health education messages to women over a three-month period. It included a series of 13 television drama programmes, broadcast at prime time on the country's most popular television channel.

It was accompanied by a series of 15-minute radio drama programmes, called Healing Hearts, broadcast daily on the country's three largest radio stations. In addition, Soul City used newspapers to provide more detailed information and to supplement the health messages conveyed by electronic media. A booklet, illustrated with characters from the television series, was serialized in the major newspapers and distributed through clinics and health service organizations.

Finally, educational packages combining audio and videotape together with written materials were produced to facilitate learning processes in both formal and informal settings. A public relations campaign strengthened the messages further by placing the issues on the public agenda by using editorial space, competitions and a range of actuality programmes in the various media.

The entire campaign was preceded by formative research to identify appropriate channels and messages. Messages were designed in consultation with the target audience and experts in the field, and materials and programmes were pretested with groups of women and men.

An evaluation analysed gender-desegregated data to assess the impact of the various channels and materials on knowledge, attitudes and behaviour. The results showed that the multimedia approach in this case was effective in reaching female audiences.

Audiovisual materials such as slides and video can assist extension workers. Women trainees, even if they are illiterate, can see and discuss innovations before putting them into practice.

Improving Extension and Training Programmes

Investing in the sharing of knowledge and learning for rural women through extension and training can be an effective means of reducing poverty and promoting food security and sustainable development. However, studies on agricultural extension have highlighted a number of weaknesses in current efforts to reach rural women. There are very few women extensionists; moreover, the attitudes and behaviour of male extension personnel can be a major barrier between extension services and women.

Extension services have often ignored the specific information needs of women as well as the fact that they may require different agricultural technologies from those suited to men. They have underestimated women's indigenous knowledge and experience and have not taken the time to listen to and learn from women themselves.

A combination of traditional and modern communication methods can help extension workers to improve the quality and outreach of their programmes with women. Fieldworkers need to abandon top-down approaches in favour of participatory communication skills and methods and establish a climate of confidence and trust.

They need to learn how to promote dialogue among women farmers, help them identify their needs and strengthen their self-confidence. Participatory communication methods can improve the linkages among women farmers, extensionists, researchers, policy-makers and planners, thereby fostering the exchange of information and knowledge and ensuring that development activities correspond to the real needs of rural communities.

Audiovisual materials such as slides and video can assist extension workers with their training activities. Women trainees, even if they are illiterate, can see and discuss innovations before putting them into practice.

Audio-visuals can compress time and space. For example, in a single session, a training group can explore an entire agricultural cycle, from sowing to harvest. Through visual materials, women can travel to places that are too distant to visit. The extensionists themselves also benefit from using communication materials. The technical information presented can be standardized and of high quality and the presentations made attractive and interesting. Audiovisual materials spark dialogue and debate and, overall, they allow trainers to be more confident and professional.

The use of mass media, such as rural radio, can reinforce and multiply the impact of extension messages and allow extensionists to reach rural people in isolated areas. Radio and television can be used to conduct distance education programmes for rural women who are unable to attend formal education and training programmes.

Developing Agricultural Technologies

Rural women play an important role in Jamaican agriculture: as farmers in their own right, in partnership with men on household farms and as the main cultivators of kitchen gardens. A challenge to extension in Jamaica has been finding creative and cost-effective ways to communicate with rural women. A pilot project, supported by the Governments of Jamaica and Canada, used various participatory communication approaches to deliver appropriately designed soil nutrient technologies to rural women.

In order to develop appropriate agricultural and soil fertility technologies for rural women, a participatory communication methodology was used that incorporated both indigenous and scientific knowledge.

The project demonstrated that women have specific information needs, and a set of participatory techniques for a gender approach to agricultural activities was developed. It also demonstrated how extension workers could select from a variety of traditional and modern communication methods according to the needs of rural women. The approaches and media applied, and the products generated, by the project included:

- a series of community video screenings, followed by discussion, showing agricultural practices in Jamaica;
- video tapes of community demonstration plots, comparing the effects of various soil nutrient applications;
- a visual baseline survey, with respondents interviewed either on video or on audiotape;
- a drama performance-for which rural women were hired as actors-to improve understanding of how gender

relationships affect agricultural decision-making (the performance was used to verify the baseline survey findings);

- oral history testimonies about each community, (these emerged from interviews and were published in local newsletters);
- a quarterly newsletter, produced to inform project participants and other audiences about soil fertility and other agricultural issues;
- participatory video training carried out in each of the communities, resulting in a series of short, humorous programmes related to agriculture and soil fertility.

Based on findings from nine months of field testing as well as on the results of the video baseline survey and a mid-term evaluation, the technology package was redesigned and a final video was produced to present soil nutrient and soil conservation recommendations.

4

Information and News Broadcasting

The modern communication system is an integral part of the development process, and can aid in the acceleration of the growth of the economy by providing the necessary motivation and information. Therefore in the Seventh Plan, all existing communication capabilities-both hardware and software-will be harnessed and also augmented to the extent required. The electronic means-radio, T.V. and telecommunications-will have to play a major role in this effort. While the communication system will be used to serve all segments of society, it will be developed to accord special priority to the rural people and to the deprived sections.

INTRODUCTION

The major thrust of the plan relating to mass, media will be to raise the level of peoples' consciousness and enrich their cultural and social life and make them better informed citizens. It will assist in stepping up the pace of development of programmes and sensitise the people towards national and international events of importance. Besides entertainment, programmes covering sports, culture and fine arts will be provided.

There will also be target-group oriented programmes i.e. for youths, women, children and weaker sections. Further the media will act as a vehicle of education and extension and so, narrow information gaps faced by the people from different walks of life. It will assist in enlarging the scope of formal education through special schemes like open universities.

The use of media will help in spreading the message of national integration and motivate the people to put in their best for achieving the national objectives. For this purpose, a skilful synthesis between traditional and folk forms of communication on the one hand, and the modern audio-visual media including satellite communication on the other, will be fully exploited. Radio, T.V. films and other forms of audio-visual media will be pressed into service for this purpose.

Sixth Plan Review

The Sixth plan outlay for plan schemes of the Ministry of Information and Broadcasting is Rs. 240.33 crores. The anticipated expenditure for the five year period 1980-85 is estimated at Rs. 244.99 crores. Details of outlay and expenditure for the four sectors are shown in Table below.

Table: Outlay Expenditure

(Rs. crores)

Sector	VI Plan outlay	VI Plan anticipated expenditure
Sound Broadcasting	122.38	84.80
Doordarshan	*86.95	133.71
Films media	23.15	18.17
Information and publicity	7.85	8.31
	240.33	244.99

* Additional schemes for TV: TV Special Programme-Rs. 68 crores; North Eastern Plan-Rs. 36.43 crores; Additional equipment for TV centres-Rs. 8.99 crores; Electronic equipment-Rs. 8.62 crores; total TV outlay-Rs. 208.39 crores.

With the completion of Sixth Plan projects, coverage by AIR has increased to 95 per cent of the population and 86 per cent by area and TV coverage to 33 per cent of population and 17 per cent of the area. A special TV expansion plan was, however, drawn up involving an additional expenditure of Rs.

68 crores to cover 70 per cent population of the country by November 1984. The Scheme envisaged provision of 13 high power and 113 low power additional transmitters. Subsequently, six more LPTs were sanctioned, in addition to three new schemes:

(1) Provision of Electronic News Gathering equipment at various Doordarshan Kendras & procurement of transportable earth terminal;

(2) Augmentation of electronic equipment at various Doordarshan Kendras, and

(3) Expansion of TV service in the North-Eastern Region.

On the completion of these schemes, there will be 186 TV transmitters of varying powers in the TV network, covering about 70 per cent population of the country. On completion of the scheme regarding TV coverage of the North-Eastern Region, about 80 per cent population of that region would get TV coverage.

In regard to schemes relating to sound broadcasting the stress during the Sixth Plan had been on the following: completing spill over programmes, consolidating and expanding existing regional services, upgrading the power of existing transmitters, providing integrated shortwave service for North-Eastern Region, setting up permanent studios at auxiliary centres, setting up of new radio stations in uncovered pockets, making a beginning towards a dedicated national channel.

Schemes relating to information and film media in the Sixth Plan aimed at building an infrastructure in the rural and remote areas and at highlighting the developmental schemes for the welfare of the poor, weaker and backward sections. The Song and Drama Division set up second Sound and Light Field Unit and a pilot project to utilise the folk forms of tribal areas. Field Publicity aimed at setting up units in all the major districts of the country. The Press Information Bureau opened new Office-cum-Information centres and took up special conducted tours of press correspondents to tribal and hilly areas.

The thrust of Directorate of Advertising and Visual Publicity's effort was towards integrated development of rural areas with emphasis on weaker sections of society like small and marginal farmers, people of tribal and hilly areas and North-Eastern Region by augmenting its production and distribution of publicity material and strengthening its exhibition units.

The plan of Films Division included increase in the number of prints for release in theatres, construction of its building at Bombay, augmentation of production facilities in Defence Film Production Unit at Delhi and opening new centres for production of films in 16 mm. specially for rural audiences. National Film Archives of India's Plan included a scheme to construct its own building to house film processing laboratory, library, museum, etc., and to set up regional archival centres. The Children's Film Society aimed at stepping up production of children's feature films and import good quality children's films. National film Development Corporation played a purposeful role for the development of good cinema and financing of theatre construction.

Seventh Plan Approach

In the Seventh Plan, the stress will be on productivity, and on providing a perspective of the new phase development. As far as possible, hardware infrastructure will be consolidated. Efforts will be made to establish and strengthen inter-linkages between the existing infrastructure and development programmes. New Management modes and organisational arrangements will be established for effective implementation.

The low power transmitters (LPTs) of Doordarshan already installed will be adapted to provide communication support to the massive development programmes envisaged in the Seventh Plan. Programme production facilities will be provided at 48 existing centres and community participation in local specific programmes will be ensured.

For All India Radio, F.M. transmitters will be used as local radio in a community-access mode with maximum local participation in programme production and for projecting the theme of national solidarity and development. The powerful Vividh Bharathi commercial channel will also be used for dissemination of vital developmental messages.

For this purpose linkages with extension staff will be established for utilisation of the broadcast message. The Film media will establish and strengthen the parallel feature film movement in the country in which films would deal with matters of social urgency in a highly artistic and creative format and be highly communicative. Production and co-production of low-cast, quality films will be undertaken. The Films Division will provide infrastructure and funds for production of documentaries. In the In formation sector, disciplines, like management, marketing, system analysis, advertising techniques and behavioural and social sciences will be inducted to make it more effective. The Field Publicity units will undertake interpersonal communication in an extension mode. The Information media units will function better as a result of overall systems planning. The facilities provides by INSAT-IB will be utilised in full by Doordarshan and Sound Broadcasting.

Sound Broadcasting

The first task of AIR during the Seventh Plan is to complete all the spill over schemes like 1000 KW medium wave transmitter at Nagpur, 250 KW short wave transmitters at Delhi and Aligarh and 500 KW short wave transmitters at Bangalore. The main thrust is to maximise the day-time coverage by providing new radio stations in uncovered pockets and to take necessary steps to compensate for the night-time shrinkage that takes place as a result of interference from the high power transmitters of neighbouring countries. Special emphasis in this regard is being given to border, tribal and backward areas. Owing to the megawatt race in the neighbouring countries, there is tremendous erosion in the service area of our medium wave transmitters.

The technology of F.M. will circumvent this problem of medium wave shrinkage and during the Seventh Plan a large number of FM transmitters will be installed. Other schemes are consolidation of regional shortwave support service, utilisation of FM service for local radio mode in the country, upgradation of power of medium wave transmitters; strengthening and consolidation of External Service Transmitters; replacement and modernisation of obsolete equipment; expansion of radio networking through INSAT; providing alternative power supply; Science and Technology; software schemes etc.

A total provision of Rs. 700 crores has been made for Sound Broadcasting including Rs. 86 crores for spill over schemes; Rs. 97 crores for modernisation and renewal of existing equipment in the network and the rest for new schemes.

Television

A three-tier service is to be introduced during the Seventh Plan period in a phased manner. A T.V. Service for the whole country with Delhi as a main production centre drawing programmes from other production centres would be set up for projecting aspects of all India interest. Each major State will have its own primary service, originating in the State in the language of the State, to be available throughout the State. Local service will be broadcast through the local transmitters. Programme production facilities would be provided at selected centres for local specific programmes. Replacement and modernisation of obsolete equipment by modern colour equipment is to be taken up on a priority basis.

Augmentation of facilities at existing centres will consist of continuing booths, continuity studios, colour OB Vans etc. Studio facilities with colour OB Vans and post-production facilities will be located at some of the capital cities. Electronic News Gathering Electronic Field Production vans are proposed for production of field programmes at major centres.

Regional ENG teams are to be stationed at some centres to cover important events of national and regional importance at short notice. The border areas are to be covered at selected places. New micro-wave links, additional end-links and uplinks are also to be set up. A staff training institute will also be set up during the Seventh Plan to train personnel for manning the new centres.

As technological advance in the hardware sector takes place, it is imperative to enrich the contents of the programme itself. Concentrated attention will be paid to software aspect of the T.V. System.

For this purpose, the creative talents in the field of culture, social changes, science and technology will also be drawn upon. Its aim would be to draw the local talent into programming ana to inculcate among the people a scientific temper and modern outlook which provides the bedrock of national integration. Care will be taken not to project themes which may have pernicious consequences of conspicuous consumerism and lead to social divisiveness.

A provision of Rs. 700 crores has been made for Doordarshan during the Seventh Plan, which includes Rs. 163.56 crores for spill over schemes and Rs. 93.98 crores for replacement and modernisation of equipment.

Science & Technology Programmes

The Research Department of All India Radio (Ministry of Information & Broadcasting) is responsible for carrying out research studies and investigations, apart from rendering specialised service to support the operational needs of the network, and also for developing equipment which are not manufactured in the country and are required on a limited scale. The activities of the Research Department cover the needs of broadcasting which includes Akashvani and Doordarshan.

The strengthening of R & D activities is proposed in the areas of:

- Propagation studies in M.F., H.F., V.H.F.; Studies relating to design and development of TV studios, transmitting equipment and aerials; Digital techniques, remote control and automation;
- Digital Television;
- Development of F.M./H.F. aerials;
- Stereophonic Broadcasting; and

- Audio and acoustic engineering studies.

In addition, several new schemes have been proposed as indicated below:

- New TV system development, e.g., digital television. MAGTV, HDTV, Video Automatic system etc. Fibre optics for transmission links.
- Microwave Broadcasting Techniques.
- Antenna systems for microwave transmitting/receiving.
- Microwave propagation studies.
- New projects under audio and acoustic engineering.
- New projects under TV Broadcasting.
- Use of micro-computers/micro processors in sound and TV broadcasting.

Significant support work relating to the area of radio and TV broadcasting is carried cut under ISRO (notably at SAC, Ahmedabad), by BEL (which is the manufacturer of major equipment needed by Akashvani and Doordarshan), NPL (Particularly on propagation studies) etc. under their own charters and programmes.

Films

There are ten units in the film sector. The Films Division will complete the 2nd and 3rd phases of its building programme. It will provide funds for the production of special films in 16 mm. specifically intended for rural audiences. Private producers will be encouraged to produce these films. It has a scheme to augment production of documentary films for the North-Eastern Region. The schemes of the National Films Archives of India include air-conditioning of their film vaults, construction of specialised vaults for nitrate films and acquisition of archival films and film materials. The Film & Television Institute of India has training schemes in various aspects of film making for colour T.V. The Children's Film Society will produce, purchase and dub children's films and organise children's film festivals. The main scheme of the National Film Development Corporation is the production and co-production of high quality, low cost films which can be used in Doordarshan and also in the video parlours. It also proposes to have a chain of theatres in State capitals and acquire playing time in theatres. An outlay of Rs. 41.5-1 crores has been made in the Seventh Plan for the film sector.

Information Media

There are eleven units in this sector. The Press Information Bureau will introduce a computerised system of indexing and strengthening of photo and feature unit and set up telephone service at regional branch offices. The Publications Division is to continue its schemes of sales promotion and publication of Yojana in different languages. The Research and Reference Division is to modernise its National Documentation Centre on mass communication.

The Directorate of Advertising and Visual Publicity has a scheme of exhibitions, development of audio-visual cell, distribution of publicity material and opening of two more regional offices. The Song and Drama division will open regional offices, strengthen the border publicity units, and set up programme designing units.

The Field Publicity Directorate is to open additional field units. Additional regional offices will be opened and equipment modernised. The Directorate's major scheme is to provide office and residential accommodation in remote areas. The Photo Division will open photo cells in State capitals, strengthen colour units at headquarters and expand its exhibition cell. One of the major schemes of the Indian Institute of Mass Communication is the construction of its building. Other schemes relate to various training courses in journalism. The Ministry also proposes to construct its own Soochna Bhavan and common office building in State capitals. An outlay of Rs. 30 crores has been provided in the Seventh Plan for the Information Sector as a whole out of which Rs. 13 crores is the building component.

Besides the Central media, the State Governments/Union Territories also have their information schemes more or less on the Central pattern, consisting of song and drama, field publicity, production of films and films shows, community listening, community T.V. viewing, printed publicity, field publicity etc. An outlay of Rs. 90.84 crores is being provided for the States and Rs. 7.06 crores for the Union Territories for this sector during the Seventh Plan period.

India has always played a leading role in the non-aligned movement. In this connection, there is a need for promoting information flow, which would project the image of the non-aligned and developing countries. This would receive requisite attention. Non-professional resources which have over a time acquired professional excellence would be mobilised to improve the quality of mass media.

Outlays

The Seventh Plan provision for schemes relating to information and broadcasting are shown in Table below.

Table: Provisions for Schemes Relating to I & B

(Rs. crores)

S. N.	Sector	6th Plan Outlay	7th Plan Outlay
I.	Sound Broadcasting	122.38	700.00
II.	Television	86.95	700.00
III.	Information & Publicity (including Films):		
	(a) Centre	31.00	71.51
	(b) States	28.46	90.84
	(c) Union Territories	3.55	7.06
	Total	272.34	1569.41

TELEVISION AND RURAL DEVELOPMENT

This chapter first provides a general overview of electronic media in rural development, illustrating how characteristics of a medium determine its strengths and weaknesses for development. Second the relation between a medium's ITPs, and the contribution of that medium to social change is treated. Third, it will be shown that the intrinsic limitations of individual media suggest a combined use of electronic media for a concerted communication effort, with the media each addressing different aspects of that effort, in line with their individual strengths, and mutually reinforcing their individual contributions. Finally, the concept of ITPs is used to show that the emphasis should not only be on electronic media as content providers, but also on their possible role as facilitators or stimulators of social change.

CONVEYING A MESSAGE

This theoretical concept assumes that messages contain a certain level of equivocality, and that some media are more capable of reducing that equivocality than others. The degree to which a medium can reduce equivocality in a message determines its richness. This in the sense that a rich medium is capable of sending messages which leave less room for ambiguity in interpretation.

The following four factors determine the richness of a specific medium: opportunities for direct and speedy feedback; possibility to use more types of signals (or cues), such as body language, volume, and intonation; use of natural language; and, the possibility to specifically adapt the message to circumstances of (individual) reception. The more complicated, and voluminous, a message, the greater the chances are of ambiguous interpretations, thus the more of the above mentioned factors a medium should be able to deploy.

RADIO AND TELEVISION

Broadcasting mass media provide information following allocation patterns, with all the attendant, intrinsic disadvantages: one-way communication with few possibilities for feedback, physical distance between sender and receiver, and reinforcement of the existing power structure. Two further weaknesses of mass media broadcasts are the difficulty of retaining the information for later use and the susceptibility, at the same time, of messages to alternative interpretations.

Radio is by far the most widely used electronic (mass) medium in rural regions of developing countries, primarily because of its versatility which allows for its use in various types of communication efforts. The presence of local radio stations and the availability of small transistor radios allow for 'easy and affordable access' in relatively large geographical areas. The extent to which local radio stations operate as independent broadcasters largely depends on the socio-political and economic context of a country, which also determine the way radio stations are allowed to be used.

Local radio stations can be considered the most important mass media as far as their contribution to rural development in developing countries is concerned. The role of these radio stations consists of providing an alternative, more independent, source of general information, as well as offering information on issues of local interest through discussions, interviews with representatives of local interest groups, and testimonies of individuals on their experiences. Simultaneously they offer local NGOs and government agencies access to mass media and often serve as intermediaries between the population and local authorities.

Although active participation of the audience in broadcasts may compensate for some of the disadvantages of broadcasting, in general, local radio stations seem to be unable to move beyond the aforementioned role. In a sense participation of the audience represents a registration pattern, which could serve to provide more meaningful information through broadcasts, thus increasing the relevance of allocation patterns. The relative independence of the local stations (of the state, but not of commercial interests, or institutions such as the church) gives them a higher level of credibility with the local population, but the essentially one-way information flow of the broadcasts limits the use of radio in rural development to very specific aspects.

TELEVISION COVERAGE IN INDIA

Radio is the medium with the largest coverage in India. The oral tradition of communication, prevalent in rural India, makes radio the main source of information. In the context of rural development a distinction between national level and local level mass media is relevant. India has various national level radio stations, such as the Aakashvani), and the privately owned FM Channels, as well as satellite-based radio broadcasters. The national level and satellite broadcasts can be received in large parts of the country, but are also a typical example of the limitations of information flows following an allocation pattern. Local radio stations, covering areas ranging from small villages to entire departments and beyond, can roughly be divided into stations with commercial objectives, and those which stress educational and developmental objectives.

The coverage of television in India is far less than that of radio, with far fewer local level television stations. However, the popularity of television is increasing, with more and more districts acquiring a satellite connection. Some of the major national level television stations are Zee Cinema, Sony TV, Sab TV, and many more, operating as satellite channels. None of those stations produces programs specifically aimed at the rural population, let alone at specific aspects of rural development.

Local television stations do exist, but in general only insert a few programs into the signal of a national level broadcaster for lack of television infrastructure and funds. Due to this relative absence of local television stations, and the dominant position of the commercial stations, the contribution of television to rural development is rather limited.

The more complex nature of television technology, and the higher costs involved with transmitting and receiving information, mean that television is by no means as widely available in rural areas as radio. Although television can be used as a centralized and a decentralized medium, the former usually prevails. Television, unlike radio, more often uses satellites, with most developing countries allowing the reception of satellite transmissions. Those broadcasts, however, are usually aimed at providing entertainment and providing an alternative source of general news, the latter depending on the leeway provided by the socio-political context. At the same time the costs of reception equipment, for example satellite dishes, and the related technical infrastructure is far more prohibitive than of radio.

Television stations, like radio stations, provide information following allocation patterns, and therefore their potential contribution to rural development is the same as that of radio. However, most television stations are based in major cities, or even in other countries, which exacerbates electronic mass media's negative factors: one-way communication, the lack of feedback opportunities and the physical distance between sender and receiver. The main advantage of television, in conveying messages, is the additional characteristic of visual information, which allows for a slightly different type of information to be provided, since less equivocal message can be conveyed by using the combination of sound and vision. However, difficulties for retaining information are similar to radio.

A MULTIMEDIA APPROACH

This concluding section will address two aspects of the use of electronic media in rural development:

- message content (media richness),
- communication process and social change.

The previous sections demonstrated that all electronic media have limitations, thus suggesting an approach combining electronic media. Basic telecommunication and the Internet are at the centre of this approach, because the organizational concept of information centers is proposed to provide access to those media. However, the choice for information centers implicates the following weaknesses:

- unfamiliarity with information centers;
- lack of credibility of centers as information source;
- low level of physical access; and,
- limited 'reach' of information centers into and coverage of remote rural areas.

Some of these weaknesses can, to a certain extent, be addressed by electronic mass media, preferably local radio stations. The easy 'access' to broadcast content, and opportunities for audience participation, could compensate for some of the weaknesses of information centers.

Stations could create awareness of centers, familiarizing people with the concept and presenting testimonials of experiences with information centers through participation in radio broadcasts. By associating themselves with information centers, 'independent' local radio stations could also lend some credibility to those centers as a reliable, trustworthy sources of information. Finally, local radio stations could keep information centers in touch with local issues, problems, and specific information demands.

The involvement of electronic mass media of course still does not solve the problem of limited access to information centers, or the limited reach and coverage of those centers. Although no combination of electronic media can completely compensate for that weakness of information centers, the combination of radio and television can provide some information available in the centers to people in remote rural areas.

Through careful use of the media richness characteristics of mass media, more complicated and technical information can be made available via broadcasts. To improve on processing and comprehension of information, groups of listeners and viewers could be established in even the smallest settlements to discuss broadcasted information during, and immediately after, reception.

Using the media richness concept implicates that the content of messages conveyed through the different electronic media should be in accordance with their specific characteristics.

Mass media, such as radio and television are most suited to convey basic, informative information on campaigns (e.g. health care, education, agricultural programs, and rural development initiatives), government and private sector financing opportunities, available (economic) development support from government institutions, NGOs and other organizations, among others. Mass media will create awareness and through audience participation, discussion forums, and testimonials, they can elaborate on initial information. Radio is more widespread and should thus be the initial medium. Television broadcasts should be added later, using the specific advantages of combining audio and visual aspects. Mass media create limited conversational patterns through audience participation, but individual and networked electronic media will have to provide more detailed and specific information, geared towards smaller groups. Individual, networked media should be used to facilitate and support conversational patterns.

This leads to the second aspect of the approach. Conversational patterns change the power structure and decentralize generation of and control over information (flows). Instead of focusing on information provision, the emphasis would shift to information exchange or interactive communication. In addition information exchange should take place at local levels, mainly using locally produced information, knowledge, and experience.

Next, to bypass existing centers higher up in the power structure, and to strengthen local level organizations and institutions, communication should preferably be horizontal. Furthermore, to increase relevance of the information and credibility of the source, communication should occur between senders and receivers similarly situated. This approach can be achieved by following the steps below:

- ownership of information centers by local organizations and institutions;
- network information centers, while retaining individual independence;
- promotion and support of independently owned and operated local mass media;
- deployment of electronic media to facilitate and support existing information exchanges at local levels; and,
- using and creating local content.

This approach supports decentralization of the power structure, to create independent information generation and storage, and subsequently facilitates, or provides conditions for, social change through local level, horizontal information exchange, complemented by information provision.

CONCLUDING REMARKS

Since the new ICTs also have significant disadvantages, in particular with respect to reach, access, cost, credibility, and familiarity, combining basic telecommunication services and the Internet with the existing electronic mass media (radio and television) is imperative to arrive at an optimal communication for rural development effort. The concept of media richness demonstrates that, with respect to content of the messages, a combination of all electronic media has distinctive advantages over the isolated use of individual electronic media. Finally, the concept of ITPs indicates that the most important contribution of the new networked ICTs is in their suitability for conversational patterns and their role in facilitating horizontal communication and in bypassing existing centers in the power structures, thus possibly facilitating social change.

AN INSIGHT INTO RURAL TV VIEWERSHIP

Television, by default, has turned out to be just the medium to access the rural middle/ upper class, if the findings of a study conducted by the Audience Research Bureau of Doordarshan this year are an indication.

As the multinationals came marching in, cities and town were deluged by a sea of consumer products. Big brand names went up in neon hoardings and flashed across millions of TV screens in back-to-back ad spots as homemakers and office-goers reached for the remote, the popcorn and the easy-chair.

Tele-watchers are quite often tele-owners and more tele-owners are to be found in the better-off States. The survey discovered that in rural India television ownership was related to the affluence of the State. The correlation also surfaced in the occupation profile of TV owners, a majority of whom held salaried jobs, owned land or were in business and trade. Agricultural workers who account for 50 per cent of the rural population owned only 15 per cent of rural TV sets.

Although, more than two-thirds of the country is rural populace, there is not much researched data available. The above study, called 'Television and Satellite Television in Rural

India', was based on field work conducted in January-April in 1997, covering 535 villages in 16 states. Over 30,000 TV households were enumerated and 7,500 respondents interviewed.

There are an estimated 22 million television sets in rural India. In terms of access to television in their homes, that means 122 million or 18 per cent of the total estimated rural population of 684 million are now able to do so. The figure has climbed by nine percentage points over DD's 1992 estimate while the number of TV homes has been growing at the rate of 3-4 million per year. Taking these figures into account, it is now estimated that the total TV homes in India stand at 55 million.

A look at the market variations in rural TV ownership reveal some interesting features. For instance, the striking differences across the states surveyed. The countrywide penetration saw TV penetration at a little over one-fifth of the rural population.

Also, not surprisingly, a high TV penetration seemed usually to partner greater rural affluence, that is more access was to be had in states which had a lower proportion of its people below the poverty line. Thus, some of the northern states such as Punjab Haryana and Himachal Pradesh over 40 per cent of the rural populace have access to TV at home. Eastern states like West Bengal, Orissa and Bihar report a penetration of under 15 per cent.

The rural affluence ranking of these six states were, respectively, 1, 6, not available, 12, 14 and 15. The corresponding percentage of penetration was 46.7, 42.2, 14.2, 12.1 and 10.1. Kerala (30.3 per cent) along with the first three states was also included in the high penetration segment.

The moderate penetration segment (17 to 23 per cent) included states such as Maharashtra, Gujarat, Andhra Pradesh, Madhya Pradesh and Assam. Interestingly, here the affluence rankings included a broad mix, with ranks 2 and 3 (AP and Gujarat) rubbing shoulders with ranks 9, 10 and 11 (Maharashtra, Assam, MP).

Analysing the data for growth in satellite television in rural India, it was found that while television ownership may be decided by economic prosperity, going for a cable connection was dictated by two added conditions: an interest in language programming and the viability of cable operation in the area. Satellite TV in India is distributed to households almost entirely through cable TV networks. Inherent hindrances in the viability of cable operation in rural areas took the form of the small incidence of television homes in any single village, the geographical dispersion of these homes, a preponderance of black and white sets and the hassles of collecting monthly subscription.

Even now, it emerged, only a tiny 2-3 per cent of the overall rural population watch satellite television at home. Change, however, was breezing in on the tailcoats of channels with Tamil, Telugu and Kannada programming. It was found that the availability of long hours of film-based programmes had motivated a sizeable number of rural homes in these language regions to acquire a cable connection.

Cable operators had been able to overcome inherent snags since operating with only one dish facing the Intelsat satellite had made it possible to keep the operation cost low and charge nominal subscriptions.

POPULARITY OF INDIVIDUAL CHANNELS

The popularity of individual channels was, on the whole, found to be similar in trends in urban India. However, while satellite TV is a threat to Doordarshan in urban India, it was far from being so in rural India, Doordarshan's strategy of launching DD2 and the regional language satellite channels is paying off by retaining some audience share for Doordarshan even within satellite homes.

In the southern states of Tamil Nadu, AP and Karnataka, it was found that Doordarshan's language channels and regional language programmes on private channels had given an impetus to cable infiltration. However, in Kerala, the topography of the state had become a deterrent to cable expansion despite similar interests in regional language programming.

Eenadu TV was found to be the largest of the satellite channels with Sun TV and then DD5 (Tamil) and DD8 (Telugu) following close on its heels. In the Hindi region comprising the north, west and Bihar, even those states that had a comparatively high television ownership like Maharashtra and Punjab, cable infiltration was comparatively still low. A possible explanation for this was the absence of a strong language factor. Gujarat in the region had the highest cable infiltration in urban areas with some percolation down to the rural areas as well.

In West Bengal the interest in DD7 (DD's Bengali channel) was high but the ownership of television sets was low, probably impending the growth of satellite television).

In this context, it was interesting to see that as much as 78 per cent of television homes in rural areas still used black and white sets. The only exception was Kerala where 65 per cent of the sets in rural areas were colour, elsewhere black and white sets dominated with over 70 per cent of the share. Most of these sets were less than five years old.

Watching TV is implicated in the disengagement of citizens from politics, the promotion of questionable images of women, and the fattening of couch potatoes everywhere. But when it comes to the medium's treatment of women, television may be getting a bum rap. A new study by Robert Jensen of Brown University and Emily Oster of the University of Chicago shows that television is having a distinctly helpful effect on women, at least in rural India, which admittedly doesn't have America's half-century of experience with the medium, or 300 channels to surf through.

The words female empowerment and television in the same sentence may bring to mind Star Jones extolling tummy tucks on The View. But for millions of women in developing countries, the benefits of TV may be substantive rather than frothy.

Attitudes about women in rural India remain, shall we say, traditional: Women are expected to cook and clean and to have lots of babies. Surveys from 2001 to 2003 show that rural

Indian women don't have a lot of control over their lives. More than half need permission from their husbands to go shopping. Two-thirds need their husbands' permission to visit friends. Spousal beating is common and accepted: Sixty-two percent of women believe that it is sometimes acceptable.

Thirty-four percent of the women surveyed believed a husband could hit his wife if she neglected the children, while nearly a third believed that showing disrespect and going places without permission warranted a beating. One fifth of women believe husbands are entitled to hit them for cooking a lousy dinner.

The usual avenue for bettering women's circumstances in the developing world is education. Women with more education have access to better jobs outside the home, better control of their fertility, and better bargaining power with their husbands. Education has other benefits, too, so it's understandably a big investment priority for most governments. But education changes attitudes slowly. So, how about TV, a quicker fix?

In the last decade, cable television has arrived in remote Indian villages, bringing with it commercial television programming heavy on game shows and Indian soap operas. Before you laugh-a feminist Days of Our Lives?-consider that the most popular Indian series take place in urban settings. Their emancipated female characters are well-educated, work outside the home, control their own money, and have fewer children than rural women. (One of the most popular shows in 2007, called Because a Mother-in-Law Was Once a Daughter-in-Law, Also, describes the life of a wealthy Mumbai family and features plots revolving around family and gender.) So, Jensen and Oster asked, does the arrival of these shows change attitudes in ways that improve women's lives?

The authors followed women in 2,700 households in villages in four states (Bihar, Goa, Haryana, and Tamil Nadu) and the capital, Delhi, from 2001 to 2003. Access to television in remote Indian villages has changed substantially in the past few years. Of the 180 villages the authors studied, 65 already had cable in 2001, and by the end of 2003, 21 more had access. Not surprisingly, when a village gets access to cable, villagers tend to watch more TV: Forty percent report watching weekly before cable came to town compared with 80 percent after.

What's the effect? In the places that didn't get cable by 2003, and in the places that already had it at the beginning of the period studied, attitudes concerning women remained relatively stable. (They were more pro-women in places that already had cable.) But in the 21 villages that got cable between 2001 and 2003, women's attitudes changed quickly and substantially.

The authors focus on three measures: autonomy (whether the woman gets to make her own decisions about shopping, health, and whom she visits), attitudes toward beating (the number of circumstances in which women view beating as acceptable), and whether women prefer having male children. After a village got cable, women's preference for male children fell by 12 percentage points. The average number of situations in which women said that wife beating is acceptable fell by about 10 percent. And the authors' composite autonomy index jumped substantially, by an amount equivalent to the attitude difference associated with 5.5 years of additional education.

So far, these results concern measures of attitude rather than behaviour-indicating, perhaps, that TV just teaches women to give the answers that surveying do-gooders want to hear. But the authors also measured the women's average number of births and the likelihood that their children were enrolled in school. When cable came to town, boys' rates of school attendance stayed the same, while girls between the ages of 6 and 10 were 8 percent more likely to go to school.

The effects on fertility were even more dramatic: For women under the age of 35, average number of births fell annually by more than half. It's possible, however, that this shows a change in the timing of births rather than overall lifetime fertility, given the study's relatively short duration.

Jensen and Oster think that TV works its magic on women by providing them a new televised set of peers and in turn changing their attitudes. Supporting this conclusion is evidence that TV's emancipatory effects were larger in places where women initially held more traditional attitudes. For example, in the places where women had formerly held high preferences for sons, the share preferring sons fell 20 percentage points with the arrival of cable, compared with a 12 percent decline overall.

Americans' average TV-viewing time of four hours a day may still be too much of a good thing. But the women of rural India, who are just getting started on their favourite cable shows, should perhaps call the TV the Empowerment Box instead of the Idiot Box.

TELEVISION AS EMANCIPATION IN RURAL INDIA

It is interesting all the speculation around the increase access in technology and new media to people in rural places and how it is or is not emancipating them. Specifically, this discussion delves into the commonly discussed question of TV series (Indian equivalent of soaps) and their effects on women in India. According to Slate, these women are being "helped" or rather, brought into the modern times (if you will) by the cable television.

A new study by Robert Jensen of Brown University and Emily Oster of the University of Chicago shows that television is having a distinctly helpful effect on women, at least in rural India, which admittedly doesn't have America's half-century of experience with the medium, or 300 channels to surf through.

So we checked out the abstract from the study and it said this: This chapter explores the effect of the introduction of cable television on gender attitudes in rural India. Using a three-year individual-level panel dataset, we find that the introduction of cable television is associated with improvements in women's status. We find significant increases in reported autonomy, decreases in the reported acceptability of beating and decreases in reported son preference. We also find increases in female school enrolment and decreases in fertility (primarily via increased birth spacing).

The effects are large, equivalent in some cases to about five years of education in the cross section, and move gender attitudes of individuals in rural areas much closer to those in urban areas. We argue that the results are not driven by pre-existing differential trends. These results have important policy implications, as India and other countries attempt to decrease bias against women.

It can be argued that there is some truth to this. I don't really prefer Waldfogel's presumptive nature of the way that things are for women in rural India, as backwards and traditional and the television is helping them come into the light. However, I think some of the trends that are happening, as a result of a change in economy and the women's movement in India, are probably reflected in television and they mutually reinforce each other.

The studies that say new technologies emancipate people in "old, narrow and backward" places are quite weary. There has been similar work done on internet access and rural women in India. Women in rural India have roles and responsibilities, extensive kinship networks, methods of healing, irrigation techniques that "modernization" sometimes wipes out. Here it can not be said that one is better than the other, it is just important to see things for what they are. Series television is very much like soap operas, they are not based in reality, the women reflect idealized and unattainable standards of beauty, and the plot lines are unrealistic and fantastical. So although they women in series may represent a more modern woman, she is also a production of capitalist desire, latching on to upper-middle class notions of success.

It is hard to judge one culture while sitting in another, wondering what exactly emancipation is for rural women in India, having some intense desire for them to be free. While ignoring how many of us are enslaved by the images we watch on television and I would hardly call that freedom.

Ultimately the study found that it was a change in attitude that is most notable, as opposed to a change in actual behaviour. I think it is safe to say that TV has the potential to change attitudes everywhere, but it is a matter of the direction that we want it to change in. Mainstream media and its reach has had truly dangerous consequences for the American imagination, so, I maybe a little skeptical of calling the TV in India an "Empowerment box."

RURAL INDIA GOES DIGITAL

A satellite-television boom in India is finally pushing multichannel TV into its vast rural hinterland and opening a new commercial battlefield in one of the world's biggest TV markets.

Places like Lodra, a village of two thousand people and a few hundred mud huts, 700 kilometers north of here in Gujarat state, typify the new phenomenon. At dusk, hundreds of people routinely gather around a TV set propped on a wooden table in the village centre. They will watch until early morning, drawn by the 36 channels relayed from a satellite to a receiving dish on the ground.

"The choice of channels puts us in a good mood after a hard day in the fields," explains farmer Madhabhai B. Thakor in a phone interview. Until last year, Mr. Thakor, like most rural Indians, he had to make do with just two of India's earnest but insipid public terrestrial channels. Now, he and his friends enjoy musicals in the local Gujarati dialect and anything with lots of fight scenes.

Nearly three-quarters of India's 1.1 billion people live in villages like Lodra, making it one of the world's least-urbanized countries. While India's cable connections have tripled over the past decade to 61 million, rural households have missed out as cable companies see no profit in stringing kilometers of wire to reach remote locations.

Enter digital television. Relying on signals transmitted from a satellite to a receiving dish and from there to a set-top signal-decoding box, rather than through cables, digital TV can transmit anywhere, delivering more channels and better picture quality.

"Digital TV is going to change the dynamics of the Indian TV marketplace," says Vivek Couto of Media Partners Asia, a research & consulting firm in Hong Kong, who sees a looming commercial battle between digital and cable companies. Mr. Couto expects India to have 12 million paying subscribers to digital TV by 2015--a huge jump from just 400,000 currently--generating 45 billion rupees, or about $1 billion, in annual revenue. Cable connections are expected to exceed 70 million by then, he says. The spread of digital might occur at an even faster clip if India's Congress Party-led coalition government endorses broadcasting-industry proposals to raise the foreign direct-investment ceiling in direct-to-home TV ventures from the current 20% to at least 49%, the level permitted in the cable industry.

There is pent-up demand for such service. India is the world's third-largest television market with 108 million TV-equipped households, a number that is growing by about nine million a year. But that still leaves half of all Indian households without a television set. Moreover, many existing TVs are old 14-inch (35-centimeter) black-and-white models that can't receive some satellite channels via cable, even if cable operators were willing to hook up remote areas for new subscribers.

So, many villages have been left with only India's famously stodgy state-owned broadcaster, Doordarshan, where the programming emphasis is on informing the rural masses about farming techniques and health issues.

"Satellite television can only rise in India, and rise very fast," says Atul Phadnis, an analyst at TAM India, a media research firm. "Direct-to-home television will be a huge catalyst."

India's pay-TV industry is focused on cable operators and has nearly $3 billion in annual revenue, according to a recent Price Waterhouse Coopers study. But satellite can go where cable hasn't, which is into the increasingly prosperous rural market.

R.V. Rajan, managing director at Anugrah Madison Advertising, a rural marketing concern in Chennai, says residents of India's countryside spend about $30 billion a year on everything from air conditioners to shampoo and household detergents. Aggregate rural spending power is growing about 25% annually.

Pradeep Kashyup, another rural-marketing guru and chief executive of New Delhi-based consultancy Mart, says rural household income has risen quickly along with India's economic expansion. Rural households now earn nearly 60,000 rupees a year, still around half that earned by urban households.

Mr. Kashyup contends that disposable income is actually higher in the countryside than in the cities because of a lower cost of living. Many villagers, he explains, own rather than rent their homes, while education and health care are mostly free. "New TV services will proliferate in the countryside very quickly," he predicts. "At the press of a button, [advertisers] will be able to reach every corner of the country."

Media companies, local and foreign, are rushing to cash in. Zee Telefilms Ltd., India's biggest media company, says it is adding 3,000 new satellite subscribers a month to the direct-to-home service it started last year called Dish TV. "Half of these are coming from small towns," says Dish TV's chief executive, Sunil Khanna.

News Corp.'s Hong-Kong based Star TV, which already operates some of India's hottest cable channels, will soon launch a direct satellite service in a joint venture with Tata Sons Ltd., the holding company of Tata Group, one of India's biggest industrial conglomerates.

Even Doordarshan, the public broadcaster, is joining the fray. It is offering a satellite service with 30 free channels, including some broadcast by southern India's Sun TV, which has agreed to join Doordarshan's digital service. The public broadcaster requires its customers to purchase only a set-top decoder and a small satellite dish for 1,500 to 2,000 rupees. Doordarshan says its satellite signals can be picked up by the basic decoders already on the market, and it says more than four million decoders already have been sold to people wanting to view its programs.

"No mass-market service can afford to ignore rural India today," says Vikram Kaushik, chief executive of Space TV, the name of the new Tata-Star TV joint venture. "There is a huge market waiting to be tapped."

Kirk Johnson, a sociologist at the University of Guam who has studied the impact of television in rural India, believes satellite TV will change social and economic patterns as well, providing poorer country-dwellers with information they can use to improve their lives.

Indeed, Mr. Thakor, the Lodra farmer, has used information gleaned from his village's new Doordarshan service to purchase a new type of cattle feed that produces more milk from his cows and makes his family an extra 45 rupees a day. He plans to use the extra cash to finance a truck purchase under a promotion he also saw on TV.

INDIA BROADCAST MEDIA

The national television (Doordarshan) and radio (All India Radio, or Akashwani) networks are state-owned and managed by the Ministry of Information and Broadcasting. Their news reporting customarily presents the government's point of view. For example, coverage of the 1989 election campaign blatantly favoured the government of Rajiv Gandhi, and autonomy of the electronic media became a political issue. V.P. Singh's National Front government sponsored the Prasar Bharati (Indian Broadcasting) Act, which Parliament considered in 1990, to provide greater autonomy to Doordarshan and All India Radio. The changes that resulted were limited. The bill provided for the establishment of an autonomous corporation to run Doordarshan and All India Radio.

The corporation was to operate under a board of governors to be in charge of appointments and policy and a broadcasting council to respond to complaints. However, the legislation required that the corporation prepare and submit its budget within the framework of the central budget and stipulated that the personnel of the new broadcasting corporation be career civil servants to facilitate continued government control. In the early 1990s, increasing competition from television broadcasts transmitted via satellite appeared the most effective manner of limiting the progovernment bias of the government-controlled electronic media. Since the 1980s, India has experienced a rapid proliferation of television broadcasting that has helped shape popular culture and the course of politics. Although the first television program was broadcast in 1959, the expansion of television did not begin in earnest until the extremely popular telecast of the Ninth Asian Games, which were held in New Delhi in 1982. Realizing the popular appeal and consequent influence of television broadcasting, the government undertook an expansion that by 1990 was planned to provide television access to 90 percent of the population.

In 1993, about 169 million people were estimated to have watched Indian television each week, and, by 1994, it was reported that there were some 47 million households with televisions. There also is a growing selection of satellite transmission and cable services available.

Television programming was initially kept tightly under the control of the government, which embarked on a self-conscious effort to construct and propagate a cultural idea of the Indian nation. This goal is especially clear in the broadcasts of such megaseries as the Hindu epics Ramayana and Mahabharata. In addition to the effort at nation-building, the politicians of India's ruling party have not hesitated to use television to build political support. In fact, the political abuse of Indian television led to demands to increase the autonomy of Doordarshan; these demands ultimately resulted in support for the Prasar Bharati Act.

The 1990s have brought a radical transformation of television in India. Transnational satellite broadcasting made its debut in January 1991, when owners of satellite dishes--initially mostly at major hotels--began receiving Cable News Network (CNN) coverage of the Persian Gulf War. Three months later, Star TV began broadcasting via satellite. Its fare initially included serials such as "The Bold and the Beautiful" and MTV programs. Satellite broadcasting spread rapidly through India's cities as local entrepreneurs erected dishes to receive signals and transmitted them through local cable systems. After its October 1992 launch, Zee TV offered stiff competition to Star TV. However, the future of Star TV was bolstered by billionaire Rupert Murdock, who acquired the network for US$525 million in July 1993. CNN International, part of the Turner

Broadcasting System, was slated to start broadcasting entertainment programs, including top Hollywood films, in 1995.

Competition from the satellite stations brought radical change to Doordarshan by cutting its audience and threatening its advertising revenues at a time when the government was pressuring it to pay for expenditures from internal revenues. In response, Doordarshan decided in 1993 to start five new channels in addition to its original National Channel. Programming was radically transformed, and controversial news shows, soap operas, and coverage of high-fashion events proliferated. Of the new Doordarshan channels, however, only the Metro Channel, which carries MTV music videos and other popular shows, has survived in the face of the new trend for talk programs that engage in a potpourri of racy topics.

DEVELOPMENT BROADCASTING IN INDIA

The advent of commercial satellite television has changed the media landscape in many Asian countries that primarily had state-run broadcasting systems. As a result, long-established broadcasters have been forced to reassess their role in a newly competitive market. This study examines the fate of one of the central practices of Third World media--the development model of broadcasting--in the face of an increasingly globalized and commercial media environment.

Specifically, this study of India's public broadcaster, Doordarshan (DD), explains how the broadcaster has been struggling to respond to transformations in the media environment. It details how its past mandate of development broadcasting has come under severe pressure as DD competes with many new satellite and cable channels offering audiences ever more choices. Beyond evaluating the Indian situation, this investigation challenges entrenched assumptions about the current demise of development broadcasting and proposes a new model of it in a competitive and globalizing media world.

Using the Indian broadcasting situation as an example has the advantage that this evaluation can be based on one of the most intensely studied media systems in the developing world. Numerous scholars have contributed to the analysis of the impact of media globalization and commercialization on Indian society and culture over the last 15 years. Such in-depth work allows the authors to move a step further to a meta-analysis of these trends with regard to the impact on development broadcasting.

After an overview of the past and current situation of development broadcasting in general, DD's specific approaches to this type of broadcasting are analysed. Findings show that DD's decision to compete with commercial broadcasters' offerings came at the cost of ignoring the constituencies and subjects it most needs to focus on. In trying to become a competitive player among the domestic and global channels, it has found itself financially challenged and, in many instances, in the role of a follower rather than a leader. The analysis then draws attention to some problematic assumptions and arguments shared in the scholarly debate surrounding its future. Finally, some solutions are proposed for an alternative model of development broadcasting. This study advocates a new type of development broadcasting that establishes a distinct brand with regard to content and identity and plays an important role in creating an informed citizenry.

TELEVISION AND DEVELOPMENT

Over the last 50 years the impetus for many third-world countries to venture into the cost-intensive development of an independent television system was driven by the perceived importance of broadcasting to national development. Starting in the 1950s and throughout the Cold War, both media scholars in the West and media planners in the third world justified and theorized the significance of broadcasting in the development process for an increasing number of countries gaining independence. In the United States, communication scholars such as Daniel Lerner, Wilbur Schramm, and Everett Rogers (1962) based in the dominant paradigm stressed that these new developing countries needed broadcasting to establish a sense of national identity and to support modernization projects and campaigns.

Likewise, in countries under the influence of the Soviet Union, the Marxist-Leninist model of journalism as an educational force supported the idea of the media as a means for development (Cambridge, 2002). Even countries in the nonaligned movement such as India favoured the development focus of the media. In general, as Eko (2003) explained:

Media were to concentrate on the task of disseminating information and messages that would improve agricultural production education, national security and other vital areas... based on the assumption that the mass media had very powerful, direct, and immediate effects on listeners and viewers.

The United Nations, especially its subdivision UNESCO, became the major international champion of development media projects.

Yet after many years of naive celebration of the importance of broadcasting for modernization, dependency theorists, especially in Latin America, successfully challenged the paradigm (for an overview see Cambridge, 2002; Reeves, 1993). Dependency theorists argued that many of these systems were government controlled, overly dependent on Western programming, and furthering the interests of the political elites, while limiting national forms of expression and the development of a national identity.

The dissatisfaction over the overdependence on Western commercial media output culminated in the controversial UNESCO McBride Report and resulted in a call for a new world information order. Yet the end of the Cold War and the neoliberal turn in the late 20th century along with intensified economic globalization seemed to make international communication policy efforts obsolete. Communication has become part of international trade agreements as opposed to political initiatives, as Hamelink (2002) pointed out. At the same time, international trade negotiations have favoured deregulation and encouraged or coerced developing countries to privatize their communication infrastructure and to allow commercial units to compete against formerly state-run institutions.

As a result, most state-owned broadcasters in the developing world were forced to adjust to a mixed economic model that included advertising and dwindling state subsidies. The new commercial media environment led to a proliferation of stations, shows, and formats, coupled with a fragmentation of audiences, and a new advertising-driven focus on affluent urban audiences. Scholars like Sinha (1995) explained that by itself, this increase in the supply of programming did not meet the development goals of an informed citizen who has access to communication technology. As he pointed out "development is not a matter, ultimately, of expanding supplies of commodities or services, but of enhancing the capabilities of people." The old paradigm of development communication was relegated to the back burner.

The globalizing and commercializing media landscape in the developing world has gained increased interest among international media scholars. After years of debating the significance of cultural imperialism, much of this work has shifted to the economic details and everyday media experiences in this new "glocalized" media world. However, this research often prioritizes the impact of change on the urban middle class or the relation between transnational media conglomerates and local production or other business aspects of the new system.

Although these studies have added a wealth of detailed new information on the impact of media globalization, international communication scholars seem to shy away from more general normative questions of what functions a broadcasting system should deliver to citizens of a given country--more generally, the relation between broadcasting and civic society in the developing world. Although some scholars have begun to address a different definition of public broadcasters in the West under the current pressures, the new role for (more or less) state-controlled public broadcasters in the third world has yet to find a place in scholarly debate.

This oversight is the starting point of this study. Using DD's experiences, it questions the role and potential of development broadcasting as the most significant and distinctive aspect of third-world broadcasting. This inquiry challenges not only the strategies of broadcasters and regulators but also some assumptions by academic media scholars that can be counterproductive to fleshing out a new role for development public broadcasting.

REACTION OF DOORDARSHAN TO COMMERCIAL COMPETITION

The case of DD is particularly interesting because unlike other countries where television was developed to serve the needs of a middle class that had the ability to buy television sets, in India, television began with a strong development mandate. However, beginning in the mid-1990s, DD tried to position itself as a competitor to both the international and domestic channels that offer a range of commercial programs. This strategy questions the role that public broadcasters like DD play in a multichannel, commercial environment and raises the broader issue of whether there is a future for development broadcasting in a commercialized global television environment.

India had taken an unusual position with regard to development broadcasting. Whereas most other postcolonial countries made development efforts only part of a mixed programming strategy, often relying heavily on imports from U.S. and former colonial Western partners, India focused its technological and programming innovations almost exclusively on rural educational programming and nation building. Television came to India in 1959 as a result of a fortuitous offer by the electronics company Phillips to provide a 500-watt transmitter at a low cost in conjunction with a UNESCO grant that was used to buy community television sets. These were set up in the area surrounding New Delhi and a weekly half-hour broadcast began. By 1965 television broadcasts had become a regular daily feature. Program content was mostly developmental in nature with some news and entertainment.

Over time, state funding for DD increased. The rationale for the expense was that it was being used to promote state initiatives of progress and integration. In 1972 additional centers were set up in Bombay, Calcutta, Madras, Lucknow, and the border towns of Amritsar and Srinagar. India's first indigenous satellite program, SITE, was launched in 1975. SITE took television to 2,400 villages in six states. Television was seen as the "open classroom" that would bring the rural masses up to speed with health, literacy, and agricultural programs. The optimistic launch of SITE as a satellite-based development model was celebrated by many communication scholars.

The acceptance of advertising on television in 1976 marked the first step toward commercialization. At the same time the number of television sets in the country continued to grow and crossed the 1 million mark in 1980. Colour television was introduced in 1982 and this development was followed by the establishment of a second channel in Delhi, Bombay, and other cities.

By the early 1980s sponsored programs were accepted. Private producers were invited to bid for slots for their programs on DD's television channel. Even in this climate of increased internal commercialization there was an attempt to maintain the development goals. One of the first soap operas on DD, Hum Log, contained messages about the need for family planning and the importance of education for women. Other popular serials during the 1980s were based on the Indian religious epics, the Ramayana and the Mahabharata.

Prime Minister Rajiv Gandhi's economic liberalization policies led to a growth both in the size of the television network and the variety of programming available. In the late 1980s a second channel targeting urban audiences called DD Metro was started in major cities. Television was now catering as much, if not more, to urban audiences than to rural audiences.

These changes were not universally seen as positive. As early as 1985, the Joshi report (1985) criticized the growing place that film-based entertainment occupied in DD's programming. It warned that the needs of the urban middle class not be allowed to dominate the programming mix on DD and reiterated the educational and development role that television had the potential to play in India.

Yet, as Johnson (2000) succinctly contended: "All of the committee's concerns have come to pass. Though several recommendations were useful, the vast majority were never fully implemented." In a critical history of Indian television, Pendakur and Kapur (1997) argued that even before the liberalization of the 1990s, the Indian state had always represented the interests of the bourgeoisie and business. Thus the process of liberalization had "greater continuities than breaks with the past."

The commercialization of Indian television broadcasting and the demise of the development mandate that had begun during the era of economic liberalization under Rajiv Gandhi accelerated with the arrival of satellite television in India. Since the launch of STAR TV in 1991, followed by other domestic and international channels, DD became concerned with losing its urban viewership to the ever-increasing international and later local competition. DD's response was to position itself as a competitor to the international and domestic channels that offer a wide variety of commercial programs. The broadcaster has been faced with choosing the direction it plans to go in the future. Yet the choices that were believed to attract urban viewers often undermined its development goals.

One of the first steps taken in response to competition was to add new channels. Channel offerings were increased from 2 in 1990 to 17 by the end of 1997 (Manchanda, 1998). The main DD feed was called DD National. DD Metro carried local news, sports, and drama; and DD3 was started as a channel carrying arts, music, news, and current affairs programming for the elite. Apart from these a number of channels in regional languages were added to broaden DD's appeal. Although Hindi is the national language, it is not widely spoken in southern India and there had been resentment at the domination of Hindi programs on DD. The regional language channels gave DD access to audiences in their own languages. Currently DD has 4 national channels and 21 regional ones.

To make its programming more competitive with commercial channels, DD entered into agreements with foreign broadcasters to carry their programming. Here DD paradoxically laid the foundation for its own future competition by providing the launch pad for commercial networks to enter the still-controlled Indian market. In 1995 CNN became the first private broadcaster to be allowed carriage on an Indian satellite following an agreement with DD to lease a channel on Insat-2B. DD received an annual payment of $1.5 million (U.S.) and up to 4 hours of telecasting time per day on the leased channel.

This agreement ended in 1997 ("CNNI Finds Satellite," 1997). Starting in 1996, DD's Metro channel carried a block of MTV programming for almost 2 years until MTV returned to India as a satellite channel. The same year a similar deal with NBC Asia gave that channel access to Indian audiences. As Jacka and Ray (1996) pointed out, "with entertainment (and viewer preference) being the sole criterion, Indian television is now the site of commercial exploitation as never before and consumer sovereignty is the guiding ethos."

DD has also tried to adopt the genres that these commercial media providers offer, such as business news programming. Rather than producing its own programming DD began allowing private channels to bid for half-hour and 1-hour time slots on its channels. DD charged a broadcast fee and bartered advertising time in the programs. By 2001, in an attempt to stop a revenue slide, it began selling 3-hour programming blocks on its channels to both domestic and foreign media companies. Most of the programming was outsourced to providers that included foreign media corporations like HFCL-Nine Broadcasting, ESPN, BBC, and Buena Vista.

However, these new financial arrangements and deals along with increasing advertising slots did not bring DD financial independence from the government. DD's advertising and sponsorship revenues for 2002-2003 fell from Rs 615 crore ($123 million) in the previous revenue year to Rs 550 crore ($110 million). Expenses for 2002-2003 were between Rs 850 and 900 crore ($170-180 million) and the shortfall had to be made up through a government grant.

To make its programming more competitive with commercial channels, DD entered into agreements with foreign broadcasters to carry their programming. Here DD paradoxically laid the foundation for its own future competition by providing the launch pad for commercial networks to enter the still-controlled Indian market. In 1995 CNN became the first private broadcaster to be allowed carriage on an Indian satellite following an agreement with DD to lease a channel on Insat-2B. DD received an annual payment of $1.5 million (U.S.) and up to 4 hours of telecasting time per day on the leased channel. This agreement ended in 1997 ("CNNI Finds Satellite," 1997).

Starting in 1996, DD's Metro channel carried a block of MTV programming for almost 2 years until MTV returned to India as a satellite channel. The same year a similar deal with NBC Asia gave that channel access to Indian audiences. As Jacka and Ray (1996) pointed out, "with entertainment (and viewer preference) being the sole criterion, Indian television is now the site of commercial exploitation as never before and consumer sovereignty is the guiding ethos."

DD has also tried to adopt the genres that these commercial media providers offer, such as business news programming. Rather than producing its own programming DD began allowing private channels to bid for half-hour and 1-hour time slots on its channels. DD charged a broadcast fee and bartered advertising time in the programs. By 2001, in an attempt to stop a revenue slide, it began selling 3-hour programming blocks on its channels to both domestic and foreign media companies. Most of the programming was outsourced to providers that included foreign media corporations like HFCL-Nine Broadcasting, ESPN, BBC, and Buena Vista.

However, these new financial arrangements and deals along with increasing advertising slots did not bring DD financial independence from the government. DD's advertising and sponsorship revenues for 2002-2003 fell from Rs 615 crore ($123 million) in the previous revenue year to Rs 550 crore ($110 million). Expenses for 2002-2003 were between Rs 850 and 900 crore ($170-180 million) and the shortfall had to be made up through a government grant.

Another move that was supposed to take broadcasting to the grassroots level is the narrowcasting experiment. As part of this experiment, 12 low-power transmitters across the country, each covering a radius of about 10 miles, broadcast programs that will appeal to the local audience. The programs contain segments on agriculture, health, education, and rural development ("DD Launches 'Narrowcasting' Tomorrow," 2002). This initiative, obviously, covers a negligible area of the country.

A major change that has taken place in the operations of DD came from the passage of the Prasar Bharati Act. Under this act, DD was converted into an autonomous corporation independent of the Ministry of Information and Broadcasting (I & B) that would be supervised by the Prasar Bharati Board. Only one member of the 15-member board represented the I & B Ministry, thus reducing government interference and oversight of DD, which was set up as an autonomous public service corporation ("Captives No More," 1997). Although the Indian Parliament passed the Act in 1990, it did not go into effect until 1997.

The implementation was delayed in response to calls for changes in the Act to reflect the new electronic media environment (Balaji, 1997). Several of the Act's main mission statements seem to reinstate the development legacy such as the objectives to "uphold the unity and integrity of the country and promote communal harmony" and to "pay special attention to the fields of education, agriculture, rural development and public health."

When S. S. Gill took over as CEO of Prasar Bharati he announced plans to make DD3 a platform for education and development programs and fulfill DD's public service goals ("Wake Up Call for Doordarshan," 1998). Yet this plan appears to have been short-lived and ended when Gill was removed from his position.

The intensified concern over competition for audiences was seen in Prasar Bharati's new chief Rajeeva Shah's plans to repackage DD1 and DD2 to arrest dwindling viewership. Shah announced that DD1 and DD2 would have a greater emphasis on entertainment. Under the revised plan, DD1 and DD2 would become 24-hour channels. Prime time on DD1 would be market driven and revenue oriented, and only non-prime-time programming would address the broadcaster's social obligations.

Only 4 years after the Prasar Bharati Board was formed, many (e.g., Gill, 2001) were sharply critical of the direction DD had taken by auctioning time to private broadcasters and concerning itself with the needs and interest of only urban audiences. Thus despite its official mission, which includes a strong commitment to educational and development programming, over the last decade, DD seems to have been mostly concerned with fending off commercial competition and declining revenues. For example, in a bid to continue to remain competitive with private broadcasters DD has decided to join the costly direct-to-home (DTH) platform ("Prasar Bharati Goes," 2003).

This investment will cost DD Rs 500 crore ($100 million) over 5 years but the channels will be kept free to air, meaning anyone with a Ku-Band dish and set-top box can pick up the signals ("Doordarshan Set to Join," 2003). This is another move that is aimed at retaining the urban, middle-class audience and will not profit poor rural audiences with lesser technological setups.

In 2002 the broadcaster launched a new channel, DD Bharati, a 24-hour art and culture channel. Anil Baijal, then Prasar Bharati CEO, claimed that this channel fulfilled its public service role. In November 2003, DD discontinued its entertainment channel, DD Metro, converting it to an all-news channel in anticipation of increased interest in news programming because of the national elections in 2004. This endeavour actually was a relaunch of DD News, which was shut down in 2001 because the amount of outsourced programming had increased and had resulted in heavy losses for Prasar Bharati.

The 24-hour channel that airs news bulletins in English, Hindi, Sanskrit, and Urdu is a terrestrial channel, which is expected to give it an edge over other all-news channels that are cable channels. At the same time, Prasar Bharati will take advantage of the "must-carry" clause that requires cable operators to carry it on their systems.

The Finance Ministry rejected a proposal from Prasar Bharati for funding the relaunch. Faced with reduced funding from the government, Prasar Bharati decided to outsource programming for at least 5 hours daily on a sponsorship basis. Its goal was to make this channel self-sufficient in 3 years. Programs likely to be outsourced include business news and programs on beauty, health, and entertainment. Once again, commercial pressures have forced it to be more market driven rather than using this channel to create a forum for discussion on issues facing the country.

The case of DD News is another illustration of the contradictory pressures facing the broadcaster. It is expected to support its operations and continue to fulfill the mission of a public service broadcaster--repeatedly upheld by Supreme Court decisions--while fending off commercial competition. In recent years there appear to be some efforts to balance these contradictory goals. On the one hand DD continues to try to become more competitive with its commercial initiatives. On the other hand there seems to be a recognition that its responsibilities go beyond purely commercial ones. In response to criticism that followed its announcement to drop Gyan Darshan, for example, DD was forced to recommit to retaining the channel's educational mission ("Educational Television," 2004).

In addition to its Gyan Darshan endeavour, DD renamed its Government Business Cell the Development Communication Division. This division serves as a production house that can meet the communication needs of various government departments and ministries as well as of a public broadcaster. In 2001 this division undertook a countrywide campaign to highlight the various schemes of the rural development ministry. It has also undertaken media campaigns on HIV/AIDS, tuberculosis, and malaria for the Ministry of Health and Family welfare.

Yet observers of the Indian media are very pessimistic about the survival chances of a development mission in a new commercialized broadcasting landscape. For example, McDowell, analyzing the results of 10 years of state regulation and privatization, argued that media policies "have not responded adequately to calls for greater attention to development uses or for greater public and non-profit access to the airwaves. A more autonomous public service television model has tacitly been rejected through these choices."

Despite the fact that the Indian government intervention repeatedly guaranteed DD a special position as compared to foreign and internal competition (thereby guaranteeing the state's continued influence on media) the broadcaster used the new situation to look and sound more and more like its commercial competitors.

Its former mandates of nation building and development seemed to have been sidelined in the process. Instead, DD now mostly creates and delivers a community of an elite, metropolitan consumer class to advertisers. Overall, the rise of commercial competition in the Indian television sector has forced DD into developing aggressive and costly counterstrategies to secure audiences and revenues. Instead of creating a distinctive noncommercial profile, DD seems to have favoured imitating commercial broadcasting.

A drastic decline in government funding accelerated this change. To guarantee ratings and advertiser support, DD expanded its range of niche channels, developed more entertainment programming with mass appeal, and forged strategic alliances with Western media conglomerates (e.g., CNN, Discovery, MTV) as another stream of revenue.

This analysis should not overlook some more positive aspects of the new commercialization and competition for DD. Overall, as even critics concur, its production values and variety of programming (although mostly entertainment-driven shows) has improved at least for urban audiences.

In its struggle for survival DD, at least to some degree, succeeded in driving back the influence of the central government in programming and executive decisions. Even if the new oversight committee, the Prasar Bharati Board, has not lived up to its mission of a public service orientation, it at least provides a starting point in this direction. Also, facing increased "glocal" regional and local competition, DD finally decentralized its heavily Delhi-based Hindi programming and opened regional outlets. At the same time media scholars have complained about the growing focus of DD on urban, middle-class audiences and the consequent abandonment of its core rural and poor audience, which relies on terrestrial service.

In general, critics also contend that the increasing commercialization of the Indian media system propagates more "Western" values, privileges consumerism as a central value of programming, homogenizes program choices, and hinders direct community access. This new urban middle-class television reality has had a detrimental impact on poor and rural audiences and women who are forced to deal with a new culture of desire and often-unachievable commercial goals.

QUESTIONING THE TRADITIONAL DEVELOPMENT MODEL

The analysis of the strategic decisions made by the Indian broadcaster illustrates why many media critics cite the increasing commercialization and globalization of the media systems as the central reason for the demise of the development postulate in India and other third-world countries. Criticism of the impact of global commercialism often implies that only a return to a less commercialized media system would allow development services to flourish again. Yet, scholarly presumptions that hark back to a nostalgic view can hinder the acceptance of alternative models.

One of these presumptions is that development broadcasting has been a successful part of development projects. Instead, many projects failed because they were not tied into a local connection and because the need for participatory communication models was not recognized. Related to this is the belief that development broadcasting is the most important part of development communication when in fact, a mix of interventions and the use of various interpersonal and mass communication systems is more effective. As Page and Crawley (2001) noted about the SITE project in India, "One of the lessons learnt was that television programmes need to be followed up on the ground. There needs to be close coordination between programme makers and schedulers and the agricultural extension workers in the field." A further assumption is that development broadcasting only entails educational and current events programming and that entertainment programs undermine the objectives of development broadcasting. Yet the reality is that entertainment programs such as soap operas have had considerable success in establishing a forum for cultural change both in Asia and in Latin America. So-called entertainment-education has become one of the more promising strategies of development communication.

A popularly held view is that fragmentation of audiences is a problem for development broadcasting. This view does not take into account the advantages of narrowcasting. Although niche development programs and channels may not gather whole nations in front of the TV they do allow programmers to cater their message toward a much more targeted group that may be underserved by the existing commercial broadcasters.

A common criticism is that the current demise of development broadcasting is undermining the public sphere. Yet, one can also argue the opposite--that a lessened development mandate means a decrease in governments' direct influence on the media--allowing for an improved civic discourse in the media.

Although the changes toward a hypercommercialized media system are an important factor of the predicament of the development model, any media-centred explanation alone is too short-sighted. To understand the demise of development broadcasting, several major social, political, and economic factors have to be taken into consideration.

First, current media deregulation and commercialization has to be seen in a much wider framework of general economic globalization. Across the developing world, planned economies have given way to neoliberal capitalism. As a result, not only the media, but economic policy in general, stipulated by the International Monetary Fund and the World Trade Organization, has focused less on poverty reduction and more on the development of a consumption-oriented middle class in developing countries.

The new commercialized media system reflects this overall policy shift. More importantly, in this environment a reversal of the advertising-driven media system is not likely. Pleas for increased government intervention to remedy the problems of this new media system are unlikely to succeed. Instead, traditional models of government-stipulated development broadcasting have to be reconfigured to adapt to this new situation.

Second, given the growing interrelatedness of global markets, nation-states have been losing their power as the main authorities of economic policy. Beyond diluting general national fiscal and trade parameters, the "withering away of the nation-state" has also undermined central governments such as the Indian one in shaping development policy. Instead, transnational trade organizations and corporations, as well as local and international nongovernmental organizations (NGOs) have moved into the void of shaping third-world development projects. Thus, development media no longer can accept governmental objectives as exclusive development goals, but have to integrate a plethora of initiatives and ideas.

Third, in the post-Cold-War world, modernization and development themselves have become contested terms. Past disastrous failures or unforeseen corollaries of large-scale, top-down development projects have led to confusion over the goals of development. Consequently, instead of uncritically accepting development campaigns, broadcasters have to find a new role such as presenting and criticizing diverse approaches to urgent societal problems.

In sum, the current decline of development broadcasting cannot be blamed only on media policy failures such as the underfunding of public or state-run broadcasting. Nor is it only a reaction to fend off commercial global competition and its preference for ratings-driven programming.

The pressure on this old mandate needs to be understood within a general socioeconomic shift that seriously challenges the assumptions, and extent of traditional development goals and the role of the media in promoting these efforts. Given the problematic history and dubious success of development broadcasting along with a current adverse socioeconomic climate, a solution for the continued existence of development broadcasting involves many more radical interventions than previously suggested.

A New Concept of Development Broadcasting

The main distinction of the development model is that this type of broadcasting gives producers and journalists a normative role in shaping and guiding the public agenda. This task mirrors the raison d'etre of public service broadcasters in the West who often have an official mandate to contribute positively to societal integration and civic discourse. Thus, it seems reasonable to evaluate if such a public service model can work for a country like India as well and whether it can guarantee the survival of development programming. Page and Crawley's Satellites Over South Asia provides a very detailed and forward-looking study of the new Asian media environment and challenges all involved parties (public broadcasters, commercial broadcasters, and audiences) to work on a new idea of broadcasting in the public interest.

They suggested reevaluating the basic function of broadcasting and recommended the provision of comprehensive service to a national audience, the obligation to provide a range of programming to reflect interests and tastes, a general mandate to provide for diversity and pluralism, a role in promoting social integration and a sense of national identity both in the political and cultural spheres, and independence both from sectarian and commercial interest.

Their model proposes the state as regulator of media policy, parliamentary commissions for accountability and diversity, autonomous public bodies as guardians of public broadcasting, and the judiciary to protect free speech. Here, Page and Crawley's (2001) arguments for a new broadcasting in the public interest mostly reflect the public service broadcasting model of Western countries, especially the BBC model in the United Kingdom. However, Western public broadcasters themselves have come under tremendous pressure fending off accusations of bureaucratic overspending and favouritism toward political interests while trying to adjust to mixed public and commercial media systems. Moreover, the extreme disparities with regard to income and access to communication technologies create a unique audience for public broadcasters in developing countries. As B. G. Verghese argued, "A large section of the Indian people are outside the market... only a public service broadcaster whose charter is to serve all people and which is not wholly dependent on ratings and commercials can really do so." Also, development broadcasting per se is not part of the mission of public broadcasters in the Western world.

Instead of imitating a flawed Western public broadcasting system, DD and broadcasters in other developing countries should work toward an independent idea of broadcasting in the public interest. Part of this distinctive model should be a commitment to development broadcasting.

Executives should understand the development mandate no longer as a burden, but as a central part of DD's brand in a saturated market. Only such a commitment will guarantee DD a special role and allow for different types of funding (e.g., memberships, government subsidies, grants) besides advertising. Yet, credibility and authority can only be sustained if these channels also work on divesting themselves of direct governmental or party influence. In India, the Prasar Bharati Act was an extremely important step in this direction. Its mandate is a call to reflect and integrate a diverse and complex group of classes and ethnicities.

The misconceptions outlined in the previous section call for overturning outdated and misguided ideas of development broadcasting. Instead of centralized, government-controlled information campaigns of dubious impact, a new type of development broadcasting has to understand itself within a broader framework of communication for development. In India, projects on DD or DD-affiliated stations have to show a commitment to being part of more complex multimedia and educational campaigns using the latest entertainment and participatory communication approaches as well as information-based programs.

One solution is to create a separate DD channel for development broadcasting as a terrestrial channel and to ensure must-carry carriage on cable systems. Because Prasar Bharati already has a guaranteed "must-carry" provision for its channels it should not be difficult to add this new outlet, which is specifically connected to the public interest. Currently cable penetration is highest in urban areas and hovers around the 50% mark. Many of the poor are still illiterate and rely on terrestrial TV for education, information, and entertainment. This separate channel could target both rural and urban audiences who are not served by the commercial counterparts with programming that is more relevant to their lives.

One central means to establish a new role for development broadcasting, in the case of India, is to provide better funding for DD, so that it does not have to undermine its identity through alliances with commercial broadcasters. In the last 10 years, DD has felt the pressure of declining revenues. At the same time, government funding for the public broadcaster has decreased from 80% to 20% of total expenditures, thus forcing a greater reliance on advertising and sponsorship revenues. Such revenues are tied to programming that is similar to what is being offered commercially and that appeals to the middle class with a disposable income to spend on consumer goods. A creative search for an independent funding stream would allow the broadcaster to be able to produce programming that meets its goals of development broadcasting.

For example, funding for this new channel outside the government structure can be provided by a DD foundation that invites contributions from national and international NGOs, transnational corporations, and government money, ensuring that none of these parties can exercise excessive influence on specific programs. NGOs will be attracted to contribute to such a foundation because it will allow them to use the broadcast media to complement their grassroots campaigns and to integrate DD's unmatched terrestrial access into their campaigns. Corporations can be enticed to give by highlighting their connection to a commendable cause. In a time when corporate social responsibility has become a major aspect of corporate image work, such a foundation provides an important outlet in a third-world country. The government should find it attractive to be able to influence development programming while being able to invest less than before.

Although this mixed funding model seems to be similar to the U.S. Public Broadcasting Service (PBS), it carefully avoids certain central flaws of this model. According to critics legislation in the United States resulted in PBS's decentralized structure and reliance on federal money through the Corporation for Public Broadcasting. This organizational structure, in turn, left public broadcasting marginalized in prime time, curtailed by constantly shifting financial sources, open to attack from politicians and the government, and forced to commercialize its programming. In contrast, DD's organizational configuration provides a very different basis. Its historic position as monopoly broadcaster, its centralized decision-making structure, and its brand recognition should work to its advantage when creating new programming and stations. Moreover, as opposed to the Corporation for Public Broadcasting as one of the central general funding institutions for PBS, the suggested DD foundation will rely on mixed funding, on separating financial from creative influence, and on concentrating on one programming type--development broadcasting. This arrangement will allow for more targeted ventures.

However, political influence and competitive pressures areas for all public broadcasters around the world--important factors to consider. Given DD's earlier problem of disproportionate government control, and the new problem of commercial diluting of the core mission, it seems that local and regional NGOs appear to be in the best position, combining local knowledge with autonomy, to take a leading role in a DD programming board to guide or implement projects and measure their success.

This DD programming board can determine urgent issues and initiate collaboration among representatives from nongovernmental and governmental development agencies along with DD producers. DD will provide two important supporting aspects. First, through its extensive terrestrial network, it can assure wide access to its programs. Second, beyond traditional development programs, DD can develop a brand identity distinctive from its commercial competition by creating better quality current events programming and development programming that helps shape a new public sphere.

DD's 24-hour news channel would provide opportunities for this kind of current event programming. Moreover, even well-produced local entertainment programming can become a forum for negotiation of social issues--as telenovelas have been demonstrating--while delivering ratings that advertisers want. Although the funding cuts by the government are a serious problem for DD, these cuts also help curb governmental influence. DD will have to rely on a mix of funding, like government subsidies, advertising revenue generated in limited hours, and probably another source such as a viewer fee or television tax. As either one of these funding options are unstable, only the mix shields against a severe financial crisis. The Prasar Bharati Board will need to take its responsibility more seriously to guarantee the outlined mission for public service broadcasting in India and not let respective CEOs arbitrarily change directions as they have done in the last several years.

DD's new approaches need not be limited to targeting underserved populations alone. What is necessary is a different concept of development broadcasting beyond public service campaigns encompassing a type of programming on all channels that makes the middle and upper class aware of the plight of the rural poor majority of the country. Such programs would help reduce the current overemphasis of media on consumption, a service that commercial channels cannot be counted on to provide. Ultimately this type of broadcasting will help to develop a civic audience that is more engaged in the pressing social issues. These productions can be guided by the principle of emancipatory journalism with journalists "who actively, explicitly, and purposefully try to expand the opportunities to emancipate the Third World from modernization." In the case of broadcasting, programming has to highlight the plight of the poor and underprivileged in the country for urban middle-class audiences. The latter aspect of creating an informed citizenry might be even more important than the earlier call for DD's actual participation in development communication. After all, a necessary condition for the survival of any commitment to social equality, justice, and development is the public consensus that these projects are invaluable and meaningful for national integration.

CONCLUSION

This analysis shows that given the current economic, social, and political circumstances, development broadcasting in its current form is unlikely to survive without significant intervention. Frustrated with the bureaucracy of government media and the excesses of commercial television, several Indian media critics have been advocating alternative models of development media beyond state and commercial influences. Often this "third way" centers on empowering community media, especially community radio. The advantage of this approach is its focus on the local and on immediate participation. Yet questions of independent funding often remain unresolved. Local and immediate participation are even more difficult to realize in the expensive television environment. Thus, the approach presented here to rescue and redefine development television is in favour of a more large-scale perspective. It presents a two-pronged solution: creating a new channel for development and creating a distinctive and complementary programming environment on all DD channels.

First, a new terrestrial channel for development communication is suggested. Instead of top-down, state-driven media campaign programming, this channel creates its programming with a mix of development communication projects initiated by NGOs as much as by the government. A new programming board brings together representatives of development experts from nongovernmental and governmental agencies as well as DD media producers to work on these campaigns, reflecting the latest multimedia and participatory approaches to development communication.

Second, DD on all its channels needs to demonstrate a civic commitment. Otherwise, the new development niche channel is at risk to become a programming outpost at the fringes of the television landscape. It can only be successful if it is integrated in a DD channel mix that in all its programming emphasizes the concepts of emancipatory journalism and civic discourse. This kind of programming should highlight the inequalities in the country, current development predicaments, and the impact of commercialization and market liberalization on Indian society.

The deregulation of media systems and demise of public funding has closed in on formerly public service or state-run broadcasters all over the world. This study more specifically engages with DD's situation and is most applicable to similar systems in Asia and Africa. More work needs to be done to be able to relate these ideas to other countries especially in Latin America.

Although the suggestions presented here focused on India, the analysis arrived at and the conclusions reached are pertinent to all broadcasting systems where commercial and public models of broadcasting collide. It is important that scholars from around the world proactively engage in a discussion on the future of broadcasting and its role as a public forum. More specifically, scholars of international communication have to move beyond lamenting the bygone era of traditional development broadcasting to create detailed new models for it that work in various countries and circumstances.

Even as globalization and commercialization have had an effect on almost every broadcasting system across the globe, each country has its unique media history, set of regulations, and infrastructure that necessitate specific, local solutions. For development broadcasting to survive, it is up to media scholars to remind policy-makers of the civic purpose of broadcasting and to provide feasible models that sustain this mandate in commercially driven multichannel systems.

Nevertheless, scholarship that ends in upholding an impermeable chasm between commercial entertainment rationales of broadcasting and educational development rationales can only accelerate the demise of broadcasting as a public service.

Only a reconfigured and integrated type of development broadcasting in India as much as in other third-world countries will ensure its continued existence in the new globalized and commercialized socioeconomic and media environment, because its role will have changed significantly.

Development broadcasting has to become an indispensable agent for creating a civic society no longer tied up in government-controlled concepts of nation building that earlier development broadcasting propagated. Rather than becoming a weak, underfunded, and deteriorating copy of commercial broadcasters, it is in this enhanced conception that development broadcasting has the potential to create its own distinct identity.

INDIA NEWS AND BROADCAST MEDIA

India News, India radio & broadcast media: The Indian national television (Doordarshan) and radio (All India Radio, or Akashwani) networks are state-owned and managed by the Ministry of Information and Broadcasting.

Their news reporting customarily presents the government's point of view. For example, coverage of the 1989 election campaign blatantly favoured the government of Rajiv Gandhi, and autonomy of the electronic media became a political issue. V.P. Singh's National Front government sponsored the Prasar Bharati (Indian Broadcasting) Act, which Parliament considered in 1990, to provide greater autonomy to Doordarshan and All India Radio. The changes that resulted were limited.

The bill provided for the establishment of an autonomous corporation to run Doordarshan and All India Radio. The corporation was to operate under a board of governors to be in charge of appointments and policy and a broadcasting council to respond to complaints.

However, the legislation required that the corporation prepare and submit its budget within the framework of the central budget and stipulated that the personnel of the new broadcasting corporation be career civil servants to facilitate continued government control. In the early 1990s, increasing competition from television broadcasts transmitted via satellite appeared the most effective manner of limiting the progovernment bias of the government-controlled electronic media.

Since the 1980s, India has experienced a rapid proliferation of television broadcasting that has helped shape popular culture and the course of politics. Although the first television program was broadcast in 1959, the expansion of television did not begin in earnest until the extremely popular telecast of the Ninth Asian Games, which were held in New Delhi in 1982. Realizing the popular appeal and consequent influence of television broadcasting, the government undertook an expansion that by 1990 was planned to provide television access to 90 percent of the population.

In 1993, about 169 million people were estimated to have watched Indian television each week, and, by 1994, it was reported that there were some 47 million households with televisions. There also is a growing selection of satellite transmission and cable services available.

Television programming was initially kept tightly under the control of the government, which embarked on a self-conscious effort to construct and propagate a cultural idea of the Indian nation. This goal is especially clear in the broadcasts of such megaseries as the Hindu epics Ramayana and Mahabharata. In addition to the effort at nation-building, the politicians of India's ruling party have not hesitated to use television to build political support. In fact, the political abuse of Indian television led to demands to increase the autonomy of Doordarshan; these demands ultimately resulted in support for the Prasar Bharati Act.

The 1990s have brought a radical transformation of television in India. Transnational satellite broadcasting made its debut in January 1991, when owners of satellite dishes--initially mostly at major hotels--began receiving Cable News Network (CNN) coverage of the Persian Gulf War.

Three months later, Star TV began broadcasting via satellite. Its fare initially included serials such as "The Bold and the Beautiful" and MTV programs. Satellite broadcasting spread rapidly through India's cities as local entrepreneurs erected dishes to receive signals and transmitted them through local cable systems. After its October 1992 launch, Zee TV offered stiff competition to Star TV.

However, the future of Star TV was bolstered by billionaire Rupert Murdock, who acquired the network for US$525 million in July 1993. CNN International, part of the Turner Broadcasting System, was slated to start broadcasting entertainment programs, including top Hollywood films, in 1995.

Competition from the satellite stations in India brought radical change to Doordarshan by cutting its audience and threatening its advertising revenues at a time when the government was pressuring it to pay for expenditures from internal revenues. In response, Doordarshan decided in 1993 to start five new channels in addition to its original National Channel.

Programming was radically transformed, and controversial news shows, soap operas, and coverage of high-fashion events proliferated. Of the new Doordarshan channels, however, only the Metro Channel, which carries MTV music videos and other popular shows, has survived in the face of the new trend for talk programs that engage in a potpourri of racy topics.

THE GOLDEN AGE OF TELEVISION IN INDIA

Growing pains loneliness and speeding globalization is stretching its realm throughout India's booming television industry. Deregulation and new technology have combined to produce an explosion of new offerings. Before the early 1990s, a single government broadcaster provided a handful of channels. Now a crowded field of domestic and global media companies, including the News Corporation, Sony Entertainment and Walt Disney, offer hundreds of channels.

Indian films, especially the flashy musicals and dramas of Bollywood, have grabbed plenty of attention in the West. But the country's lesser-known television business is more than twice as big, with an estimated $3.4 billion in revenue in 2005, according to PricewaterhouseCoopers. It is also starting to exert greater cultural influence.

Television ownership is growing fast here, and it has plenty more room to expand. There are roughly 105 million homes with televisions in India, up from 88 million in 2000. The current number of television households is about the same as in the United States, though for India that amounts to only about half of the country's households, compared with 98 percent in the United States.

Advertising spending on Indian television increased by 21 percent a year, on average, from 1995 to 2005, when it reached $1.6 billion, according to ZenithOptimedia, which tracks advertising globally. Double-digit growth rates are expected to continue for years. Such numbers are very tempting to companies like the News Corporation, Disney, Time Warner and Viacom, which are losing viewers and advertisers in their core Western markets. (In addition to the domestic market, Indian television is also delivered via satellite and cable to the global South Asian diaspora.)

The pace of change in India is supercharged because the country is catching up to, and in some cases leapfrogging, developments that took decades to play out elsewhere. "Everything that happened in the rest of the world in 10 years, is happening here in two years," said Vikram Kaushik, the chief executive of Tata Sky, a satellite-TV company that is jointly owned by the News Corporation and the Tata Group, the Indian industrial conglomerate.

In the 1990s, media companies seized on new opportunities in India after the government, which had controlled broadcasting for nearly 50 years, began releasing its grip. The first big changes in Indian television came in the early part of that decade, when cable operators used satellite dishes, illegal but tolerated at the time, to give subscribers access to news on CNN, as well as American soap operas and movies. Viewers could also watch Indian movies and music on Zee TV, then a fledgling joint venture between the News Corporation and an Indian entrepreneur.

Previously, India's ruling elite had a dual and somewhat contradictory view of broadcasting. On the one hand, politicians considered it too powerful a force to be left to the private sector, especially in the years after independence in 1947, when the nation's unity and secularism were considered vulnerable. On the other hand, television was seen as too frivolous to merit much investment at a time when politicians were focused on turning India into an industrial power.

Those attitudes began to change after a financial crisis in the early '90s forced the Indian government to devalue its currency, the rupee, and to start relinquishing its tight control over the economy. Then, in 1995, the country's highest court declared the government's monopoly over broadcasting unconstitutional. When it did yield, India went further in deregulating television than it did in other sectors of the economy. It also gave up far more control when compared with China, the country against which it is most often measured. Foreign media companies can fully own entertainment networks here; they cannot in China. (India does, however, limit foreign ownership to 26 percent of television news channels and newspapers.)

The open environment attracted the News Corporation, which entered the market in 1993 by acquiring Star TV. Star has the highest-rated shows among the private networks in Hindi-speaking parts of the country. Sony started its flagship channel here in 1995 and now has seven channels; the company owns about 61 percent of the business, with Indian investors owning the rest. The biggest Indian broadcasters are Zee and Sun TV, which dominates ratings in non-Hindi-speaking southern India.

Still, Doordarshan, the public broadcaster, remains the most widely available network, especially in rural areas, where a majority of the population lives.

To keep up with changing times, Doordarshan has retooled its programming, adding genres like soap operas and musical contests to a line-up that is still dominated by more high-minded-and what some critics would call staid-cultural programming. It has also started a satellite-TV service that has no subscription fees but also does not include the most popular private channels.

Star has been one of the few consistently profitable businesses in Indian television. Although the News Corporation does not disclose financial details of its operations here, Merrill Lynch estimates that Star accounts for 3 percent of the company's total operating income, or about $116 million in the 2006 fiscal year.

Zee, which started by offering a few hours of programming a day, now has more than two dozen channels; it started a satellite-TV service, DishTV, in 2004. "We offered an alternative to a broadcaster, Doordarshan, from which urban audiences felt disconnected," said Ashish Kaul, a senior vice président at Zee. "You cannot blame Doordarshan; it had a national obligation."

About 60 percent of the nation's television households subscribe to the cable or satellite services that carry private channels. Though Indians theoretically have dozens of channels to choose from, a handful dominate the ratings and earn most of the profits. A fragmented cable business is straining to reshape itself in response to new regulations and competition from satellite television services. The transition to digital cable, meanwhile, has so far occurred only in parts of India's four most populous cities. The changeover has been troubled by technical problems, weak enforcement of a Jan. 1 deadline and a shortage of set-top boxes.

At the same time, the newest technology operates alongside the often stark economic and social realities of India. Black-and-white televisions still account for an estimated 40 percent of all TV's in use, and about 56 percent of rural households do not have electricity, according to India's 2001 census. And because most homes in India that have a television have just one set, watching TV can be a communal activity that brings together the entire family, and often the neighbours, too.

Perhaps the most striking of the changes in Indian television is what is starting to show up on the screen.

"Dhoom Machaoo Dhoom" (Hindi for "Let's have a blast") is a Disney show aimed at teenagers, and it might look at home on the Disney Channel in the United States. It is about four teenage girls, one of them from New York, who want to start a band so they can represent their school in a talent contest. They face a number of challenges, including an arrogant classmate who is determined to derail their plans.

But the show, which went on the air last month, has an Indian twist. Priyanka, the New Yorker who has returned to her family's native land, wants the girls to perform a song they have created, rather than using a tune from a popular Bollywood movie, as the local norms dictate. In one episode, Kajal, played by Sriti Jha, complains that Priyanka doesn't understand India. "Only Bollywood works here," she insists.

The girls do not dwell on the issue, but it is an important consideration for television executives and media companies here. Indian television has a strong partnership with the film industry, whose stars appear on its shows as guests, contestants and hosts. Movies and music videos from Bollywood remain staples on television here. Yet in the last decade television has attained influence over the popular culture that is starting to rival that of the film business. And whereas filmmakers have traditionally worked in close-knit networks that operate in a single language, media companies have been exploiting the large and growing capacity of cable and satellite networks to cheaply develop customized channels and shows for different parts of the country. Zee, for instance, operates several regional-language entertainment and news channels.

"We have a vibrant TV industry," said Rama Bijapurkar, a business consultant whose clients include Disney and who also writes a column for The Economic Times. "When talking about the hinterland, TV is what Bollywood would like to be."

Nachiket Pantvaidya, an executive director at Disney's Indian operations, predicted that "Dhoom" would be a breakthrough for Indian television because it was one of the few shows produced for teenagers, and specifically for girls. He said that more than 90 percent of what Indian youths watch on TV are family dramas and other shows created for their parents. "This is a story of kids who are trying to do something out of the ordinary," Mr. Pantvaidya said. "Nobody makes TV for the real world. This kind of TV is rare."

Ms. Jha, the 20-year-old who plays one of the girls on "Dhoom," added: "This can't be compared to the whole lot of family serials. This is much more real and close to the lives of kids."

"Dhoom" is Disney's sophomore effort at producing TV shows in India-its first, "Vicky Aur Vetaal," was based on an Indian myth about a prince and a genie-like figure. The company sees television as the first step in a broader India strategy that includes films, merchandising and possibly a theme park. Last year, Disney spent $44.5 million to acquire a 15 percent stake in UTV, a production company based in Mumbai, and to buy Hungama, a television channel of children's programming created by UTV. "We decided early on that this had to be driven locally," said Gary Marsh, president of entertainment for Disney Channel Worldwide in Burbank, Calif. "If we were to truly become a global company, we had to let our regional organizations create their own programming."

India was the first country where the company developed local Disney Channel shows, something it is now doing in Britain and Japan, too.

Many of Disney's competitors have built their businesses on a similar strategy. Time Warner, which operates the Pogo and Cartoon Network channels here, is offering an Indian version of "Sesame Street" called "Galli Galli Sim Sim."

The show uses some material from the popular American show, but it is set on an Indian streetscape and is anchored by four local Muppets. A large orange-and-red lion named Boombah replaces Big Bird.

Television executives say the ventures by Disney and others aimed at youths and various niche markets are a welcome break from the way business has been done in India.

A handful of channels-which carry soap operas, reality shows, music shows and important cricket tournaments-receive the bulk of the advertising. Yet entrepreneurs continue spending millions of dollars starting copycat networks. India has more than 40 cable news channels, for example.

"Here it is, we have 200 channels of the same stuff, and people are saying let's do more of it," said Sameer Nair, chief executive of Star Entertainment, a News Corporation subsidiary. "That will churn and change." (In an indication that competition is intensifying, Mr. Nair announced last month that he would be leaving Star in March. According to news reports, he will be helping a rival Indian-owned TV company start a new entertainment channel.)

As media executives try to introduce innovative programming, exactly what can go on the air in India remains fluid. There is no overt censorship of television content, but most media companies say they aggressively police themselves to avoid running a foul of political and cultural mores.

Several movie channels were forced to go off the air for more than a week last summer when a court in Mumbai ruled in favour of a schoolteacher who had argued that films that had been rated for adult viewing only in their cinematic release could not be shown on television without being edited and recertified for a wider audience.

In some ways, television fare in India today is far more adventurous than it was even five years ago. A recent adaptation of "Big Brother," known here as "Bigg Boss," for instance, has stirred the pot by showing minor celebrities behaving badly.

Though it may seem insignificant, the show has let viewers see famous people as human beings, said Kunal Dasgupta, who heads Sony's Indian television operations, which broadcasts the show. Still, Mr. Dasgupta knows that social customs evolve slowly here. He said he was considering "with kid gloves" a proposal from an Italian company to help produce a mini series that would be based loosely on the life of Sonia Gandhi, the Italian-born leader of India's ruling Congress Party who is the widow of the former prime minister, Rajiv Gandhi.

The proposal calls for an Indian cast, but the series would take an "Italian perspective," Mr. Dasgupta said. "I find it very exciting and challenging," he said. "At the same time, knowing our own media, we could be ripped apart." He said he was "trying to see if we can get people who are really in power to accept that if we do such a thing it will be O.K."

The fact that he is even considering such a proposal is a sign of how far television has come in India. And as the country continues to experience major economic and social changes, the shape of Indian television is likely to keep evolving.

TELEVISION AND THE CHANGING FACE OF INDIA

To young women in India, TV soaps represent a medium that can influence positive change. To others, soaps are expected to impart traditional values that don't threaten Indian culture-and don't propagate what is seen as Western influences.

India's struggle to adapt to a westernizing world is still in its nascent stages. The winds of change heralded by the television make many nervous.

At 19 years of age, she is one of many students in the city's bustling university environment who come from small towns around the country.

She shares one thing in common with many of them-she has battled her family who believe she must marry young, instead choosing education and a career. Shagufta's story isn't unique, but it speaks volumes about the social changes sweeping India.

DISCOVERING OPPORTUNITIES

A year ago, she left Bhopal, a small town in the state of Madhya Pradesh, to study at India's premier undergraduate school, St. Stephan's College. Despite family pressure to marry when she graduated high school, she chose to come to Delhi to discover what the world could offer her.

Considered a rebel, her neighbours rarely allow interaction between her and their children when she returns home for vacations. These social infractions are only a minor consequence for Shagufta, who merely shrugs her shoulders and says it is her life, not one determined by her parents-or by the fear of what society will say.

As she sees it, "Things are changing. You just have to watch TV, or read the news and you know the world is no longer the same as when my mother was my age."

The battle to preserve traditional culture even finds a political platform and young women like Shagufta are still a minority.

Shagufta and her friends indulge in one addiction, other than hunting for bargains at the local Sarojini market. They gather around a large television set every week to tune into "Astitva-Ek Prem Kahani" (Self Respect-A Love Story).

A soap opera about the empowerment of Indian women, "Astitva" was launched in 2001 as a show that would break new ground. It pledged to change the way single and divorced women were seen by a conservative India.

ADDRESSING WOMEN'S ISSUES

"Astitva" promised to encapsulate the adversities and biases faced by a single woman in India's traditionally patriarchal society. It took on a lot-and has delivered very little.

In a country where women are considered over the hill by the age of 28, "Astitva" tracks the life of a mid-30s professional single woman. A gynecologist who lives in Mumbai, Dr. Simran Mathur breaks the stereotype of a traditional Indian woman.

The Plot Thickens

The character was created to represent a strong-willed professional, to whom self respect and personal ethics are more important than society's approval. An older woman by Indian standards, she falls in love and marries a man 10 years younger than her. The marriage of an older woman to a much younger man, who has an off-beat career as a photographer, would give parents, like those of Shagufta's, sleepless nights, as it did for the television character's. The marriage takes place without her family's consent, causing a split between her and her father.

The plot thickens when a few months later, she discovers she is pregnant and her loving husband is cheating on her. This set the stage for her brave decision to divorce him and become a single mother. Her father, now placated by a granddaughter, becomes her most ardent supporter.

Emancipating Indian Women

The concept of single motherhood and divorce are the antithesis of what is acceptable to conservative Indian society. "Astitva" set out to challenge that very notion. Shagufta-like many young women in India-is hooked on the show. She sees it as a sign of a changing India and the emancipation of Indian women. But the show's main audience is not young metropolitan college students. They are traditional housewives in middle India. Women like Shagufta's neighbours back home in Bhopal.

Breaking Social Taboos

The majority of India's soap opera audience lives just miles from India's largest cities while others are in remote parts of the country. These women aspire for the wealth of the urban areas, but cling to their traditional roles.

They live in cities and towns where the struggle to adapt to a westernizing world is still in its nascent stages. The winds of change heralded by the television set blaring in their living rooms make many of them nervous.

The obedient daughters, who might otherwise have chosen to follow their mothers' lead, are instead moving to larger cities to study-exposing themselves to role models well beyond their small towns. The promise of a female revolution is a fear that is now real for parents who are afraid to break social taboos.

Promoting Positive Changes

To Shagufta, TV soaps represent a medium that can influence positive change. To families like those of her neighbours, soaps are expected to impart traditional values that don't threaten Indian culture-and don't propagate what is seen as Western influences. This battle to preserve traditional culture even finds a political platform, in campaigns by national and regional politicians. Young women like Shagufta are still a minority in a country torn between modernization and ancient traditions.

Patriarchal Tones

Indian soap writers have the spectre of television ratings, fan feedback, network revenues and sponsors constantly dangling over their heads. That pressure has seen many activist-oriented soaps like "Astitva," conforming and taking on a patriarchal tone.

"Astitva" promised to encapsulate the adversities and biases faced by a single woman in India's traditionally patriarchal society. It took on a lot-and has delivered very little.

Soaps where women were to find a platform to address social change, have become more conventional. Straying husbands are excused as weak in the face of a seductress, violent sons-the product of bad mothering. And the ending? A happily ever after with an abusive partner.

Despite the publicity surrounding the show's launch as a ground breaking concept, dramatic societal changes have made its audience uncomfortable. As a result, they go searching for more traditional messages for their daughters-daughters like Shagufta, who are breaking traditions and taking the message of liberation to heart.

Sudden Changes

Families in middle India have not able to absorb this sudden attitudinal change, and have begun back tracking. An emancipated Shagufta would mean societal rejection with no chance of arranging a suitable marriage. "Astitva" has gone from being the harbinger of change, to a corrupting message from India's Westernized cities.

In the rush to maintain high ratings, the show's story-line has followed the expected trajectory of the brave central character forgiving the erring husband and his two subsequent marriages, and adopting his daughter from a third.

Broken Promises

In each of the soap operas broadcast today, the culture of joint families, female subservience and moral values are the central themes. While scriptwriters insist education, globalization or the west have not erased what makes a "true Indian woman," the now traditional patriarchal messages have found their way back into the story line.

The latest episode of "Astitva" comes to an end with the blinding of Dr. Simran and the death of her adopted daughter. Shagufta and her friends turn off the television and begin an animated discussion about the script's "black or white" portrayal of life. A disappointed soap party breaks up with the hope that the next episode will not be a complete pandering to the traditional powers that be. Shagufta's parting shot hits home- "They can't hide women like us under the carpet for much longer!"

MASS MEDIA AND WOMEN'S STATUS IN RURAL INDIA

Cable and satellite television have grown rapidly throughout the developing world. The availability of cable and satellite television exposes viewers to new information about the outside world, which may affect individual attitudes and behaviours. This paper explores the effect of the introduction of cable television on gender attitudes in rural India. Using a three-year individual-level panel dataset, we find that the introduction of cable television is associated with improvements in women's status. We find significant increases in reported autonomy, decreases in the reported acceptability of beating and decreases in reported son preference.

We also find increases in female school enrolment and decreases in fertility (primarily via increased birth spacing). The effects are large, equivalent in some cases to about five years of education in the cross section, and move gender attitudes of individuals in rural areas much closer to those in urban areas. We argue that the results are not driven by pre-existing differential trends. These results have important policy implications, as India and other countries attempt to decrease bias against women.

The growth of television in the developing world over the last two decades has been extraordinary. Estimates suggest that the number of television sets in Asia has increased more than six-fold, from 100 million to 650 million, since the 1980s

(World Press Review, 2003). In China, television exposure grew from 18 million people in 1977 to 1 billion by 1995 (World Press Review, 2003). In more recent years, satellite and cable television availability has increased dramatically. Again, in China, the number of people with satellite access increased from just 270,000 in 1991 to 14 million by 2005.

Further, these numbers are likely to understate the change in the number of people for whom television is available, since a single television is often watched by many.

Beyond providing entertainment, television vastly increases both the availability of information about the outside world and exposure to other ways of life, particularly in otherwise isolated areas. Previous work has demonstrated that the information and exposure provided by television can change attitudes and behaviour. Gentzkow and Shapiro (2005) find effects of television viewership on attitudes in the Muslim world towards the West, and Della Vigna and Kaplan (2006) show large effects of the Fox News channel on voting patterns in the United States. In the developing world, Olken (2006) shows that television decreases participation in social organizations.

India has not been left out of the satellite revolution: a recent survey finds that 112 million households in India own a television, with 61 percent of those homes having cable or satellite service (National Readership Studies Council 2006). This figure represents a doubling in cable access in just five years from a previous survey.

The study also find that in some states, the change has been even more dramatic; in the span of just 10-15 years since it first became available, cable or satellite penetration has reached an astonishing 60 percent in states such as Tamil Nadu, even though the average income is below the World Bank poverty line of two dollars per person per day.

Most popular satellite television shows in India portray life in urban settings; further, a wide range of international programs are now available. The increase in television exposure, therefore, is likely to dramatically change the available information about the outside world, especially in isolated rural areas. Indeed, anthropological case studies in India suggest that exposure to television in rural areas has an effect on behaviours as disparate as latrine building and fan usage.

In this chapter we explore the effect of the introduction of cable television in rural areas of India on a particular set of values and behaviours, namely attitudes towards and discrimination against women. Although issues of gender equity are important throughout much of the developing world, they are particularly salient in India. Sen (1992) argued that there were 41 million "missing women" in India women and girls who died prematurely due to mistreatment resulting in a dramatically male-biased population. The population bias towards men has only gotten worse in the last two decades, as sex-selective abortion has become more widely used to avoid female births. More broadly, girls in India are discriminated against in nutrition, medical care, vaccination and education. Even within India, gender inequality is significantly worse in rural than urban areas.

Given this, if satellite television increases the exposure of rural areas to urban attitudes and values, it is plausible that it could change some of these attitudes and behaviours. It is this possibility that we explore in this chapter. The analysis relies on a three-year panel dataset covering women in many Indian states between 2001 and 2003.

These years represent a time of rapid growth in rural cable access. During the panel, cable television was newly introduced in 21 of the 180 sample villages. Our empirical strategy relies on comparing changes in attitudes and behaviours between survey rounds across villages based on whether (and when) they added cable television.

Using these data, we find that cable television has large effects on attitudes and, to the extent we have information, behaviours. After cable is introduced to a village, women are less likely to report that domestic violence towards women is acceptable. They also report increased autonomy (for example, the ability to go out without permission and to participate in household decision-making). Women are less likely to report son preference (the desire to give birth to a boy rather than a girl). Turning to behaviours, we find increases in school enrolment for girls (but not boys), and decreases in fertility (which is often linked to female autonomy). These results are apparent when using regressions with individual fixed effects and when using a matching estimator.

In terms of magnitude, the introduction of cable television dramatically decreases the differences in attitudes and behaviours between urban and rural areas between 45 and 70 percent of the difference disappears within two years of cable introduction in this sample.

The effect is also large relative to, for example, the effect of education on these attitudes and behaviours: introducing cable television is equivalent to roughly five years of female education in the cross section. These effects happen very quickly; the average village has cable for only 6-7 months before being surveyed again, which implies a rapid change in attitudes. However, this is consistent with existing work on the effects of media exposure, which typically find rapid changes (within a few months, in many cases) in behaviours like contraceptive use, pregnancy, latrine building and perception of own-village status.

A central concern with the results is the possibility that trends in other variables (for example, income or "modernity") are driving both cable access and attitudes. We argue that this does not seem to the case. Changes in attitudes between the first two survey waves are not predictive of cable introduction between the second and third wave.

Further, among villages that add cable during the survey period, initial attitudes are not predictive of which year (2002 or 2003) they get access. It is difficult to identify the mechanism behind the effects in this paper precisely. However, we do find some suggestive evidence that the mechanism alluded to at the start of the paper {increased exposure to circumstances outside of the village {is operating.

In particular, we find that the effects of cable are largest in areas with initially worse attitudes towards women, i.e., those for whom cable is providing information most different from their current way of life. Although certainly not conclusive, this evidence is consistent with a model in which television changes the weight individuals put on the behaviours of their immediate peer group in forming their attitudes.

The results are potentially quite important for policy. Gender discrimination in India is a significant issue, and has been a consistent source of concern for policy makers and academics. A large literature in economics, sociology and anthropology has explored the underlying causes of discrimination against women in India, highlighting the dowry system, low levels of female education, and other socioeconomic factors as central factors.

Changing these underlying factors is difficult; introducing television, or reducing any barriers to its spread, may be less so. From the policy perspective, however, there are potential concerns about whether the changes in reported autonomy, beating attitudes, and son preference actually represent changes in behaviours, or just in reporting. For example, we may be concerned that exposure to television only changes what the respondent thinks the interviewer wants to hear about the acceptability of beating, but does not actually change how much beating is occurring. This concern is likely to be less relevant in the case of fertility or education; the former is directly verifiable based on the presence of a baby in the household, and the latter is listed as part of a household roster.

The fact that we find effects on these variables provides support for the argument that our results represent real changes in outcomes. Without directly observing people in their homes, however, it is difficult to conclusively separate changes in reporting from changes in behaviour. However, even if cable only changes what is reported, it still may represent progress: changing the perceived "correct" attitude seems like a necessary, if not sufficient, step toward changing outcomes.

HISTORY OF TELEVISION IN INDIA

State-run black and white television was introduced into India in 1959, but the take off was extremely slow for the first several decades by 1977, only around 600,000 sets had been sold. In 1982, however, the state-run broadcaster (Doordarshan) introduced color television, which dramatically increased interest in, and viewership of, television. Even with color, however, most programming remained either government-sponsored news or information about economic development. There were a few entertainment serials, which were watched with intensity. In the early 1990s CNN and STAR TV first introduced the possibility of access to non-government programming via satellite.

There was a large demand for this cable (satellite) television, which was, and continues to be, filled primarily by small entrepreneurs who buy a dish and a subscription and charge nearby homes to connect to it. This is especially true in rural villages, such as those in our sample. As we show in the data later, this means that cable access is more common in villages that are wealthier and have a higher population density, where more people can afford to pay for service and where it would therefore be more profitable to start a cable business.

However, dramatic declines in the prices of both the equipment and satellite service subscriptions (due in part to reduced tariffs and increased competition), coupled with income growth, have allowed cable to spread over time to more and more villages. In the 5 years from 2001 to 2006, about 30 million households, representing approximately 150 million individuals, added cable service (National Readership Studies Council 2006). And since television is often watched with family and friends by those without a television or cable, the growth in actual access or exposure to cable may have been even more dramatic. The program offerings on cable television are quite different than government programming. The most popular shows tend to be game shows and soap operas. As an example, among the most popular shows in both 2000 and 2007 (based on Indian Nielsen ratings) is "Kyunki Saas Bhi Kabhi Bahu Thi," (Because a Mother-in-Law was Once a Daughter-in-Law, Also) a show based around the life of a wealthy industrial family in the large city of Mumbai. As can be seen from the title, the main themes and plots of the show often revolve around issues of family and gender. Among satellite channels, STAR TV and Zee TV tend to dominate, although Sony, STAR PLUS and Sun TV are also represented among the top 20 shows. Viewership of the government channel, although relatively high among those who do not have cable, is extremely low among those who do (and limited largely to sporting events).

The introduction of television in general appears to have had large effects in Indian society.

In contrast to the West, television seems to be, in some cases, the primary medium by which people in rural villages in India get information about the outside world. For example, Johnson (2001) reports on a man in his 50's in a village in India who says that television is "the biggest thing to happen in our village, ever". He goes on to say that he learned about the value of electric fans (to deal with the heat) from television, and subsequently purchased one.

The same author quotes another man arguing that television is where they learned that their leaders were corrupt, and about using the court system to address grievances. On issues of gender specifically, television seems to have had a significant impact, since this is an area where the lives of rural viewers differ greatly from those depicted on most popular shows.

By virtue of the fact that the most popular Indian serials take place in urban settings, women depicted on these shows are typically much more emancipated than rural women.

For example, many women on popular serials work outside the home, run businesses and control money. In addition, they are typically more educated and have fewer children than their rural counterparts. Further, in many cases there is access to Western television, with its accompanying depiction of life in which women are much more emancipated.

Based on anthropological reports, this seems to have affected attitudes within India. Scrase (2002) reports that several of his respondents thought television might lead women to question their social position and might help the cause of female advancement.

Another woman reports that, because of television, men and women are able to open up a lot more." Johnson (2001) quotes a number of respondents describing changes in gender roles as a result of television.

One man notes, "Since TV has come to our village, women are doing less work than before. They only want to watch TV. So we [men] have to do more work. Many times I help my wife clean the house."

Although television overall seems to have had large effects, cable television in particular may be even more significant. This is both because it dramatically increases television viewership, and because the content is very different (again, since popular serials mostly feature urban life).

Scrase (2002) reports on respondents who note that prior to cable there was almost no entertainment, and very little current affairs, whereas the offerings on cable were broad.

There is also a broader literature on the effects of television exposure on gender issues in other countries. Many studies find effects on a variety of outcomes: for example, eating disorders in Fiji, sex role stereotypes in Minnesota and perceptions of women's rights in Chicago.

Telenovelas in Brazil have provided a fruitful context for studying the effects of television. For example, based on ethnographic research, La Pastina (2004) argues that exposure to telenovelas provides women (in particular) with alternative models of what role they might play in society.

Pace (1993) describes the effect of television introduction in Brazil on a small, isolated, Amazon community, arguing that the introduction of television changed the framework of social interactions, increased general world knowledge and changed people's perceptions about the status of their village in the wider world.

Kottak (1990) reports on similar data from isolated areas in Brazil, and argues that the introduction of television affects (among other things) views on gender, moving individuals in these areas towards having more liberal views on the role of women in both the workplace and in relationships. Interestingly, the studies in Brazil also suggest that the patterns of television viewing shortly after it is first introduced may be quite different than what is seen later on.

The evidence suggests that in the first years after introduction, interactions with the television are more intense, with the television drawing more focus (both at an individual level, and community-wide). It is during this early period that Kottak (1990) and others argue that television is at its most influential.

Most of the villages in our analysis are at this early stage of television exposure, suggesting this may be an ideal period to look for effects. The evidence described above, of course, is drawn primarily from interviews and case studies, and obviously does not reflect a random sample of these populations. Nevertheless, the overall impression given by the anthropology and sociology literature is that the introduction of television had widespread effects on society, and that gender issues are a particular focal point. Our data and setting provide an opportunity to test this hypothesis more rigorously.

DATA AND EMPIRICAL STRATEGY

Data

This paper relies on data from the Survey of Aging in Rural India (SARI), a panel survey of 2,700 households, each containing a person aged 50 or older, conducted in 2001, 2002 and 2003 in four states (Bihar, Goa, Haryana, and Tamil Nadu), and the capital, Delhi.

The sample was selected in two stages: in the first stage, 180 clusters were selected at random from district lists (40 clusters in Bihar, Haryana and Tamil Nadu, 35 in Delhi and 25 in Goa), and in the second stage, 15 households were chosen within each cluster through random sampling based on registration lists. Other than Delhi, the survey was confined to rural areas. Attrition over the panel was low, with just 108 (4 percent) of the original households dropping out by the third round.

All women in the sample households aged 15 and older were interviewed. Several sections of this survey were modelled to be compatible with other demographic surveys for India, such as the National Family and Health Survey (NFHS).

The survey collected information on a range of (current and past) demographic, social and economic variables. In addition, a village-level survey was conducted in each sample cluster, gathering information on economic and social conditions and infrastructure.

Most relevant for our analysis, the survey asked women a series of questions intended to measure various dimensions of women's status.

These questions were patterned after those used in several countries as part of the Demographic and Health Surveys, as well as in the Surveys on the Status of Women and Fertility conducted by the University of Pennsylvania Population Studies Centre.

The first set of questions deal with women's autonomy and decision-making authority.

In particular, women were asked whether they needed permission to visit the market (one question) or to visit friends or relatives (a second question). Responses were coded on a scale of 1 to 3 (do not need permission; need permission; not permitted at all). Women were also asked whether they are allowed to keep money set aside to spend as they wish.

In addition, women were asked, Who makes the following decisions in your household: Obtaining health care for yourself; purchasing major household items; whether you visit or stay with family members or friends?" The possible responses were: 1. Respondent; 2. Husband; 3. Respondent jointly with husband; 4. Other household members; 5. Respondent jointly with other household members."

Second, women were asked about son preference. In particular, women who reported wanting to have more children were asked: "Would you like your next child to be a boy, a girl or it doesn't matter?"

Finally, given the high prevalence of domestic violence in India, women were asked their attitudes towards such behaviour. Specifically, they were asked: Please tell me if you think that a husband is justified in beating his wife in each of the following situations: If he suspects her of being unfaithful; if her natal family does not give expected money, jewellery or other things; if she shows disrespect for him; if she leaves the home without telling him; if she neglects the children; if she doesn't cook food properly."

While these measures suffer from obvious limitations, in particular because they are susceptible to reporting bias, they were designed to capture as best as possible various dimensions of women's status, and to be consistent with the other major surveys on women's status.

However, recognizing the limitations, in our analysis we will also make use of measures of behaviours as indicators for, or proxies of, women's status, including fertility and girls' school enrolment. Both behaviours are linked to women's status.

Female education is generally higher in areas where women have higher status and, importantly, is itself an input to the health and education of future generations of women (and men). Lower fertility is often linked to female autonomy, in part because the value of women's time increases as the set of activities they are permitted to do goes up.

And while observed changes in fertility may represent direct changes in attitudes regarding the optimal number or spacing of children independent of changes in attitudes towards women, reductions in fertility or increased spacing is a useful outcome measure in itself because it represents gains to women, in the form of reduced health risks and increased opportunities outside of the home due to reduced child-rearing burdens.

Data on Cable Television

Crucially for this project, the village-level survey included information on cable television. Panel A of Table 1 provides information on cable availability throughout the survey.

Summary Statisticson Cable Availability

Panel A: Cable Availability by Survey Round	
Year	Number of Villages with Cable
2001	65
2002	75
2003	86
Not During Survey	94
Panel B: Cable Availability in 2001 by State	
State	Share of Villages with Cable
Bihar	7.5%
Delhi	97.1%
Goa	60%
Haryana	17.5%
Tamil Nadu	77.5%

Notes: This table shows summary statistics on cable availability, either over time or across state in therst sample year.

In the first round, 65 of the 180 villages have cable. As stated above, this was a period of rapid expansion in cable access throughout India. Thus, in our data, an additional 10 villages added cable by the 2002 survey and another 11 added it by 2003. Finally, 94 villages never get cable (no villages drop cable during the sample period). The identification of the effects of cable in the paper relies on the 21 villages that added cable in either 2002 or 2003.

For all those villages that added cable, we also gathered data on when service first became available.

There is significant regional variation in access to cable. Panel B of Table 1 shows the percent of villages/clusters in each state with cable access in 2001. Not surprisingly, the capital, Delhi, has essentially universal access.

Elsewhere, the two southern states of Tamil Nadu and Goa have very high cable penetration, at 78 and 60 percent of villages, respectively. By contrast, coverage in the two northern states of Bihar and Haryana is low (7 and 17 percent). While this variation may seem extreme, or perhaps an artifact of our particular sample of rural villages, these estimates are consistent with a 2001 national census of villages.

As noted above, television was generally available prior to cable, so it is important to explore whether the introduction of cable had any effect on the amount of television watching. Figure 1 shows this to be the case.

The figure shows the percent of people who report having watched television in the past week (unfortunately, the survey did not gather data on the amount of time spent watching). There is relatively little change in watching over time in either areas that never have cable or those that always have it.

However, in villages that get cable in 2002, the share of respondents who report watching television at least once a week jumps from 40 to 80 percent between 2001 and 2002; in villages that get cable in 2003, this share is constant between 2001 and 2002, then increases sharply from 50 to 90 percent between 2002 and 2003.

This graph suggests a strong connection between cable availability and television viewership, with a near doubling in both cases.

Consistent with the background above, cable availability is correlated with factors that make providing service profitable at the village-level, as can be seen in Table 2, where we regress whether a village has cable in 2001 on a range of village-level characteristics.

As expected, villages with higher mean income or a greater population density are more likely to have cable. Education also increases the likelihood of cable. The other clear correlate is urbanization (Table 2 includes only rural villages, so urban/rural status is not included on the right hand side. Only about half of the rural villages have cable access, while all of the urban areas surveyed do. However, the rural fraction with access has been increasing over time, again, due primarily to reductions in the costs of service (coupled with increases in income).

Village-Level Determinants of Cable Availability

Dependent Variable: Village has Cable (in 2001)	
Explanatory Variables:	
Log Average HH Income Per Capita	.0771*
	(.044)
Log Population Density	.0585**
	(.028)
Distance to Nearest Town	–.005
	(.004)
Average Education	.0584**
	(.021)
Share Muslim	.021
	(.192)
Constant	.337**
	(.166)
Number of Observations	136
R^2	.49

Standard errors in parentheses, clustered by village.

* Signicant at 10%; ** Signicant at 5%; *** Signicant at 1%

Notes: This table shows the village-level determinants of having cable an observation is a village in 2001.

The fact that cable availability is not exogenous is not necessarily a problem for the analysis here. If the availability of cable did have an exogenous driver (as in Olken, 2006) the analysis would be simple: we could just compare villages with and without cable in the cross section. Although that is not possible here, the availability of panel data allows stable village (and individual) characteristics to be differenced out. Changes in other obvious factors leading to increased cable access, such as income, can be explicitly controlled for. The primary remaining concerns are the possibility that there is some pre-existing differential trend between villages that do and don't add cable, or that the changes in cable availability are driven by some unobserved factor that also causes changes in attitudes.

Data on Gender Attitudes

The first set of dependent variables to be used are measures of autonomy, attitudes toward beating and son preference among women. The various measures of autonomy are highly correlated, but they do contain independent information.

To generate a single summary measure, therefore, we perform a principal components analysis of the decision making variables, the permission variables and the variable measuring whether the woman can keep her own money.

The first principal component of these variables captures the largest amount of variation common to all variables in the set. The autonomy measure is this first principle component, which is standardized to have a mean of zero and standard deviation of one.

The attitudes measure is simply the number of situations in which the woman reports that it is acceptable for a husband to beat his wife (0-6). Finally, the son preference variable is whether the woman reports wanting her next child to be a boy (again, this is only observed for the sample of women who report wanting more children). Panel A of Table 3 summarizes the underlying variables. Overall, the reported level of tolerance for spousal beating (which may understate actual tolerance) is high. Over 60 percent of women feel that it is acceptable for a husband to beat his wife under at least one of the six situations listed. On average, women report 1.6 situations in which it is considered acceptable; the mean among women who think it is ever acceptable is 2.6. Women are most likely to believe beating is acceptable if a wife neglects her children, goes out without permission or does not show respect towards her husband; being a bad cook, her family not sending money or, surprisingly, if she is unfaithful, are believed to be less valid justifications for violence (though one-fifth to one-quarter still feel these are sufficient justifications).

With respect to decision-making, in this table we have condensed the responses to binary indicators for whether the woman participates in the decision, either on her own or jointly with others in the household.

Summary Statistics on Dependent Variables

Panel A: Gender Attitudes			
	Mean	*Standard Deviation*	*#Obs*
Attitudes towards beating			
Beating ever acceptable	0.621	0.485	9159
# Of situations beating is acceptable	1.61	1.73	9159
Husband may hit if:			
Unfaithful	0.244	0.429	9159
Family doesn't give money	0.204	0.403	9159
Show disrespect	0.308	0.461	9159
Go out without telling	0.306	0.461	9159
Neglect children	0.336	0.472	9159
Bad cook	0.215	0.411	9159
Autonomy: Respondent can make decisions about			
Healthcare	0.566	0.495	9159
Purchases	0.556	0.496	9159
Visits to family/friends	0.549	0.497	9159
Autonomy: Respondent needs permission to visit			
Market	0.561	0.537	9159
Friends	0.675	0.496	9159
Autonomy: Money			
Resp. keeps own money	0.739	0.438	9159
Son Preference			
Want next child to be a boy	0.549	0.497	2165

Panel B: Fertility and Education			
	Mean	*Standard Deviation*	*#Obs*
Average # children	1.107	1.78	8208
Change in # children	0.142	0.352	5472
Share in school, age 6-14	0.743	0.436	8587
Share dropout, ages6-14	0.135	0.341	4455

Notes: This table shows summary statistics for the dependent variables used in the paper. All of the autonomy, beating attitudes and son preference measures are binary. Son preference is only asked of women who report wanting more children.

Overall, slightly more than half of women participate in each of the decisions. There is some overlap in these variables, though not as much as might be suggested by the similarity of their means; about 20 percent of women do not participate in any of the three decisions, 25 percent participate in one, 27 percent in two, and 29 percent in three.

In terms of permission, just over one-half of women report needing permission from their husband in order to go to the market and two-thirds need permission to visit family or friends (while not shown here, less than 4 percent are not permitted to do each of these things). By contrast, nearly three-quarters of women are allowed to keep money set aside to spend as they wish. However, by most measures, women's status and autonomy overall are quite low.

The table also reveals strong son preference, with 55 percent of women who want another child preferring that child be a boy. Note in addition that the residual is not simply preferring a girl; only about 13 percent of women want their next child to be a girl, with the remainder reporting that the sex of the child doesn't matter (about one-quarter of the sample) or reporting something else (such as "up to God").

Data on Fertility and Education

The second set of dependent variables we use are measures of fertility and education. The fertility data are based on questions on births and pregnancies asked in each survey round. In the first round, women were asked to list all children ever born to them, even if they were not currently alive or living in the household.

In subsequent survey rounds women were asked about any new births since the last survey. Finally, women were asked in each round whether they were currently pregnant. We combine these data and create a variable measuring the change in the number of children between surveys, which includes both children conceived and born since the previous survey and current pregnancies (children conceived before the previous survey but born between surveys are therefore counted in the previous survey).

It is important to include the current pregnancies in order to line up with the timing of television: the theory is that television may affect the decision to have more children, or when to have them, which will be reflected in pregnancies earlier than in births. Data on the average number of children and the average change between surveys are described in Panel B of Table 3.

Data on education are drawn from the household roster which reports information on sex, age and activities, including school enrolment, for each individual in the household. For children aged 6 to 14 at the time of the first survey, we create an indicator for whether they are in school at each survey round and, for the last two rounds, whether they dropped out in the last year. We limit ourselves to children younger than 14 at the time of the first survey because by the end of the panel, children older than that may have started to marry and leave the household, and our education data on them might therefore be less complete. The education variables are summarized in Panel B of Table above.

Correlations between Women's Status and Demographics

It is informative to explore the relationship between the outcome variables (gender attitudes, fertility and education) and various demographic characteristics. In addition to providing information about correlates of women's status, this analysis can provide a benchmark for understanding the magnitude of the relationship between the outcome variables and cable introduction, discussed in the results section.

Table 4 shows the coefficients from regressions of the measures of women's status on each of the demographic variables individually (so, for example, the coefficient of 0:137 in the first row, first column indicates that in a regression of autonomy on rural status, with no controls, autonomy in rural areas is estimated to be 0:137 standard deviations lower than in urban areas). Consistent with expectations, rural areas tend to have less favourable attitudes towards women on all dimensions, while wealthier and more well-educated people in general have more favourable attitudes.

Correlations between Outcomes and Demographics

Dependent Var.:	*Autonomy*	*Beating Attitudes*	*Son Preference*	*#Children*	*In school (6-14)*
Explanatory Variables:					
Rural Area	-0.137**	0.7460***	0.0622	0.220***	-0.0542***
Education	0.0335***	-0.0461***	-0.0316***	-0.135***	0.047***
Log HH Income PC	0.0190**	-0.0424***	-0.0176***	0.0801***	0.0171***
Age	0.035***	0.006*	-0.002	0.113***	N/A
Muslim	-0.485***	-0.529***	0.157***	1.052***	-0.137***
Hindu	-0.0318	0.195**	0.0511	-0.3907***	0.0478**
Sched.Caste	-0.130	-0.114	-0.134	0.3710***	0.017

*Significantat 10%; **Significantat 5%; ***Significantat 1%

Notes: This table reports the coecients from regressions of each outcome (Variable Autonomy, beating attitudes, son preference, number of children and whether a child is in school) on demographics. Each cell represents a separate regression, with noot her controls. Other than that demographic characteristic (and a constant).

The effects of religion and age are more mixed, with some differences across groups (for example, Hindus tend to have lower female autonomy, but also a lower acceptability of beating).

Empirical Strategy

The basic empirical strategy is straightforward. For the measures of attitudes and autonomy, we run individual-level fixed effects regressions of the status measures on cable availability (measured at the village-level). Denote the reported status for individual i in village v in year t as sivt and cable availability in the village in year t as cvt. The primary regression estimated is

$$s_{ivt} = \beta c_{vt} + \gamma_i + \delta_t + \varepsilon_{ivt}$$

where γ_i is a full set of individual fixed effects and δ_t is a full set of year dummies. This specification allows us to eliminate any fixed difference across individuals and any common trends over time; the effect of cable will be identified off of changes in village-level access to cable during the three years of the survey. The identifying assumption is that women's status in villages that added cable would not have otherwise changed differently than in those villages that did not add cable; we discuss this assumption further in the next section. The analysis includes those that do not have cable in any round, and those that have it in all three rounds; using only the former (or leaving out all of these "non-changers") does not change any of the results appreciably. All standard errors are clustered at the village level to allow for correlation in errors among individuals living in the same village. A similar strategy will be used for the analysis of fertility. Our hypothesis is that cable affects either the total desired number of children a woman wants, or the spacing of those children. For this analysis, the dependent variable is the change in the number of children a woman has between survey rounds. We will also control in this regression for whether the woman was pregnant at the time of the previous survey, to allow for the fact that some fertility spacing is generally both desirable and biologically likely. In particular, we run the following regression:

$$\Delta Kids_{ivt} = \beta c_{vt} + \phi pregnant_{iv(t-1)} + \gamma_i + \delta_t + \varepsilon_{ivt}$$

where $\Delta Kids_{ivt}$ is the change in number of children between year t-1 and year t, and $pregnant_{iv(t-1)}$ is a control for whether the woman was pregnant in year t-1 (to adjust for the fact that some birth spacing is biologically necessary). We also separately analyze the impact on the reported desire to have more children, in order to examine whether changes in pregnancies/births reflect changes in total fertility, or simply the timing of pregnancies. Finally, in the analysis of education we will focus on the same type of regression controlling for child-specific fixed effects and examining changes over time but our main interest will be in comparing the effect for girls to the effect for boys. We begin by splitting the sample, running the fixed effects regression below for boys and girls separately:

$$enrolled_{ivt} = \beta c_{vt} + \gamma_i + \delta_t + \varepsilon_{ivt}$$

Our hypothesis is that β will be larger for girls than for boys. We will also consider regressions in which the boy and girl samples are combined, and we include an interaction between gender and cable access:

$$enrolled_{ivt} = \beta_1 c_{vt} + \beta_2(c_{vt}\text{-}Boy) + \gamma_i + \delta_t + \varepsilon_{ivt}$$

In this case, the coefficient of interest is β_2, the interaction between gender and cable access. Our hypothesis is that β_2 will be negative. Finally, in addition to these individual-level fixed effects regressions, we also estimate the effects of cable on women's status using village-level matching. We apply the bias-adjusted, nearest neighbour matching strategy proposed by Abadie and Imbens (2002). This strategy matches each village in both cable regimes (adds cable; does not add cable) to the village(s) in the opposite cable regime with the 'most similar' values of a set of specified covariates. The difference in the outcome variable is then computed for each matched pair, and the estimate is given by the mean of these pair-wise differences. Since the estimator is biased when matches are not exact, as is likely, the estimator adjusts for differences in the covariates using regression functions. Since the method effectively estimates for each observation the value of the missing outcome variables for the counterfactual situation using similar-looking observations in the opposite cable regime, the key assumption is that, conditional on the covariates used for matching, getting cable is independent of the outcome variable. We match based on 2001 village-level characteristics: income, population density, distance to the nearest town, education, the fraction of people who watch TV, and the level of the outcome variable. We match using the four nearest neighbours, with matching confined to within-state only (this is particularly relevant here given the unique outlier status of Tamil Nadu discussed below).

Results

This section presents the basic results on the effects of cable. The first subsection summarizes the effects on autonomy, attitudes towards domestic violence, and son preference. The second subsection discusses education and fertility. The third subsection discusses the concern over whether the results are largely driven by pre-existing differential trends.

Beating, Autonomy and Son Preference

Before moving to the fixed effects and matching estimators, we begin by showing the relationship between the measures of women's status and village level cable access using an OLS approach. We expect there may be some bias in the OLS results, although it is difficult to definitively sign its direction. Villages with cable access are likely to be more urbanized and perhaps have more 'modern' attitudes, which are likely to be associated with more favourable attitudes towards women, suggesting an upwards bias. However, there may be other drivers of cable access that are correlated with less favourable attitudes towards women, which would push the bias in the other direction.

For example, in households where men have more power or authority, due perhaps to earning a higher fraction of the household's income, they may assert their personal preferences to a greater extent, which may include both spending on cable rather than other goods, and not allowing their wives significant autonomy. Table shows the OLS relationship between the three measures of women's status autonomy, beating attitudes and son preference and cable access. Panel A shows the results with only controls for cable access and year. The results are somewhat inconsistent. We find that cable access is associated with greater autonomy and reduced son preference. However, we also find that villages with cable have more acceptability of beating than those without it. Thus, the raw cross-sectional results yield somewhat ambiguous conclusions regarding the effect of cable television on women's status. However, part of this seeming contradiction may be driven by the uneven spatial distribution of cable access. As noted earlier, among rural areas, cable access is highest in the southern state of Tamil Nadu.

And while in general women's status is typically higher in southern India relative to the north (ex., Bardhan 1974), one apparent exception is domestic violence in Tamil Nadu. In our data, the average number of situations in which a woman reports it is acceptable for a husband to beat his wife is 2.99 in Tamil Nadu, compared to 1.4, .99, 1.9 and .90 for Bihar, Delhi, Goa and Haryana respectively. This finding is not unique to our data; results from the NFHS show that 36 percent of women in Tamil Nadu report having ever actually been beaten by their husbands, which is nearly double the national average of 19 (IIPS and ORC Macro 2000; the rates are 25, 10, 14 and 12 percent in Bihar, Delhi, Goa and Haryana, respectively). By contrast, but also consistent with what other authors have noted, in the NFHS Tamil Nadu is well above average on other measures of women's status, such as autonomy and decision-making. While there remain concerns about reporting bias for these variables, these results confirm that our data are not unique in regard to attitudes towards domestic violence in Tamil Nadu, and suggest a possible explanation for the contradictory results above is some unobserved factor or attitude perhaps unique to domestic violence that is more prevalent among households in Tamil Nadu than in other states.

Cable Television and Attitudes, OLS Regression

Panel A: Limited Controls

Dependent Variable:	*Autonomy*	*Attitudes*	*Son Preference*
Explanatory Variables:			
Village Has Cable	.6166***	.4593***	-.2896***
	(.075)	(.12)	(.046)
Constant	-.318***	1.424***	.669***
	(.049)	(.08)	(.026)
Year FE	YES	YES	YES
Number of Observations	9159	9159	1998
R^2	.05	.02	.08

In panel B, we therefore add state fixed-effects to the basic regressions, in addition to a variety of other controls, including income, education, age, and religion. The effects of cable are dramatically smaller in magnitude in all three cases. The presence of cable in a village is associated with an increase in women's autonomy/decision-making and a reduction in son preference. The coefficient on the number of acceptable situations for beating is still positive, but it is now very small, and not statistically significant. While this removes the apparent contradiction in the effects of cable on women's status, it still at least suggests that cable may not have any effect on attitudes towards domestic violence. However, there may of course remain other important village or individual omitted variables that the state fixed effects and other controls do not capture. Therefore, it is important to turn to our preferred estimation strategies. The basic fixed effects results and the identification strategy are illustrated graphically in Figures 2a, 2b and 2c. For the three measures of women's status, these figures graph the village means over time in villages that never have cable, villages that add cable in 2002, villages that add cable in 2003 and those that have cable in all three rounds. All three figures show the same pattern.

Panel B: With Controls

Dependent Variable:	*Autonomy*	*Attitudes*	*Son Preference*
Explanatory Variables:			
Village Has Cable	.1215*	.0148	-.0634**
	(.063)	(.095)	(.031)
Log HH Income per Capita	.0100	-.0007	-.0111*
	(.008)	(.01)	(.006)
Education	.0154***	-.0649***	-.0155***
	(.006)	(.007)	(.004)
Age	.0306***	-.0047	.0056*
	(.003)	(.003)	(.003)
Hindu	-.1478	-.2005	.0345
	(.134)	(.165)	(.093)
Muslim	-.2879*	-.5614**	.0649
	(.175)	(.22)	(.105)
SC/ST	.0392	-.5504***	-.1799*
	(.151)	(.189)	(.098)
Rural	-.1685	-.0393	-.0487
	(.185)	(.192)	(.105)
Constant	-.871***	2.274***	.587***
	(.258)	(.311)	(.171)
Year FE	YES	YES	YES
State FE	YES	YES	YES
Number of Observations	9159	9159	1998
R^2	.16	.22	.22

Standard errors in parentheses, clustered by village

* significant at 10%; ** significant at 5%; *** significant at 1%

Notes: This table shows OLS regressions of outcomes on cable access. Column 1 reports the effect on the first principal component of a number of autonomy measures (does the woman make decisions about her health, purchases or visits, does she need permission to go to the market or visit her family and can she keep her own money). Column 2 reports the effect on attitudes towards beating (the sum of the number of situations in which the woman reports spousal beating is acceptable). Column 3 reports the effect on son preference- the share of women who report wanting their next child to be a boy (conditional on wanting another child).

In areas that always have cable or never get cable the measures of women's status are relatively at, though trending slightly upward in some cases. However, in areas that added cable by the 2002 survey, there are large improvements in women's status between 2001 and 2002, followed by smaller gains between 2002 and 2003, suggesting the effect of cable appears very quickly. And in areas where cable is added after the 2002 survey, there is no change between 2001 and 2002, but large improvements between 2002 and 2003.

Cable television and Attitudes, Fixed Effect Regressions

Dependent Variable:	***Autonomy***	***Attitudes***	***Son Preference***
Explanatory Variables:			
Village Has Cable	.1896***	-.1880***	-.1214***
	(.044)	(.066)	(.037)
Year = 2002	-.0068	.0337	.021
	(.036)	(.044)	(.022)
Year=2003	.0573	.0252	.0326
	(.035)	(.056)	(.027)
Log HH Income Per capita	.0038	-.0066	-.0038
	(.006)	(.007)	(.003)
Income Year = 2002	.0071	-.0056	-.0027
	(.006)	(.007)	(.003)
Income Year = 2003	-.0052	-.0061	-.0031
	(.005)	(.011)	(.004)
Education Year = 2002	-.0024	-.0036	-.0005
	(.004)	(.005)	(.002)
Education Year = 2003	.0021	-.0019	-.0002
	(.003)	(.005)	(.002)
Constant	-.14***	1.76***	.619***
	(.038)	(.053)	(.025)
Individual FE	YES	YES	YES
Number of Observations	9159	9159	1998
R^2	.91	.86	.93

Standard errors in parentheses, clustered by village

* significant at 10%; ** significant at 5%; *** significant at 1%

Notes: This table shows individual-level regressions of our dependent variables on cable access. Column 1 reports the effect on the first principal component of a number of autonomy measures (does the woman make decisions about her health, purchases or visits, does she need permission to go to the market or visit her family and can she keep her own money). Column 2 reports the effect on attitudes towards beating (the sum of the number of situations in which the woman reports spousal beating is acceptable). Column 3 reports the effect on son preference - the share of women who report wanting their next child to be a boy (conditional on wanting another child).

Again, while Figure 2b may at first appear to contradict the overall relationship between cable and women's status in that acceptance of domestic violence is greater in villages where cable is available in all periods than in those that never have it, the high incidence in Tamil Nadu of both cable and the acceptability of beating is likely to be behind much of this difference. Further, three of the ten villages that add cable in 2002 and three of the eleven that add it in 2003 are in Tamil Nadu, while only four percent of the villages without cable in all periods are from that state, accounting for the higher acceptability of beating in 2001 in the villages that added cable relative to those that never had cable. This again underscores the need to consider changes in outcomes, in order to eliminate these and any other fixed differences.

The individual-level fixed effects regressions are in Table 6. All regressions include year dummies, alone and interacted with income and education, to allow for differential time trends by education and income. All three regressions show a statistically significant effect of cable television on women's status. Adding cable is associated with a .19 standard deviation improvement in the measure of women's autonomy and decision-making, a .19 reduction in the average number of situations for which beating is acceptable, and a .12 reduction in the likelihood of wanting the next child to be a boy.

For autonomy and son preference, the effects of cable are larger than the OLS estimates with controls. And in the case of attitudes towards beating, unlike with OLS, the fixed effects estimates indicate that cable does indeed improve the situation of women.

As discussed, both the beating attitudes and autonomy measure are generated from a larger set of variables measuring attitudes toward beating under various situations and different questions on autonomy. Although these composite measures are a convenient way to summarize these variables, the results are quite consistent across the individual components. This can be seen in Table below, which estimates the effect of cable access on each component variable using the fixed effect specification.

Of the twelve individual variables, nine have the expected sign (the other three are very close to zero) and seven are statistically significant.

In absolute terms, the largest effect is a reduction in the perceived acceptability of a husband beating his wife if she is a bad cook, and an increase in participation in household decisions on major purchases. We can also estimate seemingly unrelated regression models on the components of the beating attitudes and autonomy variables and test the joint significance of the effect of cable on these variables.

Doing so yields similar results: the chi-squared statistic for autonomy is 45.86, significant at greater than the 1% level, and for beating it is 22.83 (results available from the authors). Panel A of Table 7 provides the results from the matching estimator (here we show the average treatment effect; the results for the average treatment effect for the treated, in which matching is undertaken only for villages that added cable, yields similar results).

The results are remarkably similar to those from the fixed effects analysis. Adding cable is associated with a increase in the autonomy measure. The number of acceptable situations for beating declines by and son preference declines by. These results are robust to using 2 or 6 matches instead of 4.

All of these results suggest large, favourable, effects of cable on women's status. To get a rough sense of the magnitude of these effects, one option is to compare the coefficients to the effects of more traditional shifters, like education, on the same outcomes.

For example, based on the evidence in Table 4, one year of education shifts female autonomy by 0.0335. Comparing this with the fixed effect results in Table 6 suggests that introducing cable is roughly equivalent to increasing female education by about 5.5 years in terms of the effect on attitudes. Since the average education level is about 3.5 years, the effect is quite large.

Alternatively, and perhaps more in line with the theory that television leads to change by increasing exposure to urban attitudes and values, we can ask whether cable television moves the attitudes in the rural areas closer to attitudes in urban areas. We can do this by comparing the estimates of the effect of cable to the differences in the measures of women's status between households in Delhi and households in rural villages without cable, and evaluate what shares of those differences are made up for through cable introduction.

These results are shown in Table 8, which reports the average value of the dependent variables for Delhi and rural respondents, as well as the coefficient from Table 6 and the share explained. The share explained is large in all cases, varying from 42 to 70 percent, indicating that a significant fraction of the gap between urban and rural areas is closed by the introduction of cable.

These estimates of the effect of television are quite large (although, of course, the standard errors are also large, so we cannot reject somewhat smaller effects). An important issue is, therefore, whether it is plausible that effects of this magnitude would be seen so quickly. Villages that adopted cable during our survey would have had it on average for only six or seven months before they were surveyed again. Although it is difficult to directly evaluate how quickly we would expect to see effects of cable, some of the existing literature suggests that changes in attitudes and behaviours as a result of television (or media exposure in general) can be quite fast.

Johnson (2001) discusses a village that went from 2 to 25 latrines in a period of 4 years after television introduction. Pace (1993) demonstrates a large decrease in the perception of own-village status in the world with just one year of television exposure. Related, there is also a large literature showing rapid effects on attitudes arising from changes in media content (as opposed to adding television).

Effect of Cable on Beating Attitude, Autonomy Components

	Eeffct of Cable	Standard Error
Attitudes towards beating: Husband May Hit if		
Unfaithful	0.0103	0.0148
Family doesn't give money	-0.0481**	0.0196
Show Disrespect	-0.0262	0.0231
Go out without telling	0.0054	0.0119
Neglect Children	-0.0543**	0.0206
Bad Cook	-0.0750***	0.0259
Autonomy: Respondent can make decisions about		
Health Care	0.0212	0.0244
Purchases	0.0894***	0.0258
Visits to Family/Friends	-0.0048	0.0273
Autonomy: Respondent needs permission to visit		
Market	-0.0585***	0.0201
Friends	-0.0371***	0.0111
Autonomy: Money		
Resp. keeps own Money	0.0352***	0.0128

*significant at 10%; **significant at 5%; ***significant at 1%

Notes: This table shows the e"ect of cable access on the components of the autonomy and beating measure. All outcomes are binary.

In Tanzania, a radio soap opera promoting family planning resulted in between a 10 and 15 percentage point increase in contraceptive use within two years of the program being introduced, and between a 3 and 7 percentage point decline in current pregnancies. A multimedia campaign (radio and television) in Mali in 1993 promoting family planning led within just 3 months to a 20 percentage point increase in the share of individuals planning to use modern contraceptive technology in the future; a radio program in the Gambia shows similar effects within 8 months of introduction.

Finally, there is also evidence that when used as a vehicle for reaching a large number of people very quickly as in "social marketing", media can have large and immediate effects as well; for example, a television and radio family planning campaign in Nigeria increased the number of new clients at family planning clinics three to five fold within one month of airing.

All of these examples suggest that the effect of media exposure on attitudes and behaviour may happen very quickly. This makes it, perhaps, less surprising that we see such large effects of cable exposure within a short period of time.

Following on the overall results, it seems sensible to ask whether these effects differ across demographic groups for example, by age and education. To get a sense of this, we divide the sample in half based on age or education and estimate the effect of cable on the three central outcomes for each subgroup.

These results are shown in Table below. The results show consistent evidence of larger effects among the better-educated. The effects also appear to be somewhat larger among older people, although this effect is less consistent. In general, however, these results are difficult to interpret.

Effect of Cable by Age, Education

Panel A: Breakdown by Age			
Dependent Variable:	**Autonomy**	**Attitudes**	**Son Preference**
Younger	0.1170*	-0.1723**	N/A
	(.0605)	(.0724)	
Older	0.2691***	-0.2037**	N/A
	(.0639)	(.0951)	

Panel B: Breakdown by Education			
Dependent Variable:	**Autonomy**	**Attitudes**	**Son Preference**
Less Educated	0.0551	-0.0858	-0.0750
	(.0399)	(.0824)	(.0487)
More Educated	0.3888***	-0.3369***	-0.1652***
	(.0825)	(.0658)	(.0599)

* significant at 10%; ** significant at 5%; *** significant at 1%

Notes: This table shows the effects of cable broken down by age and education. In both cases, the dataset is split in half, so the younger group is the youngest half of the dataset and the less educated group is the bottom half in terms of years of education. In Panel A, the effects on son preference are not shown because this questions is only asked to younger women who are still planning to have more children.

More educated people could be more responsive because they are better at processing information, but this also may reflect the fact that they are much more likely to watch television. The results on age also have a number of interpretations: older women may have more ability to assert themselves once they come to expect more autonomy, or they may have only their husband to convince, while younger women may have both a husband and a mother-in-law. In general, without knowing something more about what actually goes on within the household, these breakdowns are interesting but difficult to draw strong conclusions from.

Education and Fertility

The results in the previous subsection point to large effects of cable television on women's status. However, one concern with these results is that we are measuring only what is reported, rather than directly observing the outcomes. It is possible that exposure to cable television gives women a different sense of what they think the interviewer wants to hear, but does not change behaviour. In this subsection we analyze the effect of cable on female school enrolment and fertility. In contrast to the measures in the previous section, these come from the household roster reports. Although it is, in principle, conceivable that respondents also misreport on these rosters, it seems much less likely to be a significant issue.

Cable Television, Education and Fertility, OLS Regression

Dependent Variable:	**Enrolled in School**		**Change in # Kids**
	Girls, 6-14	**Boys, 6-14**	**(including Current Pregnancies)**
Explanatory Variables:			
Village Has Cable	.0553*	.0441*	-.0313***
	(.032)	(.024)	(.011)
Log HH Income Per Capita	.0151***	.0113***	.0012
	(.004)	(.004)	(.002)
Household Ave. Adult Educ.	.0492***	.025***	
	(.009)	(.008)	

Child Age in 2001	-.03***	-.014***	
	(.004)	(.004)	
Hindu	-.045	-.0495	-.0209
	(.046)	(.044)	(.018)
Muslim	-.1486**	-.1429**	.0587**
	(.067)	(.058)	(.026)
SC/ST	.0875	-.0743	.0234
	(.087)	(.068)	(.013)
Rural	.0153	.0519	-.018
	(.037)	(.037)	(.014)
Education			.0013
			(.001)
Age			-.0159***
			(.001)
Pregnant Last Year			-.2139***
			(.013)
Constant	.829***	.809***	.725***
	(.085)	(.094)	(.035)
Year FE	YES	YES	YES
Number of Observations	4594	4988	5423
R^2	.09	.04	.15

Standard errors in parentheses, clustered by village

* significant at 10%; ** significant at 5%; *** significant at 1%

Notes: This table shows OLS regressions of fertility and education on cable access. Columns 1 and 2 show the effect of cable on children's school enrolment, for girls and boys respectively. Column 3 shows the effect on fertility.

Table 9 shows OLS regressions of indicators for children's current period school enrolment, and women's fertility (yearly change in number of children) on cable television access. In these regressions, cable access is positively and marginally statistically significantly associated with both female and male school enrolment. In column 3, cable access is significantly negatively correlated with fertility. However, as stated above, these regressions should be interpreted with caution, due to the possibility of significant omitted variable bias. Table 10 shows the fixed effect results on education.

In Panel A, the dependent variable is again a dummy for whether the child is currently enrolled in school. Column 1 shows that introducing cable increases the likelihood of current enrolment for girls by 3.5 percentage points (the base is 68 percent enrolled). This effect does not seem to operate for boys: the coefficient is extremely small, and not statistically significant. In both cases, the fixed effects estimates are smaller than the OLS estimates. Column 3 includes the cable variable and the interaction between cable and child gender. Though the magnitude of the difference in the effect between boys and girls is fairly large, we cannot reject that the effect is the same for both. Since there are likely to be varying costs and returns to early and later education, columns 4-9 split the sample by whether a child is 6-10 or 11-14. The differences by age are pronounced. For girls aged 6-10, the effects on schooling are large and positive, increasing the likelihood of enrolment by around 6 percentage points (from a base of 75 percent). For boys 6-10, the coefficient is negative, but it is small and not statistically significant. Thus, the gender difference is even greater in magnitude but, because of the larger standard errors from the smaller samples, in the interaction regression we can only reject the hypothesis of equality of the effects at the 10 percent level. By contrast, the last three columns of Panel A show that there is essentially no effect of cable on enrolment for boys or girls aged 11-14.

Thus, the overall effects on schooling appear to be driven largely by effects among the youngest children. One possible explanation is that educational planning is largely undertaken when children are young, so exposure to cable is too late to have much of an effect for older children. Panel B of Table 10 focuses on the likelihood of dropping out, rather than being in school, which may be the more relevant measure.

Focusing first on the full sample of children aged 6-14, cable television is associated with a large, statistically significant decline in the likelihood of dropping out for girls, whereas for boys the effect is positive and large, but not statistically significant. These effects differ greatly (13 percentage points), and in the third column, we can reject at the 10 percent level the hypothesis that the effects are the same. When split by age, cable television has a very large, negative effect on the likelihood of dropping out for girls aged 6-10 and 11-14, though the effect is only statistically significant for the former. By contrast, for boys, there is little effect among those aged 6-10, but a large, negative, but not statistically significant effect for older boys. However, while the point estimates of the magnitudes differ greatly for boys and girls, for neither age group can we reject the hypothesis that the effects of cable are equal. The results of the matching estimator presented in Panel B of Table 7 are broadly similar. Adding cable is associated with a large, marginally statistically significant increase in school enrolment for girls aged 6-10. For boys, the effects are negative, but not statistically significant. By contrast, for older children, the effects are not statistically significant for either boys or girls, and the point estimates are positive for boys but negative for girls. Thus, across the estimators, the most consistent finding is an improvement in the enrolment of young girls.

It should be noted however that while the gains for girls may reflect an improvement in women's status (either girls being more highly valued by their parents or adult women becoming more influential in household decision-making about their children's education), it is also possible that the gains arise through other mechanisms. For example, television may provide information that causes parents to update their beliefs about the returns to schooling, more so for girls than for boys (for example, Jensen (2007) finds that students in the Dominican Republic who watch television have higher perceived returns to education than children who do not watch).

Table 11 turns to the fixed effects results for fertility. Column 1 demonstrates the overall effect of cable on the change in number of children: the introduction of cable lowers the yearly increase in number of children or pregnancies by 0:09. The mean of this variable is 0:14, making this quite a large effect (in fact, much larger than the OLS effect, although of the same sign). Columns 2 and 3 divide the sample based on age, with Column 2 including only women age 35 or less and Column 3 including only women over 35.

Cable Television and Fertility

Dependent Variable:	Change in # Kids (Including Current Pregnancies)			Wants More Children
	(1)	(2)	(3)	(4)
	All	Age <=35	Age>35	Age<=35
Explanatory Variables:				
Village Has Cable	-.087***	-.1436***	-.0007	.0481
	(.021)	(.038)	(.009)	(.044)
Pregnant at Last Survey	-.6077***	-.6164***	-.5171***	-.0284
	(.025)	(.027)	(.082)	(.022)
Log HH Income PC	-.0011	.002	-.0082*	-.0063
	(.011)	(.017)	(.005)	(.008)
Year = 2003	.0695**	.115**	.0017	.0149
	(.029)	(.046)	(.015)	(.035)
Income Year = 2003	-.0128**	-.02**	-.0019	-.0108
	(.006)	(.009)	(.003)	(.007)
Education Year = 2003	-.004*	-.0063**	-.0001	-.001
	(.002)	(.003)	(.001)	(.002)
constant	.241***	.35***	.063***	.489***
	(.044)	(.067)	(.02)	(.038)
Individual FE	YES	YES	YES	YES
Number of Observations	5423	3423	2000	2251
R^2	.57	.53	.61	.87

Standard errors in parentheses, clustered by village

* significant at 10%; ** significant at 5%; *** significant at 1%

Notes: This table shows the effect of cable television on the change in number of children between years (Columns 1 through 3) and reported desire for more children (Column 4). If an individual is pregnant in year t, that is counted as an increase in a child between year t .. 1 and year t. The dataset includes two observations per person, one in 2002 and one in 2003 since we are using changes, so we need 2001 as the □first comparison year. Column 1 includes all women, Columns 2 and 4 are limited to women under 35 and Column 3 is limited to women over 35.

Since there should be little or no effect for the latter group (since fertility in India is very low among this group) this can validate that changes observed for younger women are not just changes in reporting (i.e., cable viewers report lower fertility because they learn than high fertility is less acceptable among outsiders).

Indeed, we find a significant and large effect among young women (change in number of children is decreased by 0:14 children), but no effect among older women.

This fact is not surprising given that the average increase in children in this older group is only 0:01, versus 0:21 in the younger age group. Panel C of Table 7 shows the results for the matching estimator. As above, the results are similar to the fixed effects results, with an estimated effect of-0.08 for the full sample of women and-0.12 for women 35 or under.

This short-term change in fertility could reflect either a change in the timing of births (pushing them to later), or a change in the total number of eventual births.

The results in Columns 1 through 3 of Table 11 are consistent with either result.

It is possible to get some sense of which of these mechanisms is producing the result by looking at the effect of television on the reported desire for more children (though we do not know how many more children they want). This result (the effect of cable television introduction on whether a woman, under 35, reports wanting more children) is reported in Column 4 of Table 11.

The data suggest no significant relationship between this measure of desired fertility and cable introduction. Taken together with the results in Columns 1 through 3, this may point to an effect of cable on birth timing, but perhaps not on overall fertility.

However, without data to test whether cable influences the total number of additional children a woman wants, this conclusion is only tentative. Further, delays in having children now may in fact result in reduced eventual fertility.

Effect of TV Watching, Instrumented with Cable Access

	Effect of Watching TV (IV Estimate)	Standard Error
Attitudes, Autonomy and Son Preference		
Autonomy	0.4841***	0.1352
Beating Attitudes	-0.4799***	0.1682
Son Preference	-0.3035***	0.1053
Fertility		
Change in # of Children, All	-0.2051***	0.0586
Change in # of Children, Under 35	-0.3482***	0.1152
Change in # of Children, Over 35	-0.0016	0.0209
Education		
In School, Girls 6-14	0.0700	0.0459
In School, Boys 6-14	-0.0077	0.0967
Dropout, Girls 6-14	-0.1468***	0.0521
Dropout, Boys 6-14	0.1918	0.2147

* significant at 10%; ** significant at 5%; *** significant at 1%

Notes: This table shows regressions of the outcome variables on whether the surveyed individual reports watching television in the last week. This measure of watching is instrumented with cable access. The regressions include the same controls as in the non-IV regressions in the text - income, year dummies, income and education interacted with the year dummies.

As mentioned above, it is worth noting that there are a number of mechanisms through which television access might affect fertility, including the one hypothesized here, that lower fertility is linked to higher autonomy.

For example, women may learn about birth control via informational programs on television or television may change the amount of time people want to devote to child-rearing.

The results here do not allow us to separate these mechanisms; they do suggest a causal result of television overall, but we cannot conclude with certainty that this works through increases in autonomy.

However, as an outcome in itself, delayed or reduced fertility represents a gain for women.

Alternative Explanations of the Results

While the fixed effects estimates eliminate any fixed differences that may influence both women's status and getting cable, the central concern with these results is that they may be driven by pre-existing differential trends. If areas with rapidly changing attitudes towards women (or changes in factors that in turn affect attitudes) are also more likely to get cable, we would mistakenly attribute those changes to the introduction of cable.

Similarly, the matching estimators in effect rely on the assumption that villages that look alike ex-ante but differ in whether they add cable might be expected to follow similar trajectories in women's status. While these assumptions are in their strongest form untestable, we can examine the data for any evidence of possible differential trends.

With a long panel it would be relatively easy to test for trends. Here, we have only three years, which limits the scope of this investigation. However, we can observe a short pre-trend for areas where cable was introduced in 2003. If large changes in attitudes between 2001 and 2002 were predictive of getting cable in 2003, that finding would validate the concern about pre-trends; if not, it suggests such trends may not be important. It will only be possible to perform this test for the beating attitudes, autonomy and son preference measures. In the case of education and fertility we are effectively only analyzing two changes (2001-2002 and 2002-2003) so there is no pre-trend to analyze.

To an extent, we can see the results of this test in Figures 2a-c. There is virtually no change in attitudes, autonomy or son preference between 2001 and 2002 for those villages that got cable in 2003. If there was a strong pre-trend, we would expect to see it here. To provide a more rigorous test, we consider the set of villages without cable in 2002 and test whether the change in attitudes between 2001 and 2002 are predictive of who gets cable in 2003. This regression is shown in Table 12. The results indicate that changes in attitudes between 2001 and 2002 are not predictive of getting cable in 2003.

Trends in Attitudes and Cable Adoption

Dependent Variable: Village Adopted Cable between 2002 and 2003			
Explanatory Variables:			
Change in Autonomy 2001-2002	-.172		
	(.224)		
Change in Beating Att. 2001-2002		-.0049	
		(.143)	
Change in Sex Preference 2001-2002			-.0279
			(.141)
Log Ave HH Income Per Capita	-.1316	-.1408	-.1418
	(.089)	(.089)	(.091)
Education	.0453*	.0466*	.0459*
	(.026)	(.026)	(.027)
Hindu	.0262	.0445	.0561
	(.569)	(.574)	(.577)
Muslim	.0654	.1012	.1094
	(.595)	(.601)	(.601)
Christian	1.55**	1.6222**	1.6619**
	(.763)	(.765)	(.785)
Family Size	-.1011*	-.097*	-.0948*
	(.055)	(.055)	(.056)
Main Crop is Rice	-.0808	-.0907	-.0903
	(.081)	(.08)	(.082)
Distance to Nearest Town	.0051	.0052	.0053
	(.004)	(.004)	(.004)
constant	1.516	1.526	1.507
	(1.015)	(1.02)	(1.035)
Number of Observations	79	79	78
R^2	.19	.18	.18

Standard errors in parentheses

* significant at 10%; ** significant at 5%; *** significant at 1%

Notes: This table examines the predictors of getting cable television between 2002 and 2003 and tests for whether trends in the gender attitude variables are important predictors of television introduction. The data are for 2002 and is limited to villages that did not have cable in 2002. The dependent variable is equal to 1 if the village got cable between 2002 and 2003 and 0 if they did not. The independent variables on attitudes are changes in village level averages between 2001 and 2002.

For attitudes and sex preference, the coefficients are extremely small and not statistically significant. The coefficient on changes in autonomy is larger, but the sign suggests that areas with an improvement in women's autonomy between 2001 and 2002 are actually less likely to get cable between 2002 and 2003 (although this is not statistically significant).

Although the test in Table 12 is appealing intuitively, there is likely to be a fair amount of noise in the data on changes, which pushes the coefficients towards zero. As an alternative, we can consider whether, among villages without cable in 2001 but with cable by 2003, the 2001 levels of the attitude variables are predictive of whether they get cable in 2002 or 2003. This will give us a sense of whether the timing of the introduction of cable in this sample is correlated with the pre-existing levels of attitudes. Table 13 shows these results. The dependent variable is 1 if cable was introduced in 2002 and 0 if it was introduced in 2003. All of the coefficients on the attitude variables are small, and none are statistically significant. Moreover, the direction of the effects is not consistent across the variables.

Obviously with such a short panel it is difficult to rule out the possibility of such differential trends. However, the results here suggest that, to the extent it is possible to test, there is little or no evidence that the cable results are being driven by other trends in attitudes.

We can provide some additional, though limited, evidence on whether there were pre-existing differential trends by considering the timing of cable introduction somewhat more closely.

Since it typically takes 2 to 3 months from the time an entrepreneur is ready to set up service in a village (once they have raised the funds and received a license, the equipment must be shipped, a technician must install it, and the account must be activated) to the time it is operational, if there were differential trends driving both cable and women's status, arguably they would likely be evident shortly before cable is actually turned on.

Initial Attitudes and Timing of Cable Introduction

Dependent Variable: Village Got Cable in 2002 rather than 2003			
Explanatory Variables:			
Autonomy	.1897		
	(.343)		
Beating Attitudes		.0365	
		(.153)	
Son Preference			-.1366
			(.498)
Log Ave HH Income Per Capita	.1499	.2281	.2472
	(.406)	(.388)	(.402)
Education	-.0888	-.0649	-.0561
	(.121)	(.113)	(.11)
Hindu	-2.8812	-1.9029	-1.8261
	(3.108)	(2.646)	(2.952)
Muslim	-2.8053	-1.8268	-1.6436
	(3.332)	(2.876)	(3.144)
Christian	-4.5677	-3.3486	-3.2954
	(3.989)	(3.352)	(3.485)
Family Size	-.0893	-.0129	.0195
	(.239)	(.197)	(.206)
Main Crop Rice	.4003	.2093	.1693
	(.537)	(.397)	(.431)
Distance to Town	-.01	-.0144	-.0142
	(.016)	(.015)	(.018)
constant	3.152	1.15	.948
	(5.28)	(3.6)	(3.699)
Number of Observations	21	21	20
R^2	.23	.21	.22

Standard errors in parentheses

* significant at 10%; ** significant at 5%; *** significant at 1%

Notes: The data for this table is limited to villages that got cable during the survey. The dependent variable is equal to 1 if the village got cable in 2002 (early adopter) and 0 if they got it in 2003 (late adopter). The regressors are the attitude and behaviour and control variables for 2001.

At this point, the entrepreneur will have already established that there is a local demand for cable, and may have even already signed up customers. Therefore, as a limited test, we can examine whether there were any changes in women's status already evident for villages that added cable shortly after the

2002 or 2003 surveys were conducted. Three months after the final survey, we gathered data on the month when cable was first introduced in each village (though only for those villages that added cable during the survey). These data reveal that two of the villages that added cable between the 2002 and 2003 surveys added it within two months of the 2002 survey, and three villages that had not added cable at the time of the 2003 survey added it within three months of that survey. Table 14 shows the means for the autonomy and attitudes towards beating variables for these villages (the other variables have too few observations to be meaningful for such a small sample).

Between the 2001 and 2002 surveys, those villages that added cable shortly after the 2002 survey actually exhibit if anything a worsening trend in women's status. For example, the mean measure of autonomy declined from-.27 to-.38 (in contrast to the slight improvement for those that did not add cable (figure 2a)).

Trends in Attitudes for "Early" Adopters

Changes 2001 to 2002 for Adopters 2-3 Months After 2002 Survey		
Dependent Variable:	Autonomy	Beating Attitudes
2001	-0.265	1.787
2002	-0.381	1.910
2003	-0.185	1.785
Changes 2002 to 2003 for Adopters 2-3 Months After 2003 Survey		
Dependent Variable:	Autonomy	Beating Attitudes
2001	-0.070	1.989
2002	0.036	1.984
2003	-0.114	2.105

Notes: This table shows trends in autonomy and beating attitudes for villages that adopt cable within 2-3 months after the previous survey. These "early" adopters would have the knowledge of getting cable at the previous survey. Looking at the changes therefore is a test for pre-existing trends.

Similarly, the mean number of situations where beating is considered acceptable increased from 1.79 to 1.91 (those that did not add cable were largely unchanged (figure 2c)). Similarly, if we consider the three villages that added cable shortly after the 2003 survey, between 2002 and 2003 the measure of autonomy declined from .036 to-.11, and the number of situations in which beating is considered acceptable increased from 1.98 to 2.11.

Thus in both sets of villages, we find that just before cable was added, there was if anything a slight trend towards worsening, not improving, women's status. While these samples are small, the results here, and those above, are nevertheless suggestive that there was no differential trend in women's status prior to the introduction of cable.

Overall, the expansion of cable television into new villages has arguably come about in large part due to a lowering of costs and increases in income. As costs have declined, more communities have become profitable cable markets. Overall, our identifying assumption is that villages that added cable would not have otherwise changed differently than those villages that did not add cable. While it is difficult to test this assumption with such a short panel, the tests above reveal no substantial evidence of differential trends for these two groups. Further, figures 2a-2c show there do not appear to be any real changes in women's status among groups that never receive cable (or those that have it in all three periods).

The only noticeable changes that occur in these graphs are the large, striking changes for villages that add cable, and those changes only occur after cable is in place. Otherwise, attitudes appear to be fairly stable over time.

Further, most factors that are likely to shift attitudes (and affect cable status), such as education, are fairly slow changing and could not lead to the sudden changes observed in these figures. And the most obvious shifter that might potentially change somewhat more quickly, namely income, is explicitly controlled for.

Overall, it is difficult to imagine another factor with a sharp, discrete change that drives both cable access and overall attitudes (again, keeping in mind than any fixed differences are eliminated). However, this cannot be tested, and we must maintain this assumption in order to interpret our results as the effect of cable on women's status.

Effects of TV Watching

The preceding analysis focuses on the effects of cable access on attitudes and behaviours. From an economic standpoint, however, the more interesting coefficient may be the effect of TV watching, not just the effect of having access. A simple way to estimate this effect in the context of our data is to run the same set of regressions, except with a measure of television watching on the right hand side, and instrument for watching with cable access. This is, of course, roughly equivalent to re-scaling the coefficients on access based on the first stage effect, which can be intuited from Figure 1.

In all cases, we see qualitatively similar, although larger results. This is exactly what we would expect. Adding cable has strong predictive power for watching television (with an F-statistic of 10 or more in all cases), and the coefficient is less than one, so re-scaling increases the magnitude of the effect.

As mentioned, the primary advantage of these results is that actual television exposure is a more economically interesting variable than access alone. However, the downside is that these regressions ignore potentially important social interaction effects. That is, when we are analyzing attitudes and other potentially socially constructed outcomes, the effect of introducing television to an entire area may be very different than the effect of introducing television to just one individual. Given that in our context we see only the former "experiment," it is not really possible to interpret the estimated effect of watching television as the effect we would expect to see if television was randomly introduced to only certain individuals.

Mechanisms

The results in the previous section suggest a large effect of cable television on attitudes and behaviours, but do not provide guidance about the mechanisms behind such an effect. The mechanism alluded to in the introduction is greater exposure to the outside world: cable television in rural India shows lifestyles in urban India, and the values and behaviours in urban areas are much more favourable towards women than in rural areas.

This mechanism is certainly consistent with anthropological studies, both within India and elsewhere. Perhaps the best example is Pace (1993), who describes large changes in perceptions about the outside world after the introduction of television in an isolated area of the Amazon, including changes in knowledge of facts about the world outside, as well as changes in perceptions of the status of the home village in the wider world.

To be more concrete about this mechanism, assume that an individual's attitudes are a function of upbringing (for example, the average village attitudes) and what they learn on their own later on in life, for example through interactions with peers. Television in effect may serve as a new set of information or `peers' from which individuals learn. Denote the upbringing attitude y0 and the attitudes portrayed on television as $y_{television}$. We assume that a weight α is put on upbringing, and a weight 1-α on television, which will depend on the availability of television. If there is no television available, $\alpha = 1$. Overall attitudes can be expressed

$$y = \alpha y_0 + (1-\alpha)y_{television}$$

In this simple model, if the attitudes on television are more favourable towards women than that average attitudes in your village or those you were brought up with, then introducing television will make individual attitudes towards women more favourable.

This framework suggests at least one possible test of the validity of this mechanism: the effect of television introduction should be larger in areas where y0 and ytelevision differ more. Since television content is similar in all areas, this difference will be larger when y0, the initial village level attitudes, are more gender-biased.

To test this hypothesis, we divide villages into two groups based on their average attitudes in 2001 (we do separate divisions for autonomy, beating acceptability and son preference). We then explore the effect of cable on outcomes in each set of villages. Table 15 reports these results. For all three dependent variables, we find much larger effects in areas with initially worse attitudes the effects in Columns 1, 3 and

5 are much larger than those in Columns 2, 4 and 6 (though they are only statistically significantly different for son preference).

Mechanism Test: Effect Breakdown by Initial Attitudes

Dependent Variable:	**Autonomy**		**Beating**		**Son Preference**	
Initial State	**Low**	**High**	**High**	**Low**	**High**	**Low**
Explanatory Variables:						
Village Has Cable	.2316***	.1408*	-.2559**	-.0766	-.2106***	-.0098
	(.051)	(.077)	(.1)	(.085)	(.047)	(.027)
Log HH Income PC	.009	-.0044	.0054	-.0164	-.0022	-.0051
	(.008)	(.009)	(.007)	(.011)	(.004)	(.005)
year = 2002	-.0239	.0067	.0936	-.0404	.0181	.0469*
	(.048)	(.049)	(.058)	(.073)	(.035)	(.025)
year = 2003	.0285	.0801**	-.0347	.0945	.0327	.0149
	(.055)	(.039)	(.05)	(.094)	(.035)	(.032)
Educ Year = 2002	-.0019	-.002	-.0014	-.0059	-.0046	-.0019
	(.004)	(.005)	(.007)	(.006)	(.005)	(.003)
Educ Year = 2003	.0061	-.0004	-.0005	-.0023	-.0068	.0012
	(.005)	(.005)	(.006)	(.007)	(.005)	(.002)
Income Year = 2002	.0115	.0031	-.0178**	.0087	-.0037	-.0023
	(.009)	(.007)	(.008)	(.012)	(.005)	(.002)
Income Year = 2003	-.0005	-.0092	-.002	-.0126	-.0022	.0004
	(.009)	(.006)	(.009)	(.016)	(.006)	(.004)
constant	-.676***	.44***	2.52***	.997***	.858***	.321***
	(.044)	(.077)	(.084)	(.074)	(.026)	(.03)
Individual FE	YES	YES	YES	YES	YES	YES
Number of Obs	4599	4560	4560	4599	1003	993
R^2	.89	.9	.88	.73	.88	.93

Standard errors in parentheses, clustered by village

* significant at 10%; ** significant at 5%; *** significant at 1%

Notes: This table shows the effect of cable television on individual-level attitudes, broken down by the average initial attitude level in the village. Columns 1 and 2 break down based on autonomy, Columns 3 and 4 based on beating attitudes and Columns 5 and 6 based on son preference.

These results are at least consistent with the theory that television increases exposure to a new set of peers with different attitudes, which causes individuals to change their attitudes and behaviours. However, there are a variety of other possible mechanisms that could be causing this result.

For example, the increased availability of television could affect time allocation, social interactions (for example, spending more time with others if television is watched communally, or less time if private watching displaces other social interactions) household demand for goods they see on television, or it may directly provide information that affects behaviours, such as the availability of family planning services. Depending on the model, any of these mechanisms could produce the effects observed here. Although Table 15 is consistent with the hypothesis of a change in peer groups, it is certainly not conclusive. Much more would need to be done to establish conclusively that this particular mechanism is what causes the changes in attitudes and behaviours observed in Section 4.

CONCLUSION

In this chapter, we analyze the effect of exposure to cable television on attitudes towards women in India. We argue that the introduction of cable television reduces son preference, fertility, and the reported acceptability of beating, and increases women's autonomy and female school enrolment. Overall, the effects are quite positive for women.

It is also noteworthy that the large changes observed are accomplished despite there being little or no direct targeted appeals, such as through public service announcements or explicitly socially-oriented programming (such as the 'Sabido Method' soap operas used worldwide).

It may be that cable television, with programming that features lifestyles in both urban areas and in other countries, is an effective form of persuasion because people emulate what they perceive to be desirable behaviours and attitudes, without the need for an explicit appeal to do so.

There is a significant and almost urgent focus in the policy debates in India (and elsewhere) on interventions to alter attitudes towards women and girls, especially as the availability of sex-selective abortion has resulted in sex ratios dramatically more skewed towards boys.

This paper suggests that a relatively simple and inexpensive "intervention" may actually have quite large effects on attitudes towards women. Since cable television is rapidly spreading all over India, this may lead to changes in attitudes towards women even without targeted interventions. And this can occur even in the face of poverty that keeps individual television ownership low, since people can and typically do watch with friends or relatives.

As we think about policy, however, it is worth noting that the effects estimated in this paper may be larger than what we would expect to see if cable were introduced more widely.

Although we have argued that pre-existing trends in attitudes are not driving the results, we cannot rule out the possibility that television is introduced first into areas that have the biggest potential for change; those that are receptive to television may also be receptive to changing their gender attitudes.

This means that while there is an effect of television, and the magnitude of the effect is correctly estimated within sample, the effect of further introduction may be smaller, or slower.

Nevertheless, given the magnitude of the effect estimated here, even much smaller effects could still have the potential to make a significant difference for women in India.

5

Religious Revivalism through Media

INTRODUCTION

It is a fact that television has faster and greater impact on society. In a democratic, secular and linguistically diverse country like India, television has a more significant role to play than it does now. Indian television today, has grown into one of the biggest networks in the world. It is claimed that the programme service of Indian television is aimed at the benefit of a unique pluralistic society in which the past and present, the modern and traditional blend with national languages and the multiplicity of dialects.

To address this socio-cultural mosaic, Doordarshan, the Indian television network has, over the years widened the scope of its programmes and extended its hours of transmission. But directly or indirectly, these programmes reflect certain trends. This paper presents an analysis of these trends.

Discourse analysis, a critical approach of the study of language, deconstructs the connections between language, power and ideology, which are often hidden beneath the structure of language, used in the TV serials.

According to Althusser (1986), ideology is located in the imaginary relationships of individuals with the real conditions of existence. He proposed that ideology has material existence manifest in the material practices of the people. This paper focuses on the discourse structure of language in mythological serials dubbed in Malayalam, and attempts to evaluate the language ideology of the promoters. This ideological enquiry focuses on language revivalism as well as the preponderant influence or authority of one language over another, as revealed in the TV serials.

SECULARISM VS REVIVALISM

The national television network is aimed at fostering social, economic and cultural awareness; promoting the spirit of national integration and projecting the progress made by Indians in various fields. During the last two decades successive governments at the Centre have been using mass media, particularly, television as an instrument to propagate and inculcate the spirit of nationalism.

Media persons view media as a sub-system. Because mass communication, including television, can be regarded as sub-system of culture, a sub-system represents an important variable in the process of social change.

It also represents power, and legitimizes the political and economic sub-system, thereby providing the web that holds society together. Whosoever controls the media has, to some extent, controlled the society.

Both historically and technologically, the methods and the means of communicating messages have been very crucial to the integration and the unity of a culture and society. But the recent trend is contrary. The Constitution of India declares that India is a secular country.

However, most of the programmes telecast as TV serials do not consider the values of secularism. Secularism is understood largely as a code of morality without any religion's identity in its way. This assumption on the part of the producers and administrators helps the growth of revivalism that brings in religious overtones into the present culture, presented as the exemplary model by the TV serials.

The serials on Ramayana and Mahabharata, the two great Indian epics, were the most popular programmes, till recently on Doordarshan. These serials have broken all previous records of programmes on Indian television. After the great success of these serials, other serials, namely, Sreekrishna, Ohm Namshivaya, Jai Hanuman, Japam Tapam Vritham, Jai Matha, and Jai Ganga Maiye have been telecast. All these are based on Hindu Mythology as depicted in the Epics and Puranas.

The promoters of these serials take advantage of the religious archetype of the viewers at the expense of the literary qualities of the source materials. To attract the viewers, in addition to archetypes, visual potentialities are effectively used with the help of modern technology. The promoters attract more and more regional viewers, and the serials produced in Hindi, and mostly aimed at Hindi viewers, are dubbed in the regional languages.

AUTHORITY INFLUENCE OF ONE LANGUAGE OVER ANOTHER

Language can represent not only the objective word, but it can also conceive of abstract thoughts. According to the Sapir-Whorf Hypothesis, thinking and perception are not only expressed through language, but are actually shaped by language. When the source language of the Epics is recreated by Doordarshan, it promotes authoritative influence of one language over others.

Historically, Sanskrit is considered to be the ancient language in India. Important religious, instructive, philosophical, and literary works have been written in Sanskrit. The great epics Ramayana and Mahabharata are composed in thousands of Sanskrit couplets. Vedas and Upanishads are time-honoured Hindu sacred books, which originated in Sanskrit and are rendered in other Indian languages. Consequently, Sanskrit is also perceived to be representing Hindu religion.

The Mantras of the Vedas are to be rendered in an accurate pronunciation, according to the practice and sanction of several Hindu scripture texts. All mythological TV serials appear to made it a point to ensure accuracy in rendering mantras while they depict rituals. This apparent claim enhances their prestige in the minds of the devout viewers of these serials.

Apart from other functions, the ritual forms may be used to preserve the religiosity of a social group. It is used in cultural or social practices such as wedding, upanayana, and funerals. It creates a spiritual or religious atmosphere.

Following this religious practice, the TV serials provide no translations for Sanskrit words in the original Hindi texts of the serials. The assumed reason is to create an authentic religious or spiritual atmosphere which includes, in Hindu religious contexts, maintaining the sacredness of the religious text.

Actually, Doordarshan Hindi is a stylistically Sanskritized form of the language. Critics say that the use of Hindi on national television programming has rendered Doordarshan a focal point for regional linguistic discontent. Also because television is controlled by the Centre, critics charge that Doordarshan's use of Hindi constitutes cultural "imperialism" radiating from Delhi, bringing into question the legitimacy of Federal rule.

The mythological serials that are continuously promoted now become another mode of the very same process. There is another point of view of Doordarshan Hindi by Mitra (1993), a well-known media person, who says that the present form of Hindi is an offshoot of Sanskrit and it is, therefore, able to establish a certain binding with Hindu religion as well.

In the past few years, Mahabharata on Doordarshan has also been able to reproduce Hindi as the language of Bharat (India). Almost all mythological serials on Doordarshan have been circulated using a Hindi dialect that is archetypical of north-central India. In short, these serials reproduce Hindu-Hindi authority influence by circulating Sansrktized Hindi and mythology that are typically connected with Hindu ideology and Hindu practices.

LANGUAGE REVIVALISM

Language is the central media in the process of socialization whereby people are constituted as an individual and a social subject. As Thirumalai (1988:6) writes, "there is a qualitative change in language use as the child grows, even though most of the structures are already acquired and available to him or her. The qualitative change is not simply restricted to the acquisition of some new and complex linguistic structures. The qualitative change must be seen more significantly in the ways the already available linguistic structures are put to use.... socialization is nothing but the acquisition and use of symbols."

If language is studied from the political point of view, inferences will indicate that there is always a hidden content couched in some specific linguistic terms and metaphor in the discourse. Study of these linguistic terms, metaphors, and their use will unravel the original intent.

When one deconstructs the language in the mythological serials, it could be seen that there are keen revivalistic trends in the text of the serials. The aim of television promoters is to attract more and more regional viewers.

They dub these into various regional languages. The dubbing uses highly Sansrktized terms, and tries to follow as closely as possible the original Hindi version. This type of Hindi shuns away from any naturalized Arabic and Persian loans as these are stamped as Urdu and hence unacceptable.

This dubbing technique involves modifying or adding to the sound track. Change of language is one of the most complex linguistic operations imaginable. Accents have to be matched to convey similar social effects, and words have to be found that look like the originals.

This need for keeping up the "original" flavour, seems to justify the current practice of not translating or replacing the Sanksrit words with the commonly used words from the regional languages. This helps maintain or begin a process of religious revivalism. The revivalist signs can be seen in the language aspects such as address terms and common vocabulary as discussed below.

Address Terms

The address system in the serials has a characteristic revivalistic tone. Contrived archaic Sanskrit Puranic terms are invented. Since sri is considered an honorific form, the affix forms of /sri/ is invariably appended to almost all address terms. The list of words are given below with its meaning:

Sanskrit	English	Malayalam
Pitaasri:	Father	Acchan
Maataasri:	Mother	Amma
Braataasri:	Brother	Sahodaren
Maamaasri:	Uncle	Maamen

Although the trend is to append /sri /to address terms there are some exceptions in words such as:

Thaadaa-Father (Acchan-Malayalam)

Bhavati-You/Sister (Female gender) (nee/sahoodari-Malayalam)

Bhavaan-You/Brother (Masculine Gender) (Sahoodaran-Malayalam)

Aarya-Noble (Male)

Aarye-Noble (Female)

Aaryaputra-Lord (Male)

Aaryaputri-Lady (There are no equal words from Aarya to aaryaputri in Malayalam.)

These address terms express the facet of power relations being imposed on society.

Common Vocabulary

There are a large number of words in the serials, which reflect Hindu spirituality such as:

Vidaadavu-Brahma

Sadaanda swaru:pam-one in whom goodness, knowledge and bliss are combined

Pannigrhanna-Marriage

Rishi-Saint

Devarishi-Saint of Devalokam (Saint of Gods)

Taytya-Asura

Paramapoojyan-Most respected person

Yajnakarma-Yaaga (holy sacrifice performed to propitiate gods)

Ohm sri: Sri-most honorific

Asurayooni-Female genital organ of a suravamsa

This ontological language can reflect the spiritual realm of Hinduism. There are also forms such as:

Bhakti-The practice of devotion to or love of God.

Moksha-Liberation (Shorn of any form of distinction)

Samsaaraa-The whole world of materials things (Transmigration of souls)

Nirvana-Enlightenment

Sunyataa-Against the abyss of nothingness

Here Sunyataa refers not only to nothing in the negative sense of unreality, but positively to that reality which cannot be expressed through conceptualization.

Dharma, the moral ideal and Parama, the ultimate, can also express spirituality. The word Parama is used mostly in these serials.

This noun denotes the highest status available, particularly in a Hindu religious context, and the form Parama, serves as the first element in a number of compounds. It also stands as an intensifier in such cases as the following 'Parampitaa' and 'Paramapurush.' All these words are used in the present serials and strengthen the revivalist trend at the language level.

Even though Sanskrit has a profound influence on Malayalam, this does not mean that all the Sanskrit terms used in Malayalam cannot be substituted by a native word. Use of a Sanskrit flavour as used in the serials may be intended to maintain a puranic atmosphere.

If so, can we justify that this usage functions only as genuine stylistic device? In reality, this device also has the inherent potential or assumption that the present day

Malayalam may be revised to include these terms to bring in an atmosphere of religiosity.

ARCHAISM

The uses of old or antiquated words in the TV serials come under archaism. It is a device to create an impression of a make-believe world, that is, a spiritual world far removed from present life. Archaism as an art strategy is used, generally, to create an ideal or otherwise a world of the past.

It means, then, the use of a language that is distanced from every day speech to create an impression of a world not really in existence.

These words are not used in every day speech or written prose either in Sanskrit or in any other Indian languages.

The promoters have been deliberately using archaic forms in the mythological serials to create a Hindu spiritualism. Apart from these forms, all the serials employ the word/ohm/ which artificially creates a spiritual atmosphere of Hinduism.

CONCLUSION

Power relations through the use of linguistic utterances brought out in a discourse are not something that the individuals may suddenly pull out and use. When highlighted, such utterances become a deliberate force in the hands of those who use them.

The linguistic utterances express certain specific content and ideology. Repeated use of such utterances re-inforce that content and ideology. This is what happens in the TV serials discussed in this paper.

It appears that the promoters of the mythological serials have been using their power over regional viewers and languages for purposes of revivalism. Should a government undertaking media such as Doordarshan do it?

If entertainment through mythology for purposes of culture and religion is necessary, will such presentations focus more on artistic elements of the story rather than on reviving values that may function more as an authority influence over people and other languages?

Media may be seen as a panacea for the problems of a democratic country like India. But unfortunately the Doordarshan does not seem to use its power judiciously to promote values demanded in a secular polity.

It must be remembered that the basic inspiration for Indian thought has come from the Vedas, Upanishads, Puranas and the Epics, among other sources.

These great works have exercised a great fascination for many eras on the Indian mind as reflected in the various writings in the Indian languages. However, what the language of the mythological TV serials highlights does not focus on critical Indian thought. It focuses more on other matters.

6

CONTROL IN THE MEDIA

INTRODUCTION

Newspaper and magazine journalism and production, radio and television journalism and production are regulated and given advice by government-appointed and independent advisory bodies, which seek to ensure a balance between ethical and-legal considerations and possible infringement of the right to freedom of speech in all media. Any journalist or media producer should be aware of their responsibilities either under me law or as part of self-regulation in adhering to professional attitudes and practice. The main regulatory and advisory bodies are given in this chapter.

ROLE OF PRESS COMPLAINTS COMMISSION

The Press Complaints Commission, which replaced the former and largely ineffective Press Council, is an independent self-regulatory organization dealing with complaints from members of the public about the editorial content of newspapers and magazines. The majority of its 16 members should have no connection with the press, thus attempting to ensure its independence from the newspaper industry, but in 2001 six members were editors of national and regional newspapers and magazines.

The independent chairman is appointed by the newspaper and magazine industry and must not have any vested interests or connections in the publishing industry. The public members arc appointed by an Independent Appointments Commission and once again may not have any connections with the publishing industry, other than their work on the commission. Each of the press members mast have experience at a senior editorial level. The Code of Practice, which has evolved since its introduction in 1991 to meet changing circumstances, is written by a committee of editors and ratified by the commission.

As it is not a legal document it can and has been amended to reflect parliamentary comment and advice from members of the public, newspaper editors and the PCC itself. The code sets the benchmark for the press, demanding that they adhere to ethical and professional standards by protecting the rights of the individual whilst at the same time upholding the public's interest and right to know.

The Code of Practice, which was ratified by the Press Complaints Commission on 1 December 1999, consists of 16 clauses, some of which may be excepted in the public interest, which includes detecting or exposing crime or a serious misdemeanour, protecting public health and safety and preventing the public from exposure to misleading statements from an individual or organization. Briefly the 16 clauses relate to:

- Accuracy
- Opportunity to reply
- Privacy
- Harassment
- Intrusion into grief or shock
- Children
- Children in sex cases
- Listening devices
- Hospitals
- Reporting of crime
- Misrepresentation
- Victims of sexual assault
- Discrimination
- Financial journalism

- Confidential sources
- Payment

The code performs a dual function in that it provides the press with a turn set of binding principles and guidelines as well as giving the commission a clear framework with which to deal with complaints from the public. Editors are asked to ensure that all staff observe the code, not only to the letter but in full spirit, and it is their responsibility to respond with alacrity to any complaints raised by the PCC on behalf of any individual, organization or group of people.

Editors must print in full the adjudication and in most cases complaints are resolved by the publication of an apology or correction. The outcome of each investigated complaint is published in a regular Complaint's Report, which is circulated to all branches of media, consumer, legal and public services. Some will argue that the PCC is still largely ineffective in curbing the power of the press. However, the alternative is to impose legal and statutory controls on the industry that may conflict with the freedom of the press and the public interest.

THE RADIO AUTHORITY

The Radio Authority, which was created by the Broadcasting Act 1990, commenced its licensing and regulatory role in January 1991. The members of the authority are selected from a variety of backgrounds and serve for five years. Basically, the RA has three main functions: to plan frequencies; to appoint licensees with a view to broadening listener choice and also to monitoring output; and to regulate programming and advertising. It publishes regulatory "and obligatory codes on engineering, sponsorship and advertising and programming.

It licenses and regulates all commercial radio services (not the BBC) including national, local, cable, satellite, national FM subcarrier and restricted services. The latter include short-term, freely radiating services such as 'special event' radio, hospital and campus radio and localized permanent stations. It also licenses both national and local digital services and derives its income solely from licence application and running fees. National licences, which last for eight years, are advertised in open competition and are awarded to the highest cash bidder following criteria set down in the Broadcasting Acts of 1990 and 1996.

Three licences are in existence - one for a 'non-pop' station, one for a primarily 'speech-based' station and one for an 'all-comers' station. Local licences, also of eight years' duration, are advertised in open competition in areas that the authority considers appropriate in terms of availability of a suitable frequency, projected financial stability of the proposed station and solid evidence of a serious applicant being available. Restricted Service Licences (RSLs) are issued on a temporary basis for a period not exceeding 28 days and function on low-power transmitters to a designated area of interest or for a special event. Many colleges and other institutions apply for these licences in order to give students the opportunity to gain broadcasting experience.

Long-term Restricted Service Licences (LRSLs) are intended for a single establishment such as a hospital and are often transmitted either on an induction loop or low-powered FM and AM wavebands. Cable and Satellite Licences, which are issued for a period of five years, are subject to conditions ranging from ownership, transmission details and programme content. Digital Radio Licences comprise National Multiplex, Local Multiplex and Sound Programme Services and will be awarded for periods of 12 years. The RA's advertising and sponsorship code relates to the content and presentation of advertisements and sponsorship and follows the Advertising Standards Authority's guidelines on honesty, legality, decency and truthfulness, although sponsorship proposals do not need advance clearance.

However 'special category' advertisements and national advertising campaigns broadcast on more than one station require advance clearance from the Radio Advertising Clearance Centre (RACC), a body approved by the Radio Authority. The news and current affairs code sets out rules governing the broadcasting of news and related programmes. These rules cover impartiality and accuracy, library material, phone-ins, interviews, discussions, undue editorial influence or opinion and political programming, especially at the time of elections. Finally the programme code covers such overall matters .as taste and decency; portrayal of violence, sexual conduct, terrorism and anti-social behaviour; children; religion; and sensitive areas.

The authority considers complaints from the listener and, if it decides to proceed with a complaint, will request a recording of the offending output If the station is found to be in breach of its licence agreement the RA can apply sanctions including a demand for an apology or correction to be broadcast, fires and the shortening or revocation of a licence. Findings are published in The Radio Authority and the Listener. It should be noted that technical aspects and transmission of broadcasting, including the radio spectrum, is the responsibility of The Radio Communications Agency.

THE INDEPENDENT TELEVISION COMMISSION

The Independent Television Commission, which like the Radio Authority was set up by the Broadcasting Act of 1990, replaced the Independent Broadcasting Authority (IBA) and the Cable authority. It is the public body responsible for licensing and regulating commercial television companies broadcasting in and from the UK. These include ITV, Channels 4 and 5, public teletext and a range of cable, satellite and local delivery services.

It does not regulate the BBC or S4C, the fourth channel in Wales. The Secretary of State for Culture, Media and Sport appoints the chairperson, deputy chairperson and up to a further ten members. They are supported by a full-time staff with specialist regulatory and licensing expertise as well as a range of advisors, including several specialist committees. The Central Religious Advisory Committee (CRAC) advises the ITC, the BBC and the Radio Authority on, religious matters. The Medical Advisory Panel, consisting of eminent and independent consultants gives advice on medical- and health-related advertisement. The Advertising Advisory Committee (AAC), comprising of members from the advertising industry and consumers, debates sponsorship and advertising issues. The Schools Advisory Committee (SAC), with practising teachers and national educationalists as members, provides guidelines on classroom television programmes and Channel 4 service to schools. All members of the commission must abide by government guidelines on best practice for members of public bodies, which sets out their responsibilities and their relationship with the Department for Culture, Media and Sport.

However, as well as the specialist advisory committees, the commission receives regular comment from 12 Viewer Consultative Panels (VCCs), nine in England and one each in Wales, Scotland and Northern Ireland. These panels consist of a wide cross-section of society, age and interest and are encouraged to discuss the content and range of programmes, particularly within each council's region.

The ITC licences set out conditions on standards of broadcasting and advertising, monitor broadcaster's performance against the requirements regarding programme content, sponsorship, advertising and technical performance. It ensures that a wide range of television services that are of good quality and appeal to a diverse audience is available in the UK and that there is fair competition in the provision of these services.

It investigates complaints and publishes its findings on a regular basis in its Programme Complaints and Intervention Reports and yearly in its Annual Performance Reviews. Although the-ITC does not make, broadcast or transmit programmes it regulates the standards for programme content in the ITC Programme Code, which includes guidelines on privacy, taste and decency, violence, charitable appeals, religious programmes, impartiality and commercial product placement. Minor breaches of the code will lead to advice regarding the guidelines. Serious offences will incur the issuing of a formal warning, a requirement for on-screen corrections and apologies, imposition of a fine or shortening or revocation of the licence.

It should be noted that regulation for satellite and cable programme content is different from terrestrial services in that there is no requirement for cable or satellite channels to provide a mix of education, information and entertainment. Significantly the 9.00p.m. 'watershed' is brought forward to 8.00p.m. for subscription and pay-per-view services protected by a pin system. However, licensed programme channels are still regulated by the ITC's Programme, Advertising and Sponsorship Codes and can be censured by the ITC for breaches of these regulations.

THE BRITISH BROADCASTING CORPORATION

The British Broadcasting Corporation is established under successive Royal Charters (the latest expires in December 2006), which set out its public broadcasting obligations to inform, educate and entertain. BBC services are regulated by a separate agreement under the Charter, thus recognizing the BBC's editorial independence. Twelve Governors, who are part-time non-executives, are appointed by the Crown on the recommendation of ministers.

They are men and women with a wide range of experience in arts, business, industry and public service and are trustees for the public interest in ensuring that the BBC is accountable to listeners and viewers, licence payers and Parliament..

The Governors, who meet monthly, ensure that the BBC is directed and managed in the public interest, complies with the Charter and the law and maintains the highest standards and values expected of the nation's official broadcaster. They also appoint the Director-General and the senior management of the corporation, who run the day-to-day affairs.

However, the Governors can hold management to account for their activities and are responsible for monitoring performance, setting strategies and ensuring compliance with laws, regulations and policy, which must serve audience needs and deliver good value for the licence fee. The Governors submit an Annual Report to Parliament containing their assessment of performance.

They ensure that programme makers observe the Producer's Guidelines and that the BBC's commercial aim is not subsidised by licence payers. The Governors observe the Cadbury and Nolan Codes on corporate governance and standards in public life and, in deference 10 their responsibilities, maintain an Audit Committee, a Fair Trading Audit Committee and a Remuneration Committee.

The Governors conduct formal public consultatións and seek specialist views on BBC services and programmes as part of their commitment to providing a quality service. The Governors' Programme Complaints Appeals Committee considers appeals against the findings of the BBC's Head of Programme Complaints, which in itself investigates serious complaints about BBC programmes.

The Governors are assisted in their oversight and awareness of the needs of BBC listeners and viewers in Northern Ireland, Wales, Scotland and the English Regions by National Broadcasting Councils and an English National Forum. Similarly, the Governors are instrumental in safeguarding the independence of the BBC World Service and seek advice on output and audience perceptions from the World Service Consultative Group.

THE BROADCASTING STANDARDS COMMISSION

The Broadcasting Standards Commission is the statutory body for standards and fairness in broadcasting in the UK. It is the only regulatory body that covers all commercial and public broadcasting organizations as well as cable, satellite, digital services and text. The commission consists of 13 members, representing different professional backgrounds, who are appointed by and can report directly to the Secretary of State for Culture, Media and Sport. The BSC monitors the standards of UK broadcasting and, through a programme of independent research, reports on the attitudes of the public towards issues of broadcasting standards and fairness in compliance with its published codes, which are based on research and consultation. As an alternative to a court of law it provides redress for people who believe they have been unfairly treated. Standards complaints are usually concerned with sex, taste and decency and the portrayal of violence or offensive language.

Fairness complaints are usually concerned with unfair treatment, misrepresentation or infringement of privacy. In the majority of cases the BSC, after receiving a formal complaint, has the power to demand a recording of the broadcast as well as written statements, in preparation for a hearing.

Decisions are published frequently and broadcasters must report any action taken as a result. Normally the broadcaster will transmit summaries of the findings on air and also publish them in a newspaper or magazine.

The Commission is accountable to Parliament and publishes an annual report of its work as well as a report on its financial situation, which is scrutinized by the National Audit Office.

THE BRITISH BOARD OF FILM CLASSIFICATION

The British Board of Film Classification, formerly the British Board of Film Censors, is an independent body that decides on the classification of films and video that are distributed in the UK. It has no legal status but works within the remit of established laws, particularly as regards the exploitation of children.

To maintain its independence the board does not accept funding from the film industry, although it offers guidance regarding possible classification of a film in production. Funding is obtained by the fees levied for classifying films and videos.

Films are classified into the following categories:

U (Universal)	suitable for all ages
PG (Parental Guidance)	general viewing but some scenes may be unsuitable for young children
12	suitable only for persons of 12 years or over
15	suitable only for persons of 15 years or over
18	suitable only for persons of 18 years or over
R18 (Restricted 18)	to be supplied only in licensed sex shops or cinema clubs to person of not less than 18 years.

The responsibility for showing a particular film in an area is the responsibility, not of the BBFC, but the local authority, although most accept the recommended classifications.

THE ADVERTISING STANDARDS AUTHORITY

The Advertising Standards Authority, a self-regulatory body, ensures that non-broadcast adverts appearing in the UK adhere to the rules in the British Codes of Advertising and Sales Promotion, which have been written and agreed by the industry through the Committee of Advertising Practice. The basic principles state that advertisements should be legal, decent, honest and truthful; be prepared with a sense of responsibility towards consumers and society in general; and are in line with the principles of fair competition in business.

The ASA is funded by a small levy on display advertising and direct mail expenditure and thus preserves its independence from the publishing and advertising industry. All advertisements and promotions in non-broadcast media are regulated by the ASA and include the national and regional press, magazines and free sheets.

The ASA also regulates outdoor advertising, direct marketing, sales promotions and cinema commercials, and advertisements in electronic media such as computer games, video, CD-ROM and the Internet.

Complaints, of around 12000 per year, usually fall into three categories: those that need investigating under the code; those where a complainant has misunderstood the meaning and gist of an advertisement; and those, such as television commercials, which are under the jurisdiction of the Independent Television Commission.

Most complaints are from members of the public but some are from consumer groups and competing companies. If an advertisement is found to break the codes then the ASA will ask the company to withdraw or change it, and most act upon this advice.

However, if a company or organization refuses to comply, the ASA can apply sanctions such as asking publishers and media owners to refuse more space for the advertisement unless it is changed; withdrawing trading privileges; creating adverse publicity through the media; and in the last resort, referring a persistent offender to the Office of Fair Trading (OFT), which can seek an injunction through the courts to prevent the same or similar claims being made in future advertisements.

THE MECHANICAL COPYRIGHT PROTECTION SOCIETY

The Mechanical Copyright Protection Society is one of the world's largest royalty collection societies. It is a membership organization that represents thousands of composers, songwriters and music publishers and has reciprocal agreements with equivalent organizations throughout the world.

The MCPS negotiates agreements on behalf of its members with people and organizations who wish to record music and then ensures that the copyright owners are paid for the use of their music. The society collects and then distributes the mechanical royalties that are generated by the recording of music onto many different formats such as vinyl, CD, cassette, video, broadcast programmes and multimedia.

THE PERFORMING RIGHT SOCIETY

The Performing Right Society collects royalties on behalf of music creators and publishers for the 'public performance' and broadcast of their copyright musical works. A licence is required to play music in public for commercial businesses, charities, clubs or music venues. However, a licence is not required for performances during divine services in places of worship, live musicals and operas and other dramatic productions.

There are over 40 different PRS public performance tariffs that take into account the nature and extent of the music used and the venue. Radio stations must log the titles and duration of broadcast music in order that royalties may be collected and paid to the copyright owners.

The PRS is also a member of the British Music Rights (BMR), which works to promote the interests of UK composers, songwriters and music publishers. It also funds the Performing Right Society Foundation, which aims to encourage, promote and sustain music creation and its performance at all levels.

The Performing Right Society and The Mechanical Copyright Protection Society have formed a Music Alliance of their separate societies in the UK for the benefit of composers, authors and music publishers. PRS and MCPS remain separate societies in terms of income, constitution, membership and guardianship of different rights but the alliance combines their individual strengths to the benefit of members.

PHONOGRAPHIC PERFORMANCE

Phonographic Performance Limited, a non-profit- making society, was set up by the record industry to grant licences for the broadcasting or playing of sound recordings in public.

The licence gives permission to use any or all recordings included in the repertoire of members for the stipulated purpose, as a 'blanket licence' is simpler then obtaining individual licences from all recording companies concerned. Broadcasters licensed by PPL include the BBC and commercial radio and television.

Members, which include most well known multinational and independent recording companies, assign their rights to the society so that on their behalf it collects and distributes licence fees to record companies, recording artists and musicians. Different tariffs are agreed to reflect the variety of venues and types of music being played.

It should be noted that Phonographic Performance Limited is different to The Performing Right Society in that the former distributes royalties to record companies, recording artists and musicians whereas the latter distributes royalties to composers and music publishers.

7

MEDIA AND SOCIAL CHANGE

NEW IMPERATIVES FOR INTERNATIONAL COMMUNICATION

As innumerable media corporations execute decisions made in boardrooms (where "globalization" and "deregulation" are the mantras), the challenges facing international communication scholars become veritable riddles of the Sphinx. They watch in bewilderment as transborder commercial satellites pulverize the protective, monopolistic, state-controlled broadcasting regimes of erstwhile colonies of South Asia. They ponder as the antediluvian legislation pertaining to airwaves prevalent in these nations fails in its attempts to cope with what Ithiel de Sola Pool called the new "technologies of freedom." Imagine their plight when they see the comprador bourgeoisie collaborate, nay, fraternize with the "invaders," waving market-friendly banners which spell out "joint venture."

This paper is an essay in empathy, the beneficiary being the aforementioned scholars of global media. Focusing on the Indian subcontinent, the author discusses the complex set of events leading up to the current conjuncture (the term used here in its fullest Althusserian import) in the nation's mediascape. The paper draws on literature in the field of global communication; print-media reports from the last six years; and a series of interviews with broadcast entrepreneurs, analysts, and consultants, conducted by the author in India.

It argues that the promise of global interconnectivity through new technology can fast become "technological" and "cultural imperialism" unless guided by a well-grounded understanding of global difference, national philosophies regarding the role of electronic mass media, and above all, the perils of leapfrogging developing societies into media ecologies borrowed heavily from the industrialized West. Finally, it underscores the importance of localizing the debate on globalization, allowing the concerned communities to develop and articulate broadcasting architectures most appropriate to their new role in the "global village."

The "Wonderland" of Communication Satellites

The Gulf War of 1990-91 did more than just convey images of SCUD missiles punching their targets. It also showcased to a captive worldwide audience, the technology that made this possible. Big city hotels with rooftop dish antennas were able to relay CNN's live reports to an aspiring, upwardly-mobile class of Indians. A class that would soon feature in India's own war of the airwaves.

Communication satellites are not new to India. In tune with the developmental communication rhetoric of the 1960s-1970s India conducted the world's largest techno-social experiment using a NASA satellite. The SITE project (Satellite Instructional Technology Experiment) of 1975-76 represented India's communication philosophy: a categorical rejection of the entertainment component of electronic mass media and a commitment to realizing their potential as agencies of social change. The models developed by Daniel Lerner and Wilbur Schramm served as guidelines for many of these experiments.

While television broadcasting under Doordarshan (from Sanskrit "distant vision") had already begun in 1959 as experimental programs to villages around Delhi, the SITE experiment unfolded the "national" reach of the medium for the first time. Indian broadcasting entered the satellite age with the launching of the first Indian satellite, INSAT-1A (Indian National Satellite) in April, 1982.

The viewers of CNN's live broadcast of the Gulf War in 1991 had lived through a decade of huge domestic growth in broadcasting led by a monopolistic, state-controlled

Doordarshan. Plan outlays, coupled with the nation's aggressive space research program, had assured incremental coverage of India's remotest regions. From a mere 26% of the population in 1982, Doordarshan's reach grew to approximately 80% by 1991 (Audience Research Unit 1996).

Interestingly, the avowed non-commercial objectives had given way to the immense revenue-earning possibilities of the medium. Doordarshan's commercial revenue through program sponsorships on its single national network grew from a meager Rs 159 million in 1982 to a whopping Rs 3 billion in 1992 (Audience Research Unit 1996).

According to Kiran Karnik (1997), Managing Director of Discovery Communications in India, commercialism "completely overtook" the professed developmental communication objectives. "At the end of the year," he adds, "they would not say what great programs they did, what changes they brought, what social programs they did--but this was the profit that was made, this was the ad revenue earned."

In inverse proportion, Doordarshan's credibility as an impartial information medium had plummeted. Successive governments abused the "visibility" potential of the medium, hijacking news and public affairs programming and turning them into "a-day-in-the-life-of-your-prime minister" style coverage. Pendakur (1990) charges Indian television policy of the period with serving "its own propaganda needs as well as the demands of indigenous and transnational capitalists, along with the entertainment prerogatives of the middle/upper middle classes." Urbanites cringed at its insincere attempts at developmental programming, while ruralites "wondered why items alien to their world...be repeated through loud and annoying jingles."

However, lest this criticism be construed as a dismissal of all the achievements of television in India in the eighties, it is important to highlight what Doordarshan was up against. India's prolific film-industry had created a preeminent entertainment format comprising formulaic story-lines bundled with a heavy dose of hybridized song, dance, and music. It goes entirely to Doordarshan's credit that it made sincere attempts at delivering made-for-TV fare such as pro-social soap-operas in a climate loaded with escapist entertainment formats.

THE GROWTH OF SATELLITE-FED CABLE

Three months after CNN's historic broadcast, Hong Kong-based entrepreneur Li Ka-shing launched the preview channel of his pan-Asian satellite network STAR (Satellite Television Asian Region). The company started as a 50-50 joint venture between Li and a Hong Kong conglomerate Hutchinson Whampoa. It was beaming from a communication satellite Asiasat-1, whose footprint covered 38 countries from Egypt to Japan and the Soviet Far East to Indonesia. Potential viewership of STAR was estimated to be 2.7 billion people living in the above-mentioned countries.

The five channels initially offered by STAR-Prime Sports, MTV Asia, the Chinese Channel, BBC World Service Television, and STAR Plus-were piped into urban homes in India by underground, illegal cable operators. "It came so fast," says Pronnoy Roy (1997) of India's premier news and current affairs producer New Delhi Television. "It spread all over the country through small entrepreneurial cable operators in a disorganized fashion, which was the best way it could have happened."

Amid cries of "alien invasion" and large-scale policy-paralysis, fly-by-night cable operators were capitalizing on the "hotbird" frenzy. By June 1992, a mere twelve or so months after its launch, viewership in India had gone from zero to 1.28 million households. In July 1993, News Corp's Rupert Murdoch acquired 64% stake in STAR-TV, affirming the keen interest of global media companies in India's broadcasting future.

The chaotic growth of cable is a telling comment on India's rudimentary regulatory framework. The only Act governing "wireless communication" dated back a century to the colonial government's Wireless Telegraphy Act of 1885 which prohibited "both the transmission and reception of all forms of wireless signals on Indian soil without the consent of the Government of India" (Swami 1997). Clearly lacking the political will and the administrative machinery to arrest the errant "cablewallahs," the government offered them legitimacy in the form of The Cable Television Networks (Regulation) Act of 1995. The act was narrow in its scope, requiring cable operators to register and assume responsibility for providing content under the guidelines of the "program code" and "advertising code" included in the act. Also embedded in the act was a must-carry provision, asking cable operators to "retransmit at least two Doordarshan satellite channels of his choice" (emphasis mine).

As is evident from the "must-carry" provision, Doordarshan was not prepared to relegate itself to simply being the referee. It had responded to the alarms of "cultural invasion" by launching its own line of cable and satellite channels.

By 1995, it was offering a full-blown "Entertainment Channel" (the Metro or DD2), it had added a third "Infotainment Channel" (DD3) and beefed up its regional offerings with 13 regional language channels (India has 15 recognized languages). It had floated a Movie Channel and was also eyeing the Indian diaspora with a limited duration broadcast on DD-International Channel.

For a monolithic organization mired in red-tape bureaucracy, Doordarshan had responded remarkably well to competition. Its reach, as Pronnoy Roy (1997) of NDTV stated, was "at its peak...275 million people, while the best satellite channel can reach about 75 million...only one in every four TV households have satellite and cable." Given these figures, the image of a beleaguered state-broadcaster fighting off the foreign scare is difficult to conjure. A more serious challenge to its monopoly, according to the author, was represented by:

(a) the rapid growth of the domestic private broadcast industry in news and entertainment, and

(b) the increasing awareness among foreign broadcasters of the need to Indianize their program offerings.

Murdoch's investment in STAR was an endorsement of economic projections which placed Asia among the fastest growing economies of the world. Asian cities, wrote The Economist (1993), were "fast becoming a chain of sequentially exploding firecrackers of demand for one consumer good after another." It was difficult not to be lured by the promise of playing to an audience that would comprise 60% of the world's population by 2000. English was widely spoken in the area, and the number of television channels per home averaged 2.4. STAR burst onto the market with its American software libraries and became a household name in urban India.

"But will 3 billion Asians buy Homer Simpson?" queried a 1993 Time magazine article. India was answering with a decisive "no." When the foreign channels broke into the Indian household by offering an alternative to state-controlled monopoly, they also stirred up the imagination of a culture-industry that was sitting pretty atop a 750 movies-a-year production base. Within two years of its launch, as reported by the Far Eastern Economic Review, ratings for STAR's traditional attractions, Santa Barbara and The Bold and the Beautiful, were looking "pale compared with Hindi hits," a producer at United Television, summed up the situation succinctly: "Mahabharata has 60% of the Indian audience, (while) Santa Barbara is half a percent. Sometimes it reaches even 0 percent. I rest my case."

Says Siddharth Ray (1997) of SPA, referring to a half-hearted attempt to dub English programs into Indian languages: "...this audience was not prepared to watch a blonde with a scarf who speaks Hindi." A slew of Indian channels stole a leaf from Murdoch's book and undertook the challenge of beaming into their own country through the back door shown by STAR.

The latter part of the revolution was, thus, dominated by Indian channels and software houses, programming mainly in Indian languages. Zee, launched in October 1992, led the field with its unique line-up of Hindi soaps, dramas, game-shows, and made-for-TV movies. By early-1994, Zee's prime-time audience share in three metropolitan cities was up to 37%, compared to 39% combined share of Doordarshan National Network and Metro Channel, and a meager 8% combined share of the STAR platform. SUN-TV (Tamil, one of the 15 recognized Indian languages) and Asianet (Malyalam, another recognized language) were making equally significant inroads into Doordarshan's Southern Indian stronghold. Others such as

Sony Entertainment Television, ATN, Home-TV, and EL-TV completed the roster of domestic satellite players making STAR's opening market strategy unworkable.

The response of international channels like STAR and MTV was predictable and swift. The new "foolproof formula," an Indian weekly reported, "was Indian concepts plus Indian execution equals neat Indian profits." By early 1997, STAR-TV, under the "home-grown expertise" of former Doordarshan chief Rathikant Basu, had started a daily "Hindi-band" on Star-Plus between 7 p.m. and 9 p.m., bookended by a news bulletin in Hindi and English (produced locally in India).

MTV Asia, re-entering the market after its 1994 breaking with STAR, decided to split its unified South Asian beam, creating MTV Mandarin and a dedicated Indian channel MTV India. Its biggest competitor was Channel V, STAR's hybridized music channel providing an eclectic mix of Indian film music, a fast-growing Indi-pop segment, and international hits. Speaking of a Channel V Indian top-ten show, Jules Fuller (1997), General Manager India, Channel V, said: "When we started out it was all international music, now we find at least half the chart, sometimes all the chart is Indian pop."

Between Channel V, MTV, and Music Asia (another Zee offering), the realigned objective was to cater to an indigenous market for music. Although traditionally dominated by Indian film music, the market for Indian pop was projected to rise from 6% in 1995 to 21% by 2000 due in no small part to the selling window provided by the three above-mentioned channels.

In an article written for the 1996 NATAS International Council Almanac, the author had argued against the "oversimplistic characterization of transborder satellite programming as 'cultural invasion.'" The active "local" cultural production in India, he stated, is more than likely to survive the initial onslaught of foreign programming.

Taking that argument further, not only has the local production base been revitalized, but international programmers have also been forced to approach the Indian viewer on different terms. Murdoch's 50% stake in the most popular Indian satellite channel ZEE, an 80-20 tie-up between United Television (a Mumbai-based private production house) and 20th Century Fox, are only a few examples of the recognition of the talent-base and creative potential within India. As Shashank Ghosh, creative director at Channel V, succinctly stated: "I refer to the global players as technology, and to Channel V as appropriate technology."

AMBIVALENCE IN THE NEW UNIVERSE OF CHOICE

The 250 million strong Indian middle class voted with its "zappers" to signal approval of the new age of information choices. Clearly, satellite technology had rendered domestic strategies of delinking or cultural disassociation from global capitalist media an unviable option.

However, as the dust settled in the wake of the welcome-wagon, many were left wondering: is there really much to choose from in this new universe of choice? Was satellite television merely replacing state control with market control? Media advocacy groups, critiquing the homogenous content of the multi-channel universe, were raising serious concerns about the ability of a market-driven media culture to represent the "milieu of the complex social classes" that constitute India. In the following paragraphs, the author will discuss the various divisions in the ongoing debate over the democratization of the airwaves in India.

India's policy-makers are struggling with formulating a media-policy in a climate dominated by reactive, damage-control measures. In an article titled "Cultural onslaught: mass media, globalization and the state," Sashi Kumar, president of Asianet Communication, raises a cautionary voice against the prevailing ambivalence towards the haphazard growth of the electronic media in India. Information technology, he says, travels almost instantaneously from the industrialized West to the developing world. However, "as we demur and remain tentative and reactive in our response to technology...the liberating potential of the information technology goes unrealized by default."

The term "reactive" largely summarizes the state's response to non-government satellite broadcasting. The "Statement of

Objects and Reasons" accompanying the Cable Television Networks (Regulation) Bill stated that the availability of foreign television signals has been perceived as "cultural invasion" in many quarters since their programs are "predominantly Western and totally alien to our culture." This stance has served successive coalition-based governments to cloak the official strategy vis-a-vis satellite television.

Ironically, the Indian government used the "culture" of the marketplace to dispel the "cultural invader." Media terminology such as "TRPs" (Television Rating Points), "profit centers," "SEC (socio-economic categories) Groupings," "DART" (Doordarshan Audience Research Television) has become the mainstay of the market-driven directors in Mandi House (home of Doordarshan). The state's response has been no less ambivalent than the stark contradictions between its official proclamations and actual practices. The following extract from the Press Information Bureau's annual publication pays lip-service to the electronic media: "It plays a vital role in creating awareness among the masses about policies and programs for development and helps in motivating them to be active partners in the nation building endeavour..."

The domestic broadcast industry has largely been positive in its view. Respondent after respondent interviewed by the author hailed the information revolution set off by satellite technology. The creation of new opportunities for Indian talent; the market-intelligence brought in by the foreign players; the introduction of higher technical standards; creation of a free-information society; the prospect of starting a reverse flow of Indian programming towards overseas markets-these were some benefits that the industry feels have clearly sprung from the satellite fountainhead.

Some, like Kiran Karnik of Discovery Communications, think it is a mixed-blessing. According to Karnik, satellite television has accelerated a kind of "consumerist... 'me-first' hedonistic kind of culture" which actually began with the turn-of-the-decade policy of economic liberalization. A by-product of this, he adds, and perhaps the "strongest input that has come to us from abroad," is an "immediate gratification type of culture" which has important consequence in terms of "the future orientation of India itself."

The new opportunities have resulted in a shifting cultural focus too. Amrita Shah (1997), editor of Elle Magazine India, feels that the advent of youth-targeted channels has altered how the young are perceived in society. "I think in India," she says, "we did not take young people very seriously for many years. We've always worshipped the old, the traditional. Thanks to MTV, thanks to Channel V, there is definitely...a platform given to young people."

Akhila Sivadas, coordinator of the New Delhi-based Media Advocacy Group, sees a discernible change in the representation of women on satellite channels. Targeting an urban, upwardly mobile market segment, these channels "were not only able to show women as being equals, they were also able to adopt the language of hegemony...that women could even dominate the situation." However, these images, rooted as they are "in the everyday experiences of the upper classes" are unable to deepen "insights about the process of exploitation" to a cross-section of women.

Other fora, like the New Delhi-based Forum for Independent Film and Video, seek "an alternative structure of broadcasting" which can exist outside "the point of view of the state on the one hand, and a purely commercial logic on the other." Referring to similar models of Public Broadcast Service, the forum cites three essential values for the proposed broadcasting system: Autonomy, Access, and Plurality.

Who shall be the Umpire?

In a landmark judgment (Union of India vs. Cricket Association of Bengal, 1995) echoing the 1934 Communication Act in the United States, Supreme Court judges ruled that "airwaves constitute public property and must be utilized for advancing public good." A ringing endorsement of the "rights of the listeners and the viewers," the judgment threw open the gates for a larger debate on the democratization of electronic media. The Indian Supreme Court categorically stated that "diversity of opinions, views, ideas and ideologies...cannot be provided by a medium controlled by a monopoly...whether the monopoly is of the state or any other individual, group or organization."

Further, it stated that the "broadcasting media should be under the control of the public as distinct from the government" (emphasis mine). In one stroke, the judgment called for autonomy for India's state-controlled media, and the setting up of an independent referee to regulate all broadcasters.

The Indian judiciary had set the stage for the legislative arm to put the country's broadcasting industry within a broad philosophical framework pertaining to free speech and diversity of views. Instead, the Union cabinet chose to continue along its reactive vein, obsessed with regulating technology. Out of the laborious deliberations of the parliamentary subcommittee emerged a draft document dominated by issues such as "mandatory uplinking," "foreign equity," "prohibition of exclusive rights for live broadcasting," "DTH licensing," and "cross-media restrictions."

The Broadcast Bill, currently in the stage of its legislative passage, proposes sweeping restrictions on foreign players. One of its foremost aims is to set up a Broadcasting Authority of India and make it the apex regulatory body in the country. The BAI, it is proposed, would issue licenses only to companies in which foreign equity did not exceed 49%. Licenses would be given for terrestrial and satellite radio and TV, DTH (direct-to-home) TV, and cable.

The foreign equity cap meant that channels like STAR, Sony, MTV, Discovery and other channels with dominant foreign holdings had to find Indian partners and "hand over majority control (51%) to them." Foreign satellite broadcasting could continue unlicensed so long as it (a) remained free-to-air (b) carried limited-duration advertising or (c) carried sports or international news and current affairs programming only.

Further, with the bill becoming an act in its proposed form, all licensed channels would have to uplink from India. Given the fact that the legislation came in the sixth year of satellite broadcasting, companies that had locked themselves into arrangements with nearby countries like Hong Kong and Singapore would now have to invest in brand-new uplinking facilities from India. Remarked Kiran Karnik (1997) of Discovery Communication: "this is an economic issue really, it's not a matter of great policy or philosophy." Siddharth Ray (1997) offering a dissenting view, opined that "in the long term, if you are going to make money out of this market, the market has a right to demand some investment...." An upside of the proposal is the possibility of live-event coverage and live news broadcasts for satellite channels.

Severe restrictions have been proposed in the granting of inter-category broadcasting licenses, rendering STAR's DTH plans redundant, as it could no longer be a free-to-air satellite provider and a DTH player. There are cross-media curbs proposed, barring newspapers with more than 20% interest in a broadcasting concern from applying for a license.

While the attempt to arrive at some form of regulation has been lauded by most, widespread criticism has greeted the Broadcast Bill in its proposed form. Raging debate over key provisions relating to limits on foreign equity, uplinking requirements and inter-category limitations have clouded the larger issues set forth in the Supreme Court judgment. According to Raghav Behl (1997), managing director of the leading production house TV-18: "The Broadcast Bill is a document which has been much maligned. It is a document that has gotten lost in agendas that have very little to do with broadcasting."

Others have questioned the locus standi of the Indian government in the regulatory process. "At the moment," says Karnik of Discovery Communications, "the government or the Ministry of Information and Broadcasting is both referee and player, which is quite crazy." Ideally, he adds, the government should have legislated itself out of the refereeing process by issuing broad guidelines, setting up the Broadcast Authority of India, and letting it shape the regulatory framework independent of the government.

Along with prompting the formulation of the Broadcast Bill, the Supreme Court judgment had also forced the government to resurrect a 1990 act relating to autonomy for state-controlled electronic media (Doordarshan and All India Radio). Through the efforts of a liberal Information and Broadcasting minister the act was finally notified in the Gazette (all acts of the parliament must be notified in the Gazette before attaining full stature as acts) on June 22, 1997, seven years after it was passed by the Parliament. The act would place the erstwhile government-controlled TV and radio under a Broadcasting Corporation of India to be governed by an independent board. Together, the Broadcast Bill and the Prasar Bharati Act constitute India's response to the growing demands for regulation and autonomy. In order to understand the anomalies within this response, it is important to understand the fractured political alliances within the Indian government. Since the last mid-term elections held in 1995, in which no party emerged with a clear majority to form the government, a pragmatic coalition of left and centrist parties has governed India. Certain sections of the coalition have expressed grudging to unconditional support for private broadcasting (whether domestic or foreign). However, the Left has held that "public good...would be scarcely served by private broadcasting (which) would be bound to be motivated by profit." The "Murdochites," charges Sashi Kumar, "cleverly confuse globalization with economic liberalization," often disguising their support for the latter as "advocacy of a free information regime."

The Dream of the "Global Village"

India stands at the crossroads of choice-making in the new universe of technologies. Having erupted from a single-channel, government-controlled monopoly of the airwaves into a thirty-channel cornucopia over a two-year period, it must now become a savvy regulator of its spectrum. From among the hordes of opinion-wielders, lobbyists, and power-brokers it must discern the ones most appropriate for its unique and complex citizenry.

The task is no easy one for a young democracy with an unstable political centre. Objectives are defined, redefined, and finally rendered unrecognizable by successive changes of government, shifting coalitions, or confusing diktats from the powers-that-be. All this while, the expanding global powers lobby for loosening controls and opening the market, practicing advocacy-by-proxy for the choice-deprived Indian consumer.

What are the cultural imperatives unique to the understanding and shaping of India's broadcasting future? For one, according to the author, a contextual assessment of the peculiar "information needs" and "information sensibilities" should moderate all pronouncements favouring a "consumer-take-all" approach. The critique of the proposed "global information society" can only benefit from a ground-up approach which favours the information "user" as opposed to the "provider."

Media conglomerates are putting their versions of "audience research" in place, as is evidenced by the setting up of a joint-venture between Indian Market Research Bureau and A C Nielsen for a "people meter based rating system.". To what extent this unquestioned transposition of quantitative measurement systems will be able to assess the "information" vacuum in the Indian home remains to be seen.

In discussions of a burgeoning urban middle-class of 250 million, the profile of a nation with 48% illiteracy; three-quarters of the population living in rural areas; and agriculture providing the main mode of sustenance for 65% of the population is neglected. The selective use of statistics to drive the agenda for an "information revolution" serves the purposes of the global merchant. The challenge before the international communication scholar is to enrich the understanding of the culturally, linguistically, and economically diverse information industry in countries like India.

The electronic media in countries like the United States have fulfilled market functions from their very inception. While progressive deregulation has now placed the broadcasting industry at the confluence of traditionally discrete spheres of telecommunication and computer-aided communication, there has been a concomitant deepening of concern for the user. Witness the creation of the V-chip, the new ratings system for networks and cable, and the plethora of filtering software to aid parents in shielding the young from pornography and other inappropriate content available on the World Wide Web. The enrichment of the individual user's information resources enabling him/her to identify "usable," "unusable," or "useless" information has evolved alongside the industry responsible for providing that content.

Addressing the Pre-Conference Symposium on Southern Country Interests organized by the International Institute of Communication, David Nostbakken (1994), executive director of WETV, offered a skeptical prognosis: "So before we accept that technologies of information and communication will bring positive change, we need to consider the social, cultural, and political context into which the technologies are being introduced.

Then, we must determine the kinds of actions that help to translate the improvements in communicative capacities and facilities into actual improvements in living conditions."

"When the delivery systems of the future are constructed and bandwidth becomes a commodity," wrote an analyst of European television, "power will shift to those who can create enticing things to fill it." In the preceding pages the author has described the creation of just such a delivery system in India.

As legislators, global conglomerates, and domestic media entrepreneurs struggle with evolving a regulatory framework which will allow a new democracy of the airwaves, the communication scholar must address the challenge of localizing the search for the user of information.

As the profile of this user is defined and refined, so shall the power of meaningful content in the new information age become decisive. After all, as Thoreau pointed out in Walden, the consequences of doing otherwise are appalling: "We are in great haste to construct a magnetic telegraph from Maine to Texas; but Maine and Texas, it may be, have nothing important to communicate.

We are eager to tunnel under the Atlantic and bring the old world some weeks nearer to the new, but perchance the first news that will leak through into the broad, flapping American ear will be that Princess Adelaide has the whooping cough."

THE IMPACT OF FOREIGN TELEVISION ON INDIA

Increased competition and shrinking budgets have forced public service broadcasters around the world to reconsider their role. Doordarshan, India's public service television network, shares the problems faced by its counterparts in more developed countries. Although it continues to enjoy the luxury of being the only television network broadcasting its programs from within national boundaries, it has had to change its policies and programming to compete with foreign television channels including Murdoch's Star TV.

However, it is the Indian audience that has benefited most from this competition from the skies in the form of improved quality and quantity of programs. This discussion talks about an audience survey carried out in India earlier this year to gauge television viewers' perception of these benefits. The paper also gives background on the developments in the television industry in India.

The visibility of television as a mass medium and its perceived impact on audience always generates passionate debate about the role of public service broadcasting in any country. Whether it is the Public Broadcasting Service (PBS) in the USA, BBC in the UK, ABC in Australia, the Television Republik Indonesia (TVRI) in Indonesia or Doordarshan in India, these public service broadcasters have an important role to play in their respective countries.

As with PBS's mission and the ABC's charter, Doordarshan has its own set of social objectives to live up to. In the United States, the PBS has to present programs that "educate and entertain, inform and inspire." In Australia, the ABC has to broadcast programs that " contribute to a sense of national identity and inform and entertain, and reflect the cultural diversity of the Australian community."

Similarly, Doordarshan's social objectives include that it has to:

(a) act as a catalyst for social change;

(b) promote national integration;

(c) stimulate a scientific temper in the minds of the people;

(d) disseminate the message of family planning as a means of population control and family welfare;

(e) provide essential information and knowledge in order to stimulate greater agricultural production; and

(f) promote and help preserve environment and ecological balance.

Like many public service broadcasters, over the past four decades Doordarshan has been criticised for not meeting its objectives. However, this criticism has been harsher from its viewers as Doordarshan was the only source of television in India from its beginning in 1959 until 1990.

Apart from a handful of Hindi soap operas which Indian viewers devoured, as they did not have a choice to switch channels, viewers have had to tolerate uninspiring programming for almost three decades. One of the reasons for the dismal performance by Doordarshan was lack of competition. Successive Indian governments legislated All India Radio (AIR) and Doordarshan as a duopoly. The AIR network was established in 1947. Doordarshan which was part of AIR since its inception in 1959, was separated from AIR in 1976 as the second public service broadcaster in the country.

However, in the past six to seven years Doordarshan has had to change its policies and programs to maintain its share of viewership and advertising revenue. In early 1990s following advancements in satellite technology and inadequacies in broadcast legislation in India, a number of broadcasters began telecasting their programs directly into Indian homes from foreign locations.

These broadcasters use satellite transponders to send their signals into the country, while enterprising cable operators receive these signals via dish antennas and distribute them to individual households for a small fee. As a result, Doordarshan has been forced to respond to this increased competition by increasing the number of channels and programs it broadcasts; improving the quality of its programs and trying to gain credibility for its news programs by offering prime time slots to outside producers. It has also reduced its advertising rates and launched a number of purely entertainment channels to satisfy audience demand.

Today Indian audiences have a wide variety of programs to choose from on both Doordarshan channels and other channels. They can watch numerous news and current affairs programs. Therefore, to find out how television viewers in India perceive Doordarshan's current performance. The survey included questions about the television industry as a whole: Are viewers satisfied with television programming in India at present? Are they satisfied with Doordarshan's performance at present? If television as a medium as a whole gained people's confidence as a source of credible news and information sorely lacking before 1991?

The survey also asked whether news and current affairs programs improved sufficiently to provide in-depth information "to those who may not have a formal education" due to this competition in the television industry in India. This discussion looks at the survey results and discusses the impact of foreign competition on general programming, on public service broadcasting and, particularly news and current affairs programs in India.

DOORDARSHAN-A CALL FOR CHANGE

After the demise of British rule in the Indian sub-continent, Indian politicians and people whole-heartedly embraced ideals of socialism. Hence, after independence in 1947 most of the basic industries were set up as public sectors. Since the country already had a flourishing print media that was working on the principle of "free speech and free expression for all," no need was felt to develop broadcast media at the time. Therefore, it was almost by accident rather than through planning that television was introduced in India in September 1959.

The multinational company-Philips-had been exhibiting some television equipment at an industrial expo in New Delhi. The company gifted the closed-circuit television equipment to the government at the end of the exhibition. This is when the Indian government decided to experiment with the new technology.

From these beginnings the pattern was set for the growth of television in India, which was for almost two decades dependent on equipment gifted by either foreign governments or international agencies. Since AIR engineers were deeply involved with the development of the country's first TV centre, television was perceived as an extension of radio until the 1970s when progress in space technology spurred the Indian government to experiment with television as a development communication tool.

In the 1970s and 1980s, although Doordarshan continued to expand its coverage across the country, the public service broadcaster remained torn between its role as a catalyst for social change and as a tool for government publicity. The Satellite Instructional Television Experiment (SITE) in development communication was launched in 1975. Whereas on the political front, the imposition of a State of Emergency by then Prime Minister Indira Gandhi placed Doordarshan at government's disposal.

Indira Gandhi's government suspended many democratic rights and started using both AIR and Doordarshan to publicise government policies. As the print media largely decided to black out government propaganda, Doordarshan was used to churn out dozens of programs in support of the government's 20-point development program. Meanwhile, the SITE project which involved broadcast of development oriented programs to 2400 villages in six far-flung states, lasted for a year instead of 10 years as planned. Analysts are divided about the success of the project, some contending that the project was envisaged as an experiment in satellite broadcasting rather than educational or development communication.

However, realising the potential power of television as a communication tool, the government began to adopt policies to popularise television viewing in India. This skewed Doordarshan's focus from development to commercialisation. In 1976 Doordarshan started broadcasting imported programs and accepting advertisements to support the purchase of these programs. Again, in 1982-a significant year in the history of television in India-the government allowed thousands of colour

TV sets to be imported into the country to coincide with the broadcast of Asian Games in New Delhi. There were also sponsored entertainment programs such as Hum Log and Buniyaad that added to its efforts to attract viewers in mid-1980s. Later serials based on Indian epics Ramayana and Mahabharta had a very successful run. But on the news front, viewers did not trust Doordarshan.

To boost the state broadcaster's credibility, the Information and Broadcasting Ministry of India has over the past four decades appointed a number of committees to look into its status and performance.

But these committees' recommendations have never been effectively implemented. One such international body was the Media Foundation of the Non-Aligned. The Ministry appointed the specialist organisation to convoke the broad range of public opinion about television prevailing in the country at the time. In 1986 in its report, which was based on five "feedback" seminars and a national colloquium, NAMEDIA criticised Indian television (Doordarshan) for failing in its main objective of inducing development. A contributing factor was that television remained accessible only to urban, middle and high-income groups.

The NAMEDIA report concluded:

The primary purpose of television in India is development through education, information and enlightenment, to improve the quality of life of the largest masses of the people; to bring communities and societies, regions and the states together as one nation through mutual awareness and sympathy while preserving, consolidating and enriching their unique ways of life, cultures, customs and traditions. The secondary purpose is entertainment per se or show-business.

The report also stated that "news" could not be used to promote those in power. It urged a variety of programs based on issues and current affairs, rather than just half-hour news programs, to facilitate better understanding for those without formal education. On the issue of credibility the report advocated that television in India needed an "openness" to gain credibility:

Such openness, it was considered, would not put either the government, or the ruling party or the nation in jeopardy. Squarely and properly placed in intelligent and honest context it would promote understanding and confidence and lead to greater and discriminative appreciation of issues by the people. In the longrun, it would strengthen the nation.

The NAMEDIA report stated that Doordarshan needed to establish a separate autonomous operation for producing television news:

It should have freedom of appraising news values and judgement, news selection and content, emphasis in presentation, and freedom of choice in summarising physical and human resources in making up a news programme. It should have a clear independent professional chain of command free from bureaucratic, political or other outside intervention and interference.

One of the themes which came across very clearly from the public forums organised by NAMEDIA was that television (in this case Doordarshan) in India should be free of all government control. Over the years Doordarshan, though established with high social objectives, has failed to satisfy the intellectuals as well as the common people in India.

Asok Mitra, former secretary of the Ministry of Information and Broadcasting from 1966 to 1969, in his submission to NAMEDIA recalled that in the 1960s television was considered "essential for accelerating development, modernisation and social change." He expressed his disappointment with the fact that India had followed a path similar to other Third World countries which first introduced television in the capital city and other metro cities, subserving the interests of the ruling class.

In the process of making television more attractive to the audience, government allowed more and more commercially sponsored, privately produced programs to be aired; though always retaining the final say about what was suitable for the Indian audience. Critics examining the development of Indian television say that as television grew, developmentalist alternatives were steadily eschewed, and "over the years hardware expansion was undertaken with no evidence of planning for software."

Television viewers, too, were not happy. Until 1990, most Indian viewers did not have a choice but to watch one national and one regional Doordarshan channel. In a survey in 1987, Singhal found that 90 per cent of the respondents preferred Hindi-film-based entertainment programs, whereas 60 per cent appreciated educational and development programs.

The survey of 1170 respondents showed that although 76 per cent were in favour of commercial advertising on television, 60 per cent of the low-income households, 75 per cent of viewers in lower castes and 60 per cent of non-Hindi speaking viewers felt that the "problems and difficulties of their daily life were not adequately projected" by Doordarshan. Similarly, 92 per cent of them felt that political opposition's views were not sufficiently represented, whereas 85 per cent said that Doordarshan adequately covered government policies and programs.

The fact that Doordarshan's performance did not receive many accolades was compounded by the reality that the people of India could not switch channels. Either due to its charter or due to political and bureaucratic interference, Doordarshan's performance remained unsatisfactory and it was often referred to as "the government channel" and as being "dull and boring".

Competition from the Skies and Cable Network

The impact of foreign television in India has been two-fold: viewers-at least those living in urban areas-can watch more than 40 channels and the quality of television programs has improved. People subscribing to a cable service can now choose anywhere between 40 to 50 channels to watch. As an alternative to three half-hour news programs in three different languages, they can choose between the two 24-hour news channels (BBC & CNN) and up to 20 news and current affairs programs on various cable and foreign television channels everyday. Since the 1991-92 invasion from the skies by foreign television networks, Doordarshan too has expanded its service from 2 to

18 channels with a claimed viewership of 448 million at the end of 1997.

The first competition for Doordarshan came in the form of illegal distribution of television signal by cable and foreign television channels in late 1980s and early 1990s. With the introduction of VCRs in India, some dynamic entrepreneurs in Bombay in 1984 launched cable network. Instead of people watching programs on their VCRs at home by buying or borrowing videocassettes, the cable operator in the area/block connected their television set to a community network for a small fee. This way all those connected to the local cable network could watch one or two movies, sitcoms in a regional language and perhaps a pirated foreign program everyday. According to a survey cited by Rahim, there were about 3500 cable TV networks in India in May 1990. Another advertising group estimated that more than 330,000 households in four metros of Bombay, Delhi, Calcutta and Madras had cable connections with a total audience of 1.6 million.

Legally, there is no prohibition on receiving a TV signal in India.

Therefore, other television channels and networks owned by Indians or foreigners have been able to beam their programs into the country from the skies using satellite technology without violating any Indian law or regulation. However, there is legal uncertainty over its distribution. Until 1995, the Indian Telegraph Act 1885 governed the laying of cables on public property. It required the cable operator to apply for a licence to do so.

The success of cable operation was due to a number of reasons: on one hand the urban middle class had spare time and resources to seek more entertainment; on the other, "the government channel" remained slow in satisfying that demand. Being hooked up to a cable network became fashionable among the hotels that catered to tourists' needs. In fact, cable networks spread across smaller Indian cities during and after the Persian Gulf crisis in February 1991, when everybody was nervous about the war. One of the US television networks did offer the Indian government broadcast rights to its service at the time.

Doordarshan declined the offer. Nevertheless, dish antennas picking up CNN and other satellite broadcast service signals sprouted everywhere, defeating the Indian government's attempt to protect the politically stifled public service broadcaster.

In the Far Eastern Economic Review, Hamish McDonald wrote that Doordarshan's credibility was undermined by its Gulf War coverage which was noted for its "state news, lack of visuals, use of ancient library footage and poor audio quality.". Although the war ended within weeks, people's desire for foreign programs had been aroused and they wanted more. Entrepreneurs took advantage of this market opportunity and started installing their cable networks in every block of big cities where people were willing to pay between Rs 50 and Rs 150 (Aus$2-6) a month for the connection. In May 1991, the Satellite Television for the Asian Region (STAR) TV launched its operation from Hong Kong beaming multi-channel television over a South Asian footprint via Asiasat.

The television scene in India or for that matter in Asia has not been the same again. By the end of 1991, experts in the communication field began speculating the effect satellite television, in this case STAR TV network which at the time included BBC news service, would have on television programming in Asian countries. Columnists Margaret Scott and Hamish McDonald in the Far Eastern Economic Review wrote that: Social, political and commercial surprises of immense proportions are bound to follow. For starters, using satellite for transborder television defies the tradition that national sovereignty includes state control over television within a nation's borders... Nowhere will the impact be more profound than in news coverage, for most of the countries under Palapa's and AsiaSat-I's footprint have spawned heavily regulated television industries, often government owned.

The small-time entrepreneurs who recognised the demand for more television in India spearheaded the massive, largely illegal proliferation of cable networks in India, rather than a single cultural imperialistic aggressor such as Rupert Murdoch. Cable operators began operating with two dishes-one pointed at Palapa for CNN and the other at AsiaSat for STAR TV (plus BBC)-and included them both in their menu of channels for sale. The scene described by commentators at the time (1991 year-end) was something like this: In crowded bazaars like Delhi's Lajpat Nagar or Bombay's Lemington Road, shops are busy taking orders for indigenously made satellite dishes. Rolls of cable are piled on pavements. All around Indian cities, private cable television operators are stringing coaxial cables along the road and up light poles. For a small monthly fee, people could watch 24-hours a day the U.S. open (live), Prime Sports (the wrestlers of the WWF), MTV (music videos), American soap operas such as Santa Barbara and The Bold and the Beautiful, morning cartoon shows and BBC's World News Service-all part of STAR TV network. Ninan says the impact of television in India in the 1990s has been accentuated by the rapid nuclearization of Indian middle class homes, the trend of the working mother, and the consequential rise in "latch-key children."

Television viewing in India had been on the rise since the introduction of Hindi soap operas in the late 1980s. However, the television scene changed sensationally after the advent of STAR TV and subsequently the launch of other foreign and local channels. TV homes have more than doubled in the last seven years from about 30.8 million in 1991 to 65 million by 1998. At the same time, according to the Indian readership survey, cable and satellite homes have grown from 1.28 million in June 1992, 9.30 million in June 1995, to 11 million in December 1996.

Doordarshan's Audience Research Unit puts the total number of cable and satellite homes at 14.2 million in December 1996; and Joshi estimates that there are about 15 million homes with cable connection.

An overwhelming number of viewers (90 per cent) in Hyderabad-a city in south of India-in July 1992 were thoroughly dissatisfied with programs and cited that as the reason for the switch-over to cable TV.

Abdur Rahim, who measured the impact of cable on television and VCR viewership, interviewed 250 people including

200 cable and satellite TV subscribers about a year after the launch of STAR TV. Many (62 per cent) felt that Doordarshan was wasting public money on "unimaginative", "absurd" and "silly" programs. The cable subscribers who participated in the study considered cable TV not as "more than television" but as "more of television." Viewers preferred cable TV channels to Doordarshan for both entertainment and news programs. Rahim found that BBC was the most popular channel because of the quality of its news programs.

RESEARCH METHOD

We carried out a survey in Bombay and New Delhi in January 1998 to explore people's response to the impact of foreign television and cable networks in the past five to seven years. The study was conducted in these two cities as the subscription to cable/foreign television channels remains an urban phenomenon.

Self-administered questionnaires were delivered to 350 sample households and later collected in-person. In this way, the survey participants could seek clarification if they did not understand a question.

This took into account the fact that English is a second or third language for Indians and even though they understand English, some of the complex questions can be confusing. This also prompted respondents to complete the questionnaire on time. A pilot survey was conducted in Bombay to fine-tune the questions, where 20 university students answered the questionnaire.

The stratified sampling method was used to ensure comparison between different groups of population. Three audience groups were chosen: 1. University students in Bombay, 2. Bombay residents and 3. New Delhi residents. The important variables included age, education and income levels, as these can influence the consumption habits among audiences. An effort was made to select different suburbs in Bombay to have approximately equal representation of various income groups in the survey. Questionnaires were given out in areas with low, middle and high-income groups in Bombay, which was the main location for the survey. No such distinction was made in New Delhi or when asking university students to answer the questionnaire.

The questionnaire included a combination of closed and open-ended questions. Besides asking audiences to indicate their level of satisfaction with television programs, they were given an option to comment on the reason/s for their satisfaction/dissatisfaction. They were also asked of their perception of the quality of present day programs compared to those broadcast in 1991-92, and to name their favourite news programs and channels.

RESULTS

In all, 350 questionnaires were given out to households. Of these, 291 were completed (51 by university students, 205 residents in Bombay and 35 residents in New Delhi). Overall, 3 to 6 per cent did not answer one or the other question. There was a higher number (40.7 per cent) of respondents in the age group of 18-24 years.

However, this group includes most of the university students. The over representation of younger people in the audience sampling was not planned, but can be explained by the fact that when a questionnaire was given to a household, it was generally answered by the younger member of the family. Reasons for this could be their better knowledge of English and interest in television programs.

As many as 99.3 per cent of the respondents watch television, whereas 97.9 per cent watch television at home, indicating a very high level of television adoption among the urban population in India. Most people (80.6 per cent) said they watched television every-day of the week. More than 82 per cent watch television from one to four hours a day. It is significant to note that about 80 per cent of the cable subscribers watch television for one to four hours a day. Overall, about 68 per cent subscribe to one or more cable services. Those who do not subscribe to a cable service gave a range of reasons from "parents do not allow," "it distracts from studies" to "not interested".

Table: Distribution of respondents by age

Audience/age groups	*Bombay residents %*	*University students %*	*New Delhi residents %*	*All groups %*
Under 18 years	23.5	13.7	20.6	21.4
18-24 years	35	72.5	26.5	40.7
25-34 years	20.5	11.8	5.9	17.2
35-44 years	13	2	20.6	11.9
45-54 years	6	0	11.8	5.6
55 years & over	2	0	14.7	3.2

Table: Distribution of respondents by income

Annual household income in rupees	*Bombay residents*	*University students*	*New Delhi residents*	*All groups*
More than 110,000	23.3	18.6	59.4	26.9
109,999-80,000	13	30.2	25	17.2
79,999-51,000	32.1	23.3	9.4	28
50,999-26,000	20.7	16.3	6.3	18.3
25,999 or less	10.9	11.6	0	9.7

Table: Distribution of respondents by education

Education level	*Bombay residents*	*University students*	*New Delhi residents*	*All groups*
University graduate	55.6	77.6	61.8	60.1
Secondary	34.3	17.6	20.6	29.9
Primary School	6.1	2	8.8	5.7
None of the above	4	2	8.8	4.3

In response to the question about "how many Doordarshan channels and 'channels other than Doordarshan' can you watch daily?", the response is so spread out that it is almost unquantifiable. Responses ranged between 1 to 100 channels. However, most of the television viewers watch either 1-3 channels (42.8 per cent) or 4-10 channels (47 per cent) regularly.

Table: Average number of television viewing hours per day

Audience	*All areas (in %)*	*Cable Subscribers %*
1 hour	20.8	21.2
2 hours	29.6	26.4
3 hours	18.3	18.1
4 hours	13.7	14
5 hours	6.3	8.3
6 hours	4.9	6.2
7 hours	1.8	1.6
8 hours	1.4	1
10 hours	1.8	2.1
12 hours	0.7	0.5
15 hours	0.4	0
19 hours	0.4	0.5
Total =	100	100

An overwhelming number of respondents have one or more favourite television programs.

The 10 most-favourite programs are Hindi soap operas (known as serials in India), viz., (in order of preference): Amanat, Hum Paanch, Aahat, Just Mohabbat, Hasratein, Banegi Apni Baat, Boogie Woogie, Teacher, Thoda Hai Thode Ki Zaroorat Hai and Dastaan.

The (English) News and Aaj Tak (a Hindi news & current affairs program) on Doordarshan channels are the 12th and 13th most-favourite programs respectively.

This indicates that the television audience in India still prefers Hindi-entertainment programs to other programs.

Similarly, the most favourite television channel is Zee TV-Star's Hindi channel 8; then in order of popularity Sony TV, Star Plus, Discovery, Star Movie, ESPN, Star Sports, DD2, DD1 and BBC.

Table: Number of channels regularly watched

Audience	*All areas (in %)*	*Cable Subscribers %*
1-3 channels	42.8	36.5
4-10 channels	47	51.8
11-20 channels	7.7	9.1
21-30 channels	1.1	1
More than 30	1.4	1.5

An impressive 78.7 per cent of the respondents regularly watch news and current affairs programs on television.

The most viewed news and current affairs programs are: Aaj Tak (a Hindi news & current affairs program on Doordarshan channel DD2) followed by The (English) News (on Doordarshan channel DD1), Zee News (A mix of Hindi and English news and current affairs program on Zee TV), Star News and the English news channel-BBC World service.

More than two-thirds of the respondents rely on television and newspaper for their daily news updates. However, the newspaper still remains as the source of news on which most people depend, followed by television.

Table: Source of news

Audience/Sources of news	*Bombay Residents %*	*University students %*	*New Delhi residents %*	*All areas %*
Television	74.1	86.3	85.7	77.7
Radio	9.3	17.6	5.7	10.3
Newspaper	80	86.3	94.3	82.8
Magazine	19	27.5	14.3	19.9
Internet	2.4	2	0	2.1

Relatively higher numbers of respondents are satisfied with programs on "channels other than Doordarshan" for their technical quality, entertainment value, credibility of information and overall performance. For overall performance, 91.1 per cent said they were satisfied with "channels other than Doordarshan", whereas 67.6 per cent were satisfied with

Doordarshan channels. A striking majority (84-85 per cent) of the respondents said that Doordarshan programs had improved over the past five to seven years.

Table: Source of news on which people most depend

Sources of news/Age	*Under 18*	*18-24*	*25-34*	*35-44*	*45-54*	*above 54*	*Overall %*
Television	34.6	50	40	43.3	62.5	33.3	44.8
Radio	0	0	3.3	3.3	0	0	0.4
Newspaper	65.4	49.1	57.1	53.3	37.5	66.7	54
Magazine	0	0.9	2.9	0	0	0	0.8
Internet	0	0	0	0	0	0	0

A similar number of respondents wanted Doordarshan to improve further. Opinion varied about how Doordarshan programs should change from "needs to broadcast more entertainment programs" to "improve technical quality" and "show more educational and meaningful programs."

Table: How should Doordarshan programs be different?

How different should DD programs be?	% of response
More entertainment programs	24.4
Improve technical quality	20.3
Improve news and current affairs	11.6
More educational & meaningful	10.9
More variety, less repeats	7.2

Hindi entertainment channels such as Zee TV and Sony TV are among the most popular cable/foreign channels. However, BBC still gets the highest score for credibility of news and information. More than 70 per cent of the respondents feel that Doordarshan covers local, regional and national issues better than international issues; whereas an almost equal number feel that channels other than Doordarshan cover all these categories of issues well. About 90 per cent of the respondents state that channels other than Doordarshan cover national and international issues better than Doordarshan. Once again, Zee TV is considered the best cable/foreign channel to cover local, regional and national issues, whereas BBC remains the best channel for covering international issues.

An impressive number of respondents feel that programs on Doordarshan channels represent Indian cultural values, whereas only about half of those feel that programs broadcast by "channels other than Doordarshan" represent Indian culture. As can be observed from the responses, younger generation is more satisfied with Doordarshan for representing Indian cultural values in their programs. However, more than two-thirds of respondents also think that foreign programs are good for the country as they are "informative and cover global issues".

Opinion is divided over the question of government censorship of programs. Most people are concerned about the broadcast of "vulgar programs" and "the need to preserve Indian culture"; however they "do not want the government to censor programs for political reasons". A majority of people said that programs are "not biased" on television. However, more viewers feel that programs are "not biased" on "channels other than Doordarshan", compared with Doordarshan. Most of the respondents commented that Doordarshan programs were still "government oriented", whereas "other channels" provided "more variety and entertainment".

Significantly higher number of people are satisfied with the quality of news in January 1998 (93 per cent) than before cable and foreign television channels became popular in 1992 (64.1 per cent). Cable subscribers are marginally more satisfied with the quality of news today than before. However, an overwhelming majority of respondents feel that news program have improved in technical quality, entertainment value, credibility and coverage of current affair issues.

Discussion

The survey results support the research hypothesis that increased competition in the television industry in India has immensely benefited the audience by providing them with better quality and quantity of programs and channels. Although the primary focus of programming provided by all channels has been entertainment, news and current affairs have not been far behind. Today, audiences have an option to switch between channels and watch a wide range of programs, and they do exercise this choice as is evident from the survey results.

The profile of an Indian television viewer is one who watches one to three hours of television daily and three to four channels regularly. Although the typical Indian viewer still prefers Hindi-entertainment programs, he or she watches a number of news and current affairs programs on anywhere between two to 10 different channels every week.

The survey shows that respondents are very discerning in comparing the quality of programs offered by all channels. Although they are satisfied with the programs on offer as of today on all channels including Doordarshan, Indian viewers still want Doordarshan to further improve as they perceive that Indian cultural values are better represented by an Indian television network.

This is one of the reasons why "other channels", which began their broadcast by showing re-runs of Western soap operas from yester-years, have been Indianising their menu of programs. Not surprisingly, Star network's Hindi channel-Zee TV-which essentially broadcasts Hindi-entertainment programs is the most popular among Indian audiences. Other channels including Doordarshan have tried to adopt Zee's success formula to achieve the same result.

One of the focus areas of the survey was to find out if viewers can rely on television as their source of news. With the addition of two 24-hour news channels and a vast range of news and in-depth current affairs programs, Indians are relishing the visual feast of watching live telecast of news events around the world. The respondents in Bombay and Delhi overwhelmingly indicate that they are keen to watch news and current affairs programs on television, and choose a combination of Hindi and English news and current affairs programs from both Doordarshan and "other channels".

A new language called Hinglish – a mixture of Hindi and English is becoming popular in India. Joshi refers to this language as the Bombay Hindi language. Channels such as Zee TV present news programs in this new language where a news story is told in both Hindi and English: sometimes even a sentence can have both Hindi and English words so that everybody can understand it.

This relaxing of standards to reach a mass audience is one of the surprising outcomes of the recent expansion of television industry in India. Yet Indian viewers still want to watch more of local or regional language news and current affairs programs. This is evident from the fact that channels covering local issues in local languages such as Sun TV in Tamil Nadu and Eenadu TV in Andhra Pradesh have achieved some degree of success against other more popular national channels such as Zee TV and Sony TV. Indian viewers are beginning to trust television as a source of news along with newspapers, which still remains popular.

One of the areas of dissatisfaction with the television industry had always been the technical quality of the programs telecast by the public service broadcaster. Although India has not lagged behind in venturing into satellite technology, during the first three decades of development of television, a number of factors from the quality of equipment used to produce programs to the quality of television sets at the receiving end diminished the entertainment value of television programs. However, with the advent of Star TV channels in 1991 and falling prices of television sets, Indian audiences today enjoy technically superior programming.

In the survey, the audience indicate that though they are satisfied with the improvements in Doordarshan's technical and entertainment quality of programming, they still consider "other channels" to be better. Overall, urban Indian viewers are more satisfied with television programming at present than five to seven years ago. However, a future potential study could be to gauge the impact of foreign television on the rural population of the country. Because of time and resource constraints, this audience survey had to be restricted to two cities. But the study does allude to the improvements in programming for all viewers as competition from foreign and other cable channels has caused Doordarshan to improve its reach and programming. It could be deduced that as a result, today the Indian rural population is better off than before as they can view better Doordarshan programs. Cable networking has already spread to smaller cities and towns of India, and will soon reach the rural population.

There is no doubt that Doordarshan has a significant role to play in India, particularly in providing information and entertainment to the masses and, representing Indian cultural values. The network has to satisfy other social objectives such as disseminating the message of family planning and national integrity.

Television audiences across the world not only want to receive important information from their television sets, but also want to be entertained. Indian audiences in that respect are no different. They also want their television to be a window to the world via a variety of news and current affairs programs – local, regional, national and international. In the case of India, it is the other channels including both owned by foreign or Indian private businesses which have provided them with that opportunity. As a result, the national public service broadcaster has improved its performance. On the other hand, the presence of Doordarshan has made other channels Indianise their programs rather than feed the starving Indian audience old Western sitcoms.

TV AND SOCIAL CHANGE IN RURAL INDIA

The wave of ICT innovation, that started in the United States of America in the eighties, hitting Japan and Europe rather soon in the nineties, has found new territory to flood.

India and China are preparing themselves to surf the waves, so many people and magazines tell us.

The Europe based Doors of Perception Conference, has been asking questions in the middle of these tumultuous movements "What is this stuff for?" By doing so, debates were triggered, many best practices shown, a powerful network evolved. A network in which business, design and underground meet, all being there not to miss the next ripple in the waters, all there to show and benchmark their own work, find new people and/or companies to work with. It has been driven by a social agenda, an agenda in which the ameliorating quality of life was in the centre of attention. Always seeking the high ground in which public and commercial domain meets, in which design and serendipity exchange.

In December 2003 the Doors of Perception Conference organized for the second time its Indian edition, Doors East 2003 in Bangalore. Starting with a two day workshop in which over 40 people participated (25 from India, 15 from USA and EU) and resulting in a conference with 30 speakers and over 350 people participating.

The workshops and conference took place in the National Institute for Fashion and Technology (NIFT), partner of the Dutch Amsterdam Fashion Institute (AMFI).

In Confrontation with Indian Reality

India has 18 formal languages, and many more are spoken. The complexity of Indian society with its rich 6000 years of history, many religions, many geographical distinct areas and very fast entrance into the 21st century is very hard to grasp in such short time. The sensory experience of India with its colours, its smells, its tastes is impressive and changes perception of the world.

Bangalore, the India's Silicon Valley where the conference was held, is heavily polluted. CEO's of big companies run the city, up to the point that parks in town are taken care of by large companies. In return they can work by the law that says that if you can prove you need a certain piece of land for the development of industry, with or without houses on it or parks for example, it can be taken.

Bangalore is polluted, but even more so is Delhi. When the pollution of Delhi reached the unbearable point, all public utility vehicles (buses, taxis, rickshaws) were obliged to start running on gas. This sort of happened overnight, and the way gas is distributed is so dangerous that people leave the bus or rickshaw outside the gas station when it is time to fill up. And still, one can't see the sun in Delhi because of the smog, although it is improving people assure me.

One third of India lives below the poverty line. According to Ravi Sundaram, urbanist at the school of architecture in Delhi, per year 60.000 new poor people move into Delhi, the city expands exponentially.

Next to huge office buildings you will find people living in tents. They have to find ways of livelihood, somehow, to survive. It is raw capitalism in its worst form.

Women's participation in public life is everywhere, but hardly in power. Shree Venkatram (journalist) wrote a report on women's presence in media in India over the last 50 years. She analysed 18 English and Hindi newspapers and found this presence has been ameliorating with 1,3% per year. Today women's presence is 13%, mostly in the adds though, Indira Gandhi being the only woman who made it to the front page till today.

Bangalore, India's Silicon Valley

Bangalore in the South, has a very pleasant climate. It is the booming city of ICT. Many small and large companies are all present. You find yuppie life with trendy cafes and nightclubs, next to Bollywood cinemas and little old fashioned food places everywhere. Of course, there are poor neighbourhoods with very poor people, but the city as a whole drives on industry and you can feel it everywhere.

The Door East Conference

Focus of the Doors East conference was 'Mobility, Geography and Access'. The overall evolving theme for me though, was the realization and the endeavour to understand the development of service design and service economy. Service design, as we understood it, has different meanings in different areas of application. To develop content is different from developing technological infrastructure, to sell goods is different from selling services.

In USA and EU the development of content is a constant area of concern. E-learning, my field, has many initiatives to make it flourish. But we yet have to find the workable service model that will be sustainable in the structural development of content as well as in the development of infrastructure that will deal with authorship and privacy in a convincing way.

Presentations of the western participants dealt a lot with how to move the private, public and commercial domains forward in cohesion: how to develop strategy, how to create support, how to design innovation in schools and design new schools. It were all questions we are familiar with over here.

Nevertheless it is interesting to hear how other people and institutions go about things. I realized again that the way we deal with things at the Hogeschool van Amsterdam is pretty impressive.

I enjoyed presentations of some of the new interaction designers exploring for example, the body as interface for information, fluid time interfaces to monitor the going bad of milk-instead of just a date that is never correct anyway, elaborate time banking and car sharing designs as a service for mobile phone companies. My presentation raised questions derived from the experience of the 10 year innovation of the Hogeschool van Amsterdam and the experience of being part of the Digital University of the Netherlands.

The Indian presentations did not talk strategy, they talked business, but on issues we usually talk strategy. The given complexity of Indian society demands from any initiative to be extremely simple to be able to survive. What really cracked my brain was that I found in India, that a service economy is very much in place (one does not iron ones own clothes, it gives someone the opportunity to earn some money, etc).

Also, the development of content and integration of ICT is realized in apparently economically sustainable service models. Since Indian society is a complex one, simplicity of the ideas is actually very impressive and attractive. The buzzwords of the conference were corporate citizenship and social entrepreneurship.

Corporate Citizenship

In the workshop a variety of new Indian best practices was presented. Being a European participant, it struck me the very first day how socially driven projects were financed and organized in commercial ways. And in the conference this insight became even deeper when the Indian labs of the 4 of the big companies (Philips, Siemens, Nokia and Hewlett Packard) presented details on how they have been doing deep research into the lifestyles the poorest sections of society.

They did not only talk about their research but also about their difficulties in communicating with the mother companies about the results they find and designs they develop.

This trend started about two years ago. Realizing that the markets of the wealthy parts of this world are more and more saturated with technological devices, facing the burst of the ICT bubble and facing world recession, companies have become aware that the majority of the people on our planet are poor. And this is a huge potential, provided one changes the models of doing business. Poor people do not have the money to purchase tech-gadgets. Nevertheless, the services that are facilitated via those gadgets can be sold for millions time a few rupi's. This will make a huge market in the end, so the companies argue.

The business models that they are exploring are inspired by a new Indian tradition of innovation that have been first heard of in the Doors of Perception conference 4 in 1996 when Sam Pitroda (well known Indian businessman) talked about his plan to make sure a public phone system would be available in every village all over India. Pitroda gathered over 300 students one summer and made a complete roll out plan for putting wires in the ground to make sure every village would have this public phone.

He assumed that once there was a public phone in every village, all villages would have a chance to participate much better in the market place (making deals, finding out about market prices, communicate about transport and huge amount of personal communication that also helps to develop rural areas in unforeseen ways).

He also assumed this huge scheme would be profitable, since in every village one person would be the service deliverer of this public phone service.

This person will find a living and the people from the village only have to pay a few rupees for the call they make. STD (Standard Trunk Dial) as it is called today, is indeed found all over India, in rural areas and also all the cities. It is a model that builds upon the already existing service infrastructure that is part of communities.

It took some years, but then in the Indian models of innovation it is remarkable that one does calculate at least 5 to 6 years before profit will happen. A very different time-frame than the figures that were shouted at the time of the hype in ICT in USA and EU, where investors and banks were going down to 6 months time to market and another 6 to make sure you were successful.

Even Nokia, well known for its really short time-to-market which their modular building nearly developed into an art form, is now looking for ways to connect to this new scheme of innovation. You do not sell your goods, you design a framework in which other people will deliver services, the goods being the carrier of the service to be delivered.

We are used to the fact by now here in the west, that when we order a hamburger it will consist of meat from Argentina, pineapple from Israel, flour made of wheat from Russia, sauces made in Italy and wrapped in paper produced in China. We also know the coca cola model, the Amazon model of internet business, and the American callcenters based in India. We have not seen these service networks evolving on a scale like the present.

Strangely enough, they have a social agenda we only knew from NGO's and charitable bodies. Now the social reality is the driver of new economic models, since in India everybody is convinced of the fact that sustainability in social terms can only be achieved when it is based on solid economic business structures. In education for example the innovation is financed with venture capital and the government hardly participates.

Off the record in the conference a lot of stories were shared about changes in companies from within. How do boards change opinion, how can one be effective, how and when to seek confrontation. It gave me a feeling of hope that maybe we are entering a new paradigm in doing business, when so many people are actually concerned and want to make a difference and are willing to work hard to find new forms.

Social Entrepreneurship

As a result of this new market strategy of the big companies providing technological service infrastructure, smaller initiatives are evolving, calling themselves social entrepreneurs. Jiva and N-Logue, two Delhi based companies, were part of the workshop. They have attracted serious venture capital to develop e-learning and e-health services to poor people mostly living in rural areas. Jiva 8 years old now was founded by Indian expatriates who came home to make a difference in their country. Jiva does three things: health, learning and social entrepreneurship. In 1995, Jiva first started exploring the health market and they were making money rather soon with providing an ayurvedic (traditional Indian medical and lifestyle system) internet shop.

They then took it further with the ambition to provide cheap and effective health-care to rural villages. In December 2003 they won the World Summit Award (at the World summit on the Information Society held in Geneva 10-12 December 2003) with their 'Teledoc' project.

Teledoc provides a mobile phone interface for doctors and health workers to diagnose people who are ill and who are elsewhere. The doctor sits behind a computer anywhere, and the local health worker (the one who runs the service), talks to the patient and fills in standard forms that the doctor sees on his screen. If necessary a man on a scooter will bring medication to the village (creating another job..).

First aid and simple advice can be delivered efficiently at low cost. Health workers are trained by Jiva, establishing a relationship of trust between villagers and the health worker, between the health worker and the doctor. Creating this trust is the most critical success factor in this service model. Having developed this model together with 10 villages and Nokia, they are now preparing to 'roll out', as one of Jiva's founders, told me.

Jiva created a similar long term innovation scenario with their schooling department. Inspired by the development life long learning and the rise of the information society, Jiva has developed a learning to learn methodology for India. In 1999 Jiva started a school in an outskirt of Delhi and with a team of 10 designers and copywriters all the time present in the school and working with the teachers for over 6 years. Today they publish books, have internet sites and train teachers (IRL and on-line).

Since one and a half year they are now rolling out: today 500 village schools work with this methodology and it takes 54 hours to train teachers to change from the old way of trespassing curriculum to the new learning to learn strategies of learning. They plan to intensify the rolling out. The design team will stay in place, only working harder to unfold new parts of the curriculum to transform. And also here, Jiva is starting to earn money with their publications and with the training of teachers, with the continuous back up service they provide for teachers.

While Jiva specializes in development of content services, N-Logue focuses on creating small entrepreneurs in villages who deliver internet services including web cam connections via the already existing STD telephone infrastructure. They roll out a standard technology set (PC, printer, web cam), including training for the service deliverer, for a fixed start up price for which they take the risk for success.

Their service includes agricultural college, online clinics, marketing data, financial services (incl. microcredits, banking) and travel services. Over 8500 villages have been connected in the last two years as was presented in the doors east conference. The person running the service knows how to operate the machine.

Creative Resource

The creative aspect of service design in India is very much dominated by pragmatism and standard procedures.

Nevertheless there are many design schools in India, and some really good designers. Being very well educated theoretically and being aware of western and Indian traditions, most designers look for ways of integrating these old and new cultures. There is a tremendous respect for the Indian heritage and big concern that it will evaporate with the evolving media-society.

The Bollywood industry has become a commercial culture that is appreciated highly. But for young musicians, writers, designers and artists, there is very little space to develop new work. Visiting the Sarai medialab in Delhi was therefore very interesting. Sarai is a medialab in Delhi that is connected to the Waag Society in Amsterdam. They do social research, innovate design practice, publish, organize events and concerts and run a medialab. Two years ago they started two other medialabs in some poor neighbourhoods of Delhi, to foster creative resources. The medialabs in these localities are called Cybermohallah's. In these creative spaces young people between 15 and 20 years old, spend 3 to 6 hours a day.

These media labs are not a school, not a computer training, nor a job creation facility. They provide a creative space where young people write and visualize and critic each others work and discuss the notions and perceptions that underlie their work. In one Cybermohallah 15 young people will participate.

People from Sarai-being the 'motherlab'-will visit once a week to have conversation, and take time for this conversation, as well as to tackle technical or design issues. As Jeebesh Bagchi (one of Sarai and Cybermohallah's founders) formulated it: paper, pencil, conversation and duration will make creativity flourish. And that is what we need.

In another two years Sarai intends to start another 5 Cybermohallah's, creating in this way a new youth culture and influence the way people inside and outside the localities perceive of life in these localities. Building a creative resource and knowledge base eventually.

Two books have been published that are very impressive. Especially since the stories the young people write examine in detail experiences of day to day life in a very revealing way.

The human experience in walking down the street, in realizing time passes by, in describing the fight-known-all-over-the-planet in a family negotiating what television program to watch.

The focus on creative resources is rather courageous in a country with so many people living below poverty lines. Why not make schools or jobs for those young people? Sarai takes the perspective that culture has always been this driving force in change and crisis, culture is an expression of wealth as it is of poverty. It is an expression of the human condition. Whether one is rich or poor, stories and songs and drawings will help to transcend the day to day life.

The raw capitalism in India does not take this into account, being very conservative. To see the results and the success of the Cybermohallah's, to read the work and meet young people, gave me great inspiration. And the realization that creative resource always needs fostering and space for self organization at the same time.

The trust that Sarai puts in these young people, that no one considers to be good for anything else than work force, is more than worthwhile and already does and will pay off in the future in unforeseen ways today.

Conclusion

The confrontation with raw capitalism is intense for everyone coming from social democracies in the west. To see though that out of this raw capitalism now has evolved a social agenda in unforeseen ways till now, was very provoking. We are aware of the big difference big companies like Shell can make in peacemaking process like in South Africa. This new trend though where big companies look for poor people markets is very worthwhile following.

Local resonance and transparency of models appears to be a requirement though. Local resonance being the basis for trust for any one person to be able to express and act upon this. Transparency requiring simplicity and at the same time facilitating different forms in different places. The local has to resonate in the global.

Talking to the Jiva people they emphasized how the building of a trust relation is crucial for their success. The issue of trust has been on the ICT agenda because of e-cash and electronic banking. But mostly it is a non issue in today's world. Trust is a two way thing, one can not build trust without listening.

To create business models that actually take into account this local resonance's in the context of establishing trust relations was one of my deep insights in India. We do develop learning to learn methodologies, talk about question-based design of curricula, but we always define how other people will act. Taking the scale of higher education institutions in the Netherlands into account, it would be a challenge to analyze and design learning environments from the perspective of trust relations and from the perspective of an infrastructure that allows local resonance's to be distinct.

Possibly this change of capitalism from within will actually make a huge difference in the decades to come. Social equality, creative development, eco-awareness and more still have to be put on this new market's economic agenda though. And the question is whether this will be possible at all. But if this happens, India's wave of innovation will effect us all in ways we will inevitably learn to appreciate. Conferences like Doors East are the bridges that make this learning possible.

CHANGING RURAL SOCIETY: MYTH AND REALITY

Communication for social change is part of an evolution of communications methodology that can help accelerate global development. The process began in the first quarter of the 20th century with the use of publicity tools to bring attention to social problems such as hunger and disease.

It grew to a reliance on public relations as a means of identifying stakeholders and creating programs to fit the audience's interests. More recently, social marketing took centre stage-where sophisticated marketing and cause related advertising tools were applied to influence individual and societal behaviours-such as convincing couples in poor nations to use contraceptives.

This was followed by development communications and strategic communications, the latter which rightfully considers communication to be a process rather than as a series of products.

In the pages that follow, the two authors argue that communication for social change is a distinct way of doing communications-and one of the few approaches that can be sustained. Such sustainability is largely due to the fact that ownership of both the message and the medium-the content and the process-resides with the individuals or communities affected.

We believe that this approach can help make greater contributions to the pace of development. From this basic assumption we move to questioning "how" and "if" and "where" we might find interesting work and committed individuals to test the effectiveness of this approach.

In order to do this work, the Rockefeller Foundation has brought together a group of social activists, academics, filmmakers and journalists, funders, electronic communications experts, service providers and professional communicators. The ideas expressed in this position paper reflect discussions held at two conferences-one at the foundation's Bellagio Study and Conference Centre on Lake Como, in Italy, and the other in the fall of 1998 in Cape Town, South Africa.

In Bellagio we committed to a new agenda for global communications: communication that is empowering, many-to-many (horizontal versus top-down), communication that gives voice to the previously unheard, and that has a bias toward local content and ownership. The group's action steps, agreed upon at the end of the meeting, include a commitment to convince others of the value of this approach (broadening the debate), to publicize writings about the effectiveness of this work, and to continue to study the prospects in a global setting.

During the Cape Town gathering, we continued the inquiry with an expanded group of people. There we developed a concrete and comprehensive definition of communication for social change, put together an outline for the skills and attributes needed to do this work, began work on the skills/resources training "toolbox" or "practitioner's kit" or "knowledge transfer", reached agreement on measurements, and identified organizations and people that we'd like to engage in helping us do this work and to advocate for its effectiveness. What follows is further explanation of the value and benefits of the discipline of communication for social change.

AN ENVIRONMENT FOR NEW THINKING

This initiative is based on a simple premise: that recent developments--in communications technologies, in political and media systems, and in emerging development problems--suggest a greatly enhanced, radically different role for communication in development programming.

Communication programming has, very simplistically, tended to fulfill three roles in development thinking and practice:

First, its role has been to inform and persuade people to adopt certain behaviours and practices that are beneficial to them: for example, to inform people how to protect themselves from HIV and to persuade them to use a condom; to persuade them of the importance of vaccinating their child and to inform them when and where they can do so; to persuade them that simple sugar and salt solutions can cure diarrhoea and to inform them how to make them up; to persuade them to have fewer children and to inform them how to do so.

Second, it has been used to enhance the image and profile of the work of organizations involved in development with a view to boosting the credibility of their work, raising more funding and generally improving public perceptions.

Third, it has been used on a more targeted level within communities to enable community consultation over specific initiatives.

The communication for social change initiative believes that all these roles are important and communication work in general remains underfunded and undervalued. We argue that these traditional approaches to communication are generally insufficient in addressing the reality of the development problems that exist, and they do not always reflect the complex changes in the communications environments taking place in many developing country societies.

We argue in this position paper that communication can play a much greater role in enabling people to take control over their own lives, in enabling people and societies to set their own agendas in relation to political, economic and social development; and in enabling, in particular, the voices of the economically and politically marginalized to be amplified and channelled to mainstream public and political debate.

We argue that the interaction between communication and the social well-being of people in developing countries will be radically redefined over the next few years. Global economic liberalization of communications, the deployment of the Internet, mobile telephony and other new technologies and the changing political environment in most developing countries are all coinciding to make the cusp of the new millennium a defining moment which will determine how successfully all countries, especially developing nations, adapt to and exploit these changes.

Information in society does not simply enable people to know what they should do or think.

Information is power--it enables people to make sense of their lives and it enables them to shape their aspirations. Ultimately it can enable them to take control of their lives. In many areas of the world, people have precious little access to information outside their community that enables them to make such "sense."

In other societies, despite a multitude of information outlets, people who are historically marginalized and excluded remain "voiceless" and "invisible" because those who control information channels refuse to share access equitably. Communication for social change principles focus on using direct, many-to-many communications which spring from the affected communities. The problems inherent in this work are those which have plagued communication practice for decades: how to assess impact beyond counting products produced or net impressions received; how to program communication for social change work on the micro community level and on the macro multinational level, often simultaneously; and how to transfer knowledge and skills to those most in need of "training" who often live and work in hard-to-reach areas. We also struggle with ways to capture the best learning-those cases that illustrate the power of communication for social change yet are not overly simplistic.

Language is also a challenge: the notion of how to explain this work in terms that can be readily accessible and used by grassroots activists as easily as by professional communicators. These are all issues that the groups assembled for the Rockefeller Foundation conferences grappled with. This paper reveals some preliminary thoughts on solutions. Others, such as site-based knowledge transfer, are in the early exploratory stages and will require more study, testing and applications, especially in developing nations with scarce human and financial resources.

Yet nothing in our questions should suggest lack of conviction nor should they prevent us from energetically embracing the potential of communication for social change to fulfill critical gaps in the development process.

What is Communication for Social Change?

The traditional understanding of the role of communication in development is one that seeks mainly to change individual behaviours. This behaviour change communication can be broadly defined as a process of understanding people's situations and influences, developing messages that respond to the concerns within those situations, and using communication processes and media to persuade people to increase their knowledge and change the behaviours and practices that place them at risk.

Communication for social change, on the other hand, is defined as a process of public and private dialogue through which people define who they are, what they want and how they can get it. Social change is defined as change in people's lives as they themselves define such change. This work seeks particularly to improve the lives of the politically and economically marginalized, and is informed by principles of tolerance, self-determination, equity, social justice and active participation for all. This approach attempts to rebalance strategic approaches to communication and change by taking the overriding emphasis...

Away from people as the objects for change ... and on to people and communities as the agents of their own change.

Away from designing, testing and delivering messages...and on to supporting dialogue and debate on the key issues of concern.

Away from the conveying of information from technical experts... and on to sensitively placing that information into the dialogue and debate.

Away from a focus on individual behaviours...and on to social norms, policies, culture and a supportive environment.

Away from persuading people to do something ...and on to negotiating the best way forward in a partnership process.

Away from technical experts in "outside" agencies dominating and guiding the process...and on to the people most affected by the issues of concern playing a central role.

THE STARTING POINT

The starting point for this inquiry is the growing evidence that, as a generality, the "communications environment" in which most people on the planet live has changed radically over the last decade. It has changed both in relation to the information people have access to, and the opportunities people have to communicate their own perspectives on issues that concern them. This new communications environment is shaped by three main interlocking trends:

I. Media liberalization and deregulation

II. New information and communication technologies

III. The changing global political and economic context.

In general, and with important exceptions, these trends are tending to decentralize communications in developing countries, with a trend towards a more fragmented, more horizontal, people-to-people model of communication, and away from a highly centralized, vertical model.

In industrialized countries, media liberalization suggests more choice for consumers, which should, theoretically, mean increased access. Yet the way it plays out in countries like the United States is in encouraging the growth of huge media monopolies that result in far less community input to programming. With deregulation, public service programming has become just a fading memory, and station ownership has leaped beyond the realm of possibility for most community-based organizations or individuals of color.

This new communications environment has, we argue, important implications for development programming, an importance that is compounded by the emergence of new development problems--such as HIV/AIDS--that demand new approaches to communication. Our inquiry suggests that there are many opportunities to be seized, as well as real challenges to be faced in understanding and acting upon these changes.

Liberalization and Deregulation

Most people on this planet receive most of their information on issues beyond their immediate communities from the print and broadcast media.

Fifteen years ago, much of humanity had one main source for this information--their governments. The means were stolid, formulaic broadcast and print media that had been established with the express purpose of telling people what they should know and think.

Two general trends have changed this. First, following the end of the Cold War, a combination of internal pressure from their citizens and external pressure--often in the form of conditions set by donors--have led governments to relax censorship and freedom of speech laws. Second, this pressure for political liberalization has been combined with economic liberalization and deregulation of national media industries.

The result in many of those countries with tightly controlled media has been a blossoming of dynamic, generally populist and highly commercial newspapers, television and radio media in most developing countries, and flourishing of new community media in some. Meanwhile, old monopoly state-run media, particularly broadcasters, have tended to languish, losing their audiences to more dynamic competition. They also face declining government support and funding.

The implications of these changes for those involved in communication are challenging.

Monopoly broadcasters have presented a convenient way of communicating simple messages to huge audiences through one medium. In much more fragmented media environments, this opportunity no longer exists and reaching the same audience requires putting messages out through many different media, and adapting it to many different audiences.

Perhaps more importantly, the creation of these more complex and dynamic communications environments raises the deeper question of just what information do people have access to, and does it empower poor people and give them a greater voice--or does it move them further to the economic and social margins?

At their worse, new communications environments have done the latter. They have shifted from providing stodgy and dogmatic government propaganda to providing a uniform diet of often Western popular music. In some countries, state-controlled news has been replaced by no news, or information that is sensational, inaccurate or irrelevant to the daily lives of much of its audience, or news that is derived entirely from international sources.

Often operating in anarchic regulatory environments, commercial and private stations have little obligation to provide anything other than entertainment. At its very worst, media have encouraged intolerance, sectionalism and tribalism, the most extreme example being the "hate" radio of RTML in Rwanda which played a key role in the massacres in that country.

At their best, however, commercial, community and, in some cases, newly invigorated state-run news and media organizations have managed to attract large audiences with compelling, popular and informative programming. In Kampala, Uganda, the FM station Capital Radio attracts some of its highest audiences for its Capital Doctor program, which provides advice and information on issues of sex, HIV/AIDS and other health issues. In South Africa, a form of "edutainment"-

"Soul City," set in a Johannesburg township--has become one of the most popular soap operas in the country, yet has succeeded in educating people about diarrhoea, HIV/AIDS and other issues.

Again in South Africa, deregulation has spurred the creation of more than 80 community radio stations broadcasting in 15 languages. Community stations have made serious inroads into the broadcast markets, often stealing audiences from the well-established public broadcasting stations. Community broadcasting provides communities with information that is relevant to their lives, as well as a voice through which people can make demands.

In Cape Town, the tiny community radio station, Radio Zibonele, drew on their audience's anger to play a key role in mediating and resolving the township's gang warfare surrounding the taxi business.

In fact, the success of community radio proves, in some small way, the ready market for communication for social change principles to be applied in diverse circumstances throughout the world. In addition to sub-Saharan African nations, community radio has succeeded where little else can from northwest Canada to southeast Asia.

The print media too is changing under similar pressure, with more entertaining, more populist and often more trenchant coverage of news issues. These changes have demonstrated how in the print media in particular, poor reporting undermines many other forms of social and political discourse; high quality reporting can play a major role in promoting and stimulating constructive public debate. Well-informed, investigative reporting in particular can provide a key element of public accountability, both for national governments, for international institutions, and for NGOs and other civil society organizations.

Finally, the last decade has seen an explosion in satellite broadcasting. Take the South Asia region, home to one-fifth of the world's population which is today within the footprint of at least 50 broadcast satellites. In India, Pakistan and Bangladesh alone there are more than 70 million households with television sets, adding up to a total viewership of 300 million. By 2007, there will be 550 million television viewers in these countries. Half of them will be hooked up to cable-able to watch the 350 channels that will be available to them by then.

These changes do not apply to all people in all countries, but in one form or another they do affect the vast majority of people in the great majority of countries.

They present many problems; reaching lots of people with prepared messages is becoming more difficult and more expensive. They also present substantial opportunities: to work with communities to enable them to amplify their voices, to enable access to the information that can empower them, to help shape communication environments that can work for people, not against them.

New Information and Communication Technologies

The current revolution in information technologies represents probably the most profound set of technological developments human society has experienced since the industrial revolution.

The innovations of the Internet--and particularly e-mail--have transformed communications capacities in countries with often dilapidated telecommunications infrastructures; and have opened up access to much more information about global issues. The falling costs and increased access to telephony mean that an increasing number of people have the capacity to communicate rapidly beyond their immediate communities, thus opening up new economic opportunities and opportunities for social and political discourse. For many participants in this communication for social change initiative these technologies represent a huge opportunity:

Centralized control of information by governments or commercial interests becomes much more difficult. Increasingly, political systems can neither control the information their citizens receive nor monitor or constrain how they communicate with each other.

Technology is--for good and ill--increasing access to the kind of information that is uncensored and unfiltered. Technology is growing most rapidly in those areas where its demand is most clearly defined by the users.

The capacity of people to access information is substantially increased.

The capacity of people to organize, advocate and lobby beyond physical boundaries is greatly enhanced.

The capacity for people and organizations in developing countries to communicate information--their aspirations, demands, experiences, analysis--becomes cheaper, more powerful and far more pervasive.

Nevertheless, we also recognize the limitations of these technologies. In particular, the "information gap" between rich and poor is stark. One of the least expensive of the information and communications technologies (ICTs)--the telephone--illustrates just how far apart the rich and poor worlds are in access to such technologies.

One quarter of the countries in the world still have fewer than one telephone line per 100 people. The majority of the population in developing countries--60% of the total--live in rural areas. Yet in these countries, more than 80% of main telephone lines are in urban areas.

The distribution of new ICTs is no more equal.

Eighty four per cent of mobile cellular subscribers, 91% of all fax machines and 97% of Internet host computers are in developed countries.

Telecommunications is nevertheless becoming cheaper, more reliable and more accessible and will continue to do so.

Despite the constraints, it seems likely that we are seeing the emergence internationally of organizational structures that are increasingly based on networks, rather than hierarchies. It is this revolution which represents most powerfully the increase in horizontal, people-to-people communication, and which provides profound new opportunities for more inclusive public and policy debate.

A Changing Political and Economic Environment

The collapse of the Soviet Union and the end of the Cold War have had far reaching effects, a full exploration of which is beyond the remit of this paper. However, two key issues should be mentioned.

The first is the growing, though uneven, democratization and political liberalization that has swept much of the developing world over the last decade. Many of the highly centralized one-party states or dictatorships have given way to multi-party democracies, or at least to more open political systems.

This political liberalization has been matched by a still more pervasive economic liberalization and we have seen the rapid emergence of a new global economy. As Manuel Castells argues, "for the first time in human history the entire planet is capitalist, since even the few remaining command economies are surviving or developing through their linkages to global, capitalist markets."

As all governments are finding, including China's, maintaining strict and centralized control of information in a market economy (which, in turn, needs to rely on communications technologies) is both difficult and often inefficient.

The fragmentation and decentralization of information outlined above is potentially countered by the greater concentration of ownership in communications and media industries ushered in by globalization. According to UNESCO's World Communication Report 1997, "international [media] conglomerates are emerging with the purpose of controlling not only the transmission system (manufacturing, network, cable, satellite etc.) but also the programs they convey."

An increasing spate of mergers and acquisitions over recent years has seen the emergence of a handful of "world companies" who now dominate global media markets. Time Warner Inc., News International, Sony, Finivest and Bertelsman each have annual sales well in excess of $10 billion, an increasing percentage of which is generated outside the United States. This concentration is compounded by convergence of media and telecommunications industries leading to still greater concentration of ownership.

Such concentration may not matter and may be offset by the more horizontal and decentralized models of communications outlined above.

But both these trends--towards a decentralization of information production away from government, and a concentration of ownership of the means of communication in the hands of transnationals--should matter to anyone involved in communication. These trends are bound up intimately with questions of who controls the information that people receive.

Communication and emerging development problems These changes to communication environments come at the same time as important changes in how we think about development. Some of the most important emerging development challenges of the last decade have raised new questions.

Issues such as HIV/AIDS, reproductive health and reproductive rights, and others such as tobacco use have highlighted more intensely than ever how disease and poor health are linked not only to poverty and poor nutrition, but also to prejudice, to social, political and economic inequality, and to social dislocation. They have focused an especially strong spotlight on social and political environments where issues of sex and sexuality are habitually hidden or are difficult to debate in public.

Such complexities are forcing societies globally to change--to question long cherished, deeply rooted social, political, and religious mores and practices. A whole range of issues--from HIV to reproductive rights, from domestic violence to female genital mutilation--have crystallized the need for much wider social and political change. Such change is informed by what happens both within countries and by international debates, but if it is to be sustainable, change has to emerge from within societies.

The means of how societies change, and who drives such change is contentious and difficult. Part of such change will come from education about issues such as condom use--but much of the more deep seated changes that need to take place in societies, such as the improvement in the status of women, need to emerge from advocacy and vigorous public debate within and between societies.

Such debates depend fundamentally on communication: on communication within societies, within families, within communities, through political discourse; and on communication between societies, at the levels of the individual, of the community and of the global society. The capacity of people to communicate is intimately bound up with their capacity to effect change.

In short, a new model of communication could be emerging from a mixture of political, technological, economic and social change. It is decentralized, pluralistic and democratic; it seeks to empower rather than persuade people; it fosters debate among and between citizens, among and between communities, and between people and government. This model envisages increasingly horizontal communication allowing people to communicate with each other easily and inexpensively. It also involves the steady disintegration of traditional monolithic vertical lines of communication, where governments owned radio and television stations in order to control flows of information.

CREATING AN ENVIRONMENT FOR CHANGE

The Rockefeller Foundation has responded to a growing body of opinion and evidence that the role of communication in developing country societies is changing, and that the strategies of those working in development needed to change with it. The Foundation's inquiry is based on the premise that the changes that are taking place in communication and society may have profound implications for donor and development strategies, but that this premise remains poorly researched and articulated. Communication for social change programming suggests a major shift in development. Above all it is about enabling publics and communities to articulate their own agendas for development--at the community, the provincial, the national and the international level. Programming in this area is about making connections--at these different levels and between them. It involves making connections between global trade policies and local communities, and it involves making connections between many different kinds of activities--between the issues themselves (such as HIV/AIDS, domestic violence) and the means that exist for debating and discussing them: community radio, women's radio listeners groups, an informed and responsive national media, quality media programming (e.g., Soul City), telecommunications.

It involves framing and phrasing debates in language and forms that are inclusive. It involves a responsibility of academics in particular, but those concerned with development in general, to communicate research and information not only to their peers, but to the wider public within developing countries. It involves "returning" research and analysis to where it originates. Perhaps, above all, it suggests that the key role for donor and development institutions is to create an environment for change. It suggests a role that sees these organizations continuing to inform and create development strategies, but also in creating the conditions where developing country societies can assess, challenge and adapt such strategies and begin to create strategies for themselves.

It provides new opportunities pto open up development decisions and programming to public debate and dialogue, and to enable publics--and not just experts--to be more proactive in shaping debate on development issues.

THE PROCESS OF INQUIRY

The Rockefeller Foundation has been engaged aggressively in intellectual inquiry about the power of communications for nearly 60 years. In the late 1930s, program officer John Marshall formed the Rockefeller Communications Seminar whose goal was to promote a theoretical framework about the role of mass communications in American culture. Under Marshall's guidance, the foundation funded one of the country's first efforts to quantitatively document the effect of radio on listeners. The work expanded in the 1940s to include support for Paul Lazarsfeld, who began the new field of communication and attitude research. In this time-frame, the foundation also funded the creation of the first communications journal, Public Opinion Quarterly.

It is from this historical base that the current communications efforts to promote an enhanced discipline known as communication for social change grows.

The Rockefeller Foundation, like most other progressive U.S.-based foundations, is in the business of positive social change-change in attitudes, in behaviours, in utilization of technology, and of access to opportunities to enhance lives.

While a key player in the development arena, the foundation's focus remains predominantly on science-based knowledge.

Yet at the core of much of the foundation's current portfolio is the need to affect individual and community norms and behaviours-the type of change that requires sophisticated, sustained communication.

Three years ago we began to ask the tough questions: how can we demonstrate that communication-planned and implemented strategically-can indeed bring about desired social change? Can we prove that such communication thinking and work is as systematic, scientific, sustained and measurable as other social sciences?

And can we move beyond publicity and promotional activities to a new way of thinking and delivering communication that starts with the identified community or stakeholder's needs, engages the recipient of the communication in decision making and, most importantly, can be sustained and replicated. The answers are "yes", "maybe" and "watch us."

We began this inquiry the way much work starts at this foundation-with a group of people coming together at a Bellagio conference. While this may not have been a unique method, the process of discovery we used-search conference methodology-yielded encouraging results. We brought together disparate types with little in common except our belief that communication MUST be done differently. We, individually and collectively, knew that we were on the cusp of an evolutionary turn in the history of communication for development.

We felt that our work had to be bigger than embracing electronic technology or providing access to those in "unwired" parts of the world. We also believed, with some certainly, that the discipline of communication can be ill-defined, misunderstood, undervalued and often ignored for its contributions to the development process.

What we're about today is, hopefully adding to the discourse rather than muddying it. In the process of figuring out what to do and where to start, we realized that the type of communication work that needs to be done is not often done-especially in poor areas of developing nations most in need.

It seems that a particular niche for this network will be in identifying needed skills, developing ways to transmit training and to reach those people and communities most likely to have scarce resources.

Going forward we will work with such people and communities to bring communication for social change to them. We come to this work humbly confident that ultimately, development-in virtually any sector-cannot happen without innovative and sustained communication processes.

Where is Good Work Happening?

One question that we're asked frequently is "what does communication for social change look like? Who is practicing it, or where is the greatest potential?"

In looking for examples of good work, it's important to keep in mind the key principles of communication for social change: it empowers individuals and communities, it engages people in making decisions that enhance their lives, it is many-to-many, it relies on democratic ideals, it allows previously unheard voices to be heard, and both the process of communications and the content of the messages are controlled by the receiving communities. This can be heady stuff-at times bordering on the ideal rather than the practical. Yet even so, we've found examples of innovative social communications work in several locales.

As we work in the United States, Africa and Asia, for example, it appears that the most likely practitioners of communication for social change are small struggling organizations with few resources.

Communication for social change in some respects becomes a means of survival.

Without the benefit of large communications staffs or budgets, and facing media that are hesitant to cover social issues in substantive ways, some small NGOs and community-based organizations have figured out how to use the people most affected by their work to make the communications process work.

In Africa and Latin America, the community radio movement stands out.

By definition, community radio stations cannot succeed without local control, citizen participation, local issues-based programming and open access. Yet radio remains essentially a top-down methodology; that is, someone decides what will be broadcast, it airs, and is received passively by listeners.

The better community radio stations, such as Cape Flats' (South Africa) Bush Radio, Radio Zibonele in the Khayelitsha community of Cape Town, South Africa, and Alexandra Township's community station focus on audience participation.

New programming stems from the suggestions listeners make when phoning into the stations, or when they are working there as volunteer staff. Critical issues facing the communities are discussed-and problem solving happens in real time-on the air.

Outreach is daily and continuous-the community radio stations are vital parts of the neighbourhoods where they operate. They don't just "cover" issues-they lead the residents in collective decision making.

A KEY CHALLENGE: CAPTURING IMPACT

Recognition of the role of communication in achieving social change is not necessarily new nor surprising, but it receives comparatively little funding. While the case for this kind of programming--for the reasons already given--is building, there remain significant obstacles to it attracting major support.

Much of this work involves stimulating dialogue and debate within communities and the public, and--when it works best--ensuring that the engine of change is the community and public itself. As a consequence, much of this work is unpredictable and risky. Because dialogue and debate are the immediate objectives and are difficult to measure or attribute to any particular intervention, and because it is recognized that social change is likely to take a long time, this work is very difficult to assess and evaluate.

Indeed, many of the communications initiatives that are currently funded--particularly around behaviour change--attract support less because they are perceived as addressing the main problem, but more because they can be claimed as having changed something.

In the field of HIV/AIDS, for example, much of the funding for communications initiatives has gone into attempts to change individual behaviours. Much of this work has had substantial impact but it has not, as many of its practitioners would acknowledge, sought to change the underlying factors that are driving a still escalating epidemic: poverty, social exclusion, prejudice and discrimination, migration and poor health systems. Such problems are fundamental. Communication for social change programming can constitute only part of the real solution; it can help enable people to shape their own agenda, articulate their own priorities and aspirations of how to address the epidemic, and ensure that donors are following and responding to public and policy debates within developing countries as well as shaping such debates.

Evaluation of impact in this area remains difficult but not, we conclude, impossible. It does, however, mean that we must develop new methodologies.

MEASUREMENTS AND EVALUATION

Donors have a right and an obligation to demand evidence that their funds have been spent wisely, that they have achieved what they were meant to, or that there are good reasons for any changes or lack of achievement.

However, there are other reasons why impact needs to be measured.

1. *Accountability*-understanding the impact of communication interventions is an essential component of being accountable. The primary accountability is to the people engaged in the communication intervention. Being involved with them in aspects of their lives requires that accountability. They are also the people, proportionate to their means, who will invest the most resources.
2. *Progress*-understanding what is happening and whether it is what people want to happen.
3. *Improvement*-information from any measurement and evaluation is crucial to both large strategic decisions and to fine tuning communication interventions in order that better value is gained from the investments that are made.
4. *Motivation*-a sense of achievement is crucial to motivation. Good motivation is an essential element of any endeavour, including communication for social change programs. The people involved draw energy and drive from knowing that progress is being made. Not knowing can lead to the opposite.
5. *Credibility*-Good data on the impact of communication for social change interventions can only enhance the credibility of this field and the investments-from local to international-that are made.

The long-term goal of all development action is to see positive change in the issues of concern. We all want less poverty, increased employment, better gender equality, to eradicate HIV/AIDS, more girls in school, higher educational achievement, lower child and maternal mortality rates, better nutrition, fewer accidents and no violence. That is the crucial measure of success.

Such changes can take five years or a decade, but generally much longer. People involved in communication for social change initiatives need more immediate data that indicates whether what they are doing is making a contribution to the overall change process.

It is not possible to run a program for 15 years before assessing impact and then finding that the wrong things were done. More immediate information on the contribution of communication to change is required.

Although communication for social change activities tend to have less specific and immediate objectives and targets, they nevertheless need to develop a similar set of indicators both to measure and indicate progress and to drive the nature of the programming. We are at the start of this work, but the Cape Town meeting, drawing on the information, analysis and perspectives above, made some suggestions of indicators.

Expanded Public and Private Dialogue and Debate

Dialogue and debate are crucial. They indicate that people are engaging in the issues of concern, are motivated to look at them, and that at least some of the parties to the debate and discussion are challenging the orthodoxy that may be contributing to the matters of most concern. For example, the role of women in politics; the need for a more open approach to sexual health issues; equal rights for boys and girls; and land redistribution. Increased accuracy of the information that people share in the dialogue/debate Accuracy of information is important.

There are two types of information. First where there is specific, proven data such as would exist in relation to a particular medical issue. Second, accurately reflecting the background information, perspectives and views of the parties to a debate over a more complex issue such as girls in school.

The more accurately the data and the perspectives are reflected in the dialogue-from among friends to public policy debate-the more likely is the chance of positive change. The means available that enable people/communities to feed their voices into debate and dialogue.

Increased leadership and agenda setting role by disadvantaged people on the issues of concern Whatever the focus of the communication for social change action the people at the centre of the issue[s]-those whose everyday lives are most affected-should be involved in the major decisions related to the initiative. This will ensure relevance and meaning-a vital component for any intervention.

Resonates with the major issues of interest to people's everyday interests Communication for social change interventions need to be positioned in ways that resonate, make sense to them, to which they can relate. Of course this is a basic tenet of all communication, but it can be easily forgotten in the midst of complex detail relating to an issue such as breast feeding and HIV/AIDS.

If the positioning of the issue does resonate there is a greater chance of momentum and action. And it is not possible to focus on all the many and varied aspects of a concern. Rarely can the issue that resonates be chosen in advance. It will emerge and then needs to be accentuated.

Linked people and groups with similar interests who might otherwise not be in contact One of the main turning points for any change process is when different groups form alliances with a common overall objective and a loose coordination framework. Each group does its own thing, but in the knowledge that it contributes to a greater effort. Therefore activities that link people together and help working alliances can be interpreted as contributing to positive change.

CONCLUDING OBSERVATIONS

Throughout the NGO community in industrialized and in less wealthy nations, the potential both to apply communication for social change methodology and to encourage its use is great. The change communication principles seem obvious to those of us in development, philanthropy and social services. They speak to the very essence of our work-that is, to helping create locally-based solutions to critical social ills.

Yet throughout time, obvious "fixes" have been the ones most often overlooked. "Of course innovative communication techniques are essential" we hear frequently.

"Of course we have to empower those 'on the ground' to have greater control of their own stories and how they are communicated. Of course 'horizontal' communication is more effective than top-down," we all opine. Yet "how" remains a mystery in far too many instances. Or more precisely, we're not sure "how to make it work."

Key to answering the "how" question, we believe, is in finding smart practitioners and thinkers throughout the world who are able to reach others, train others, test the change communication principles, encourage ongoing site-based work, and evaluate its effectiveness.

The strategy for moving this initiative forward has five prongs:

1. Reaching clarity of terms and defining, or perhaps refining, the field;
2. Identifying and describing the skills, attributes and resources necessary for communication for social change. During the Cape Town conference, participants discussed both the form and content of the skills development process.
3. Developing the systems and exchange mechanisms needed to spread the change communication work globally;
4. Maintaining the network of supporters and enrolling others; and,
5. Using concrete measurements to evaluate effectiveness and the reach of communication for social change.

We are well along on the first prong. We believe we have many good ideas for the second and third ones. Each day we're thrilled by another expression of interest that we receive; the word is getting out, which only fuels our evangelical spirits.

And, as this paper suggests, there are different ways of doing evaluation that should further the communication for social change agenda.

Yet, many questions remain: can we create a "transfer of knowledge" or type of curriculum that can be transported worldwide easily and economically? What's in such a curriculum? Who are the trainers? How will they receive the information? (Is, for example, Internet-based training a viable option?) Can we establish regional centers of learning that are based on local realities? How do we reach people in those areas of the world most in need of this knowledge but who have the smallest number of resources to access such training?

Or should we, perhaps, be worrying less about skills and more about personal attributes? Going forward we must debate answers to these questions and test possible solutions on a community-specific basis.

BIBLIOGRAPHY

Albarran, Alan B.: *Management of Electronic Media*, Belmont, Wadsworth/Thompson Learning, 2002.

Arant, David: *Perspectives: Ethics, Issues and Controversies in Mass Media*, St. Paul, Coursewise Publishing, 1999.

Berry, David: *Ethics and Media Culture*, Woburn, Focal Press, 2000.

Blanchard, Margaret A.: *History of the Mass Media in the United States, An Encyclopedia*, Chicago, Fitzroy Dearborn Publishers, 1998.

Bliss, Edward: *Now the News: The Story of Broadcast Journalism*, New York, Columbia University Press, 1991.

Briggs, Asa and Peter Burke: *A Social History of the Media from Gutenberg to the Internet*, Malden, Blackwell, 2001.

Cannadine, David: *History and the Media*, New York, Palgrave Macmillian, 2004.

Cannadine, David: *History and the Media*, New York, Palgrave Macmillian, 2004.

Chermak, M.: *Victims in the News: Crime and the Indian News Media*, Boulder, Westview Press, 1995.

Christians, Clifford G.: *Media Ethics: Cases and Moral Reasoning*, Boston, Allyn & Bacon, 2004.

Earl, R.: *Writing for Mass Communication*, White Plains, NY: Longman, 1996.

Ehrlich, Matthew C. *Journalism in the Movies*. Urbana: University of Illinois Press, 2004.

Ericson, Richard: *Crime and the Media*, Brookfield, Dartmouth Publishing, 1995.

Fallows, James: *Breaking the News: How the Media Undermine American Democracy,* New York, Pantheon, 1996.

Folkerts, Jean, and Dwight L. Teeter, Jr.: *Voices of a Nation: A History of Mass Media in the United States,* Needham Heights, Allyn & Bacon, 1997.

Freedman, Warren: *Press and Media Access to the Criminal Courtroom*, New York, Quorum Books, 1988.

Gordon, A. David: *Controversies in Media Ethics,* White Plains, Longman Publishers, 1999.

Hudson, Robert V.: *Mass Media,* New York, Garland Publishing, 1987.

Jewkes, Yvonne: *Media and Crime,* Thousand Oaks, Sage, 2004.

Land, Mitchell : *Contemporary Media Ethics*, Spokand, Marquette Books, 2006.

Langman, Larry: *The Media in the Movies,* Jefferson, NC: McFarland & Company, 1997.

Langman, Larry: *The Media in the Movies,* Jefferson, NC: McFarland & Company, 1997.

Limburg, Val E.: *Electronic Media Ethics,* Boston, Focal Press, 1994.

Louis, A: *Ethics in Media Communications*, Belmont, Wadsworth, 2003.

Merrill, John C.: *Journalism Ethics: Philosophical Foundations for News Media,* New York, St. Martin's Press, 1997.

Michael, Dillon: *Media Ethics Goes to the Movies*, Westport, Praeger, 2002.

Mouritsen, H.: *Case Studies in Media Management*, Boston, McGraw-Hill, 2001.

Patricia, A.: *Police and the Media,* Springfield, Thomas Books, 1987.

Patterson, Philip : *Media Ethics: Issues and Cases,* Boston, McGraw Hill, 2002.

Peter, Burke: *A Social History of the Media from Gutenberg to the Internet*, Malden, Blackwell, 2001.

Ripley, Jr. Casey: *The Media and the Public,* New York, H.W. Wilson, 1994.

Robert, V.: *Mass Media,* New York, Garland Publishing, 1987.

Robert W. Snyder: *Defining Moments in Journalism*, New Brunswick, NJ: Transaction Publishers, 1998.

Sohn, Ardyth: *Media Management: A Casebook Approach,* Mahwah, Lawrence Erlbaum Associates, 2003.

Surette, Ray: *Justice and the Media*, Springfield, Thomas Books, 1984.

Ward, Hiley H.: *Mainsteams of American Media History,* Needham Heights, MA: Allyn & Bacon, 1997.

Warner, Charles: *Media Management Review,* Mahwah, Lawrence Erlbaum Associates, 1997.

INDEX

D

E

G

H

I

J

M